# The Maoist Movement in India

# The Maoist Movement in India

*Perspectives and Counterperspectives*

EDITOR
## Santosh Paul

Routledge
Taylor & Francis Group
LONDON NEW YORK NEW DELHI

First published 2013 in India
by Routledge
912 Tolstoy House, 15–17 Tolstoy Marg, Connaught Place, New Delhi 110 001

Simultaneously published in the UK
by Routledge
2 Park Square, Milton Park, Abingdon, Oxfordshire OX14 4RN

First issued in paperback 2015

*Routledge is an imprint of the Taylor & Francis Group, an informa business*

© 2013 Society for Economic and Political Reconstruction

ʌɟǝıɔos  society
ɔıɯouoɔǝ ɹoɟ  for economic
ןɐɔıʇıןod puɐ  and political
uoıʇɔnɹʇsuoɔǝɹ  reconstruction

*Typeset by*
Star Compugraphics Private Limited
5, CSC, Near City Apartments
Vasundhara Enclave
Delhi 110 096

British Library Cataloguing-in-Publication Data
A catalogue record of this book is available from the British Library

ISBN-13: 978-1-138-66292-6 (pbk)
ISBN-13: 978-0-415-63406-9 (hbk)

*Dedicated to my mother and father for having given me a secular, liberal and leisured education*

# Contents

# List of Plates

# List of Abbreviations

| | |
|---|---|
| AFSPA | Armed Forces (Special Powers) Act |
| AICC | All India Congress Committee |
| AICCCR | All India Co-ordination Committee of Communist Revolutionaries |
| AMS | Adivasi Mahila Sangathan |
| AOB | Andhra–Orissa border |
| APCC | Andhra Pradesh Congress Committee |
| APGenco | Andhra Pradesh Power Generation Corporation Limited |
| APL | Above Poverty Line |
| ATS | Anti Terrorist Squad |
| BJP | Bharatiya Janata Party |
| BPL | Below Poverty Line |
| BRICS | Brazil, Russia, India, China and South Africa |
| BSF | Border Security Force |
| BSP | Bahujan Samaj Party |
| CAF | Chhattisgarh Armed Force |
| CEO | Chief Executive Officer |
| CISF | Central Industrial Security Force |
| CM | Chief Minister |
| CNM | Chetna Natya Manch |
| COBRA | Commando Battalion for Resolute Action |
| CPI | Communist Party of India |
| CPI(M) | Communist Party of India (Marxist) |
| CPI (Maoist) | Communist Party of India (Maoist) |
| CPI (ML)/CPI (M–L) | Communist Party of India (Marxist–Leninist) |
| CRPF | Central Reserve Police Force |
| CRZ | Coastal Regulation Zone |

| | |
|---|---|
| CSPSA | Chhattisgarh Special Public Security Act |
| CVC | Central Vigilance Commissioner |
| DAKMS | Dandakaranya Adivasi Kisan Mazdoor Sangh |
| DGP | Director General of Police |
| DK | Dandakaranya [forest] (in Maoist party-speak) |
| FIMI | Federation of Indian Mineral Industries |
| GoI | Government of India |
| GDP | Gross Domestic Product |
| GI | Galvanised Iron |
| GPS | Global Positioning System |
| IBM | Indian Bureau of Mines |
| IBSA | India, Brazil, South Africa |
| ICAR | Indian Council of Agricultural Research |
| IDP | Internally Displaced Persons |
| IED | Improvised Explosive Device |
| INSAS | Indian Small Arms System |
| IPC | Indian Penal Code |
| IPL | Indian Premier League |
| ITBP | Indo-Tibetan Border Police |
| JD(U) | Janata Dal (United) |
| JNM | Jan Natya Manch |
| JNU | Jawaharlal Nehru University |
| JPC | Jharkhand Prastuti Committee |
| JS | Janatanam Sarkar |
| KAMS | Krantikari Adivasi Mahila Samity |
| LMG | Light Machine Gun |
| LTTE | Liberation Tigers of Tamil Eelam |
| MCC | Maoist Communist Centre |
| MCCI | Maoist Communist Centre of India |
| M–L | Maoist–Leninist |
| MLA | Member of the Legislative Assembly |
| MML | Mysore Mineral Limited |
| MP | Member of Parliament |

| NABARD | National Bank for Agriculture and Rural Development |
| NASA | National Aeronautics and Space Administration |
| NBA | Narmada Bachao Andolan |
| NGO | Non-Governmental Organisation |
| NHRC | National Human Rights Commission |
| NREGA | National Rural Employment Guarantee Act |
| NREGS | National Rural Employment Guarantee Scheme |
| NTRO | National Technical Research Organisation |
| NTUI | New Trade Union Initiative |
| OMC | Orissa Mineral Corporation |
| PDS | Public Distribution System |
| PIL | Public Interest Litigation |
| PLGA | People's Liberation Guerrilla Army |
| PM | Prime Minister |
| POTA | Prevention of Terrorist Activities Act |
| PPP | Purchasing Power Parity |
| PSU | Public Sector Undertaking |
| PU | Party Unity |
| PUCL | People's Union for Civil Liberties |
| PUDR | People's Union for Democratic Rights |
| PWG | People's War Group |
| RJD | Rashtriya Janata Dal |
| RPC | Revolutionary People's Committee |
| RSS | Rashtriya Swayamsevak Sangh |
| SC | Scheduled Caste |
| SCB | Soil Carbon Bank |
| SEZ | Special Economic Zone |
| SHC | Soil Health Card |
| SLR | Self-Loading Rifle |
| SP | Superintendent of Police |
| SPO | Special Police Officer |

| | |
|---|---|
| ST | Scheduled Tribe |
| TADA | Terrorist and Disruptive Activities (Prevention) Act |
| TB | Tuberculosis |
| TOI | *The Times of India* |
| TPC | Tritiya Sammelan Prastuti Committee |
| UAPA | Unlawful Activities (Prevention) Act |
| UN | United Nations |
| UNEP | United Nations Environment Programme |
| UP | Uttar Pradesh |
| UPA | United Progressive Alliance |
| USSR | Union of Soviet Socialist Republics |
| VHP | Vishwa Hindu Parishad |

# Preface

The peasant revolt in the Naxalbari subdivision of Darjeeling district in the year 1967 is still a potent symbol of agrarian revolt in 2012. The current Maoist movement is a continuation of the armed struggles of the extreme left in the 1960s and 1970s. The Red Army's takeover of China coordinating a series of peasant revolts has inspired Maoist movements all over the world. Kanu Sanyal, one of the founders of the Naxalite movement, was echoing the Red Army phenomenon when he called for 'liberat[ing] the rural areas through revolutionary armed agrarian revolution and encircle the cities, and finally, to liberate the cities and thus complete the revolution throughout the country'.[1]

The situation is alarming enough for policymakers to adopt new and radical approaches to resolve the problem. Over 2,600 civilians and security force personnel were killed between 2008 and 2010.[2] The inability to redress the economic factors is the dominant cause for the sustained violence which has affected 182 districts and several states in what is now called the Red Corridor. The liberalisation of the economy has put India on a fast track in the years 2000 and 2011, clocking a Gross Domestic Product (GDP) growth of a quarterly average of 7.45 per cent. It is ironic that despite almost 8 per cent growth we have not been able to contain economic disparities, nor have we been able to raise the income levels to alleviate poverty.

---

[1] Alex Peter Schmid and A. J. Jongman, *Political Terrorism: A New Guide to Actors, Authors, Concepts, Data Bases, Theories and Literature* (New Brunswick, NJ: Transaction Publishers, 2005), p. 571.

[2] *The Times of India*, 'Maoist violence claims 2,680 lives in 2008–10', 9 March 2011, http://articles.timesofindia.indiatimes.com/2011-03-09/india/28671947_1_incidents-of-naxal-violence-school-buildings-telephone-exchanges (accessed on 19 March 2012).

The problem undoubtedly has its roots in social and economic deprivation. At the heart of the conflict is a battle for land. The government is aware and has been taking steps. The National Rural Employment Guarantee Act (NREGA) is a substantive measure to contain economic deprivation. Similarly there is a rethink on the issue of land acquisition. Again, it remains to be seen if the forthcoming policies will in any manner ameliorate the condition of those living in the tribal belts where people are being displaced for mining activities.

As I conducted the study, I was overwhelmed by the extensive scholarship available on this subject. The objective of the Society for Economic and Political Reconstruction (SEPR) in compiling this valuable anthology of essays, articles, interviews and writings on the subject of Maoism is to provide a new perspective to this complex socio-economic and political problem. To this end, this anthology brings together writings from economists, journalists, political scientists, film-makers, judges, lawyers, food experts, and environmentalists. This volume could enable evolving of cohesive and multipronged solutions within the confines of democracy. Besides, it could also be a continuous guide for policymakers and legislators and those of us who are interested in finding a solution to this problem.

There is no alternative to the printed word in a meaningful exchange of ideas. The printed word is any day far more durable and enduring vis-à-vis other transient media. The debates on Maoism on television, due its format, are unable to come to grips with the problem. Opinions rendered end up in oversimplification of the issues and shallow hysterics. By the end of the programme there is inevitably no solution in sight, differences are even wider, the protagonists more hardened about their opinions and the viewer forgets everything upon switching to the next channel.

SEPR attempts to bring the debate on Maoism into the national consciousness through this collection. The aim is to encourage collective introspection and assimilation of ideas from every spectrum of opinion. It is also important to inform the reader that the Society's first express aim is to 're-affirm the faith in constitutional democracy and human freedom as the only political option to better the human condition economically, politically and socially'.[3] It is also important to remember that India has for over six decades successfully worked a democratic constitution. It is with these objectives in mind that this anthology is being published.

**Santosh Paul**

---

[3] Clause of the trust deed of the Society for Economic and Political Reconstruction.

# Acknowledgements

I would like to convey my gratitude to all the authors who were kind enough to give permission to publish their articles in this anthology: Samir Amin, Aditya Nigam, Jairus Banaji, Jairam Ramesh, Prakash Jha, Swaminathan S. Anklesaria Aiyar, M. S. Swaminathan, Chetan Bhagat, Swapan Dasgupta, Gurucharan Das, Nirmalangshu Mukherji, V. K. Mehta and Justice Krishna Iyer. I am extremely grateful to newspapers, magazines and journals — *The Times of India, The Economic Times, The Hindu, Hindustan Times, Daily News and Analysis, Outlook, India Today, Monthly Review, The Platypus Review, Seminar, Press Trust of India, Tehelka, Economic and Political Weekly, Congress Sandesh* — for giving me the permission to reproduce writings which have appeared in their publications.

My special thanks go to Meera Mathew due to whose efforts this book has come to be published. I would also like to express my gratitude to Arvind Gupta, Mohita Bagati, Madasamy, Ravi and Ganesh for having lightened my work during the tortuous task of getting the book published. Finally, I'd like to thank my wife Sabina Paul and my father for having taken care of everything and helping to make this volume possible. I am grateful to Nilanjan Sarkar who enabled me to conceptualise this book and encouraged me to go through the rigours of getting this book published.

I would like to express my gratitude to my publishers Routledge who have spent over a year meticulously going through every single detail. Without their enthusiasm, this book would have never seen the light of the day. My special thanks goes out to the editorial and commissioning teams for going through the drafts threadbare and making corrections, modifications and amendments to ensure that the work is flawless to the extent possible.

If there are any mistakes, the fault is entirely mine.

The Society for Economic and Political Reconstruction gratefully acknowledges permissions granted by individuals and institutions to reproduce copyrighted material in this volume. For articles and write-ups from newspapers, magazines and periodicals, permission to reproduce them in most instances has been sought from the publisher and not the author, following Section 17 of the Copyright Act, 1957. Author permissions have been sought where copyright lay solely or jointly with the author. Every effort has been made to cite the owners of copyright with respect to the text reproduced in this book. Perceived omissions if brought to notice will be rectified in future printing:

**Aditya Nigam**, 'Rumour of Maoism', *Seminar*, no. 607, March 2010. Reproduced with permission of the author and publisher.

**B. K. Handique**, 'No Back Door Entry to Private Firms for Mining', *Hindustan Times*, 15 September 2010. Reproduced with permission of Press Trust of India.

**Chetan Bhagat**, 'The Wrong Diagnosis', *The Times of India*, 17 July 2010. Reproduced with permission of the author.

**Digvijay Singh**, 'I Have Differed with Chidambaram on His Strategy, But We Remain Friends', *Outlook*, 24 May 2010. Reproduced with permission of the publisher.

**Dola Mitra**, 'The Path Rarely Taken', *Outlook*, 26 April 2010. Reproduced with permission of the publisher.

**Gurcharan Das**, 'No Ifs or Buts, Defeat Maoist Violence', *The Times of India*, 25 October 2010. Reproduced with permission of the author.

**Jairus Banaji**, 'The Maoist Insurgency in India: End of the Road for Indian Stalinism?', *The Platypus Review*, no. 26, 6 August 2010, pp. 1–3. Reproduced with permission of the author and publisher.

**Jairam Ramesh**, 'An Eco-Visionary Par Excellence', *Hindustan Times*, 5 June 2010. Reproduced with permission of the publisher.

**Jairam Ramesh**, 'Cannot Deny Links Between Forest Departments and Mining Lobbies', *Hindustan Times*, 15 May 2010. Reproduced with permission of the publisher.

**'Justice Krishna Iyer's Plea** to Manmohan Singh on Behalf of Binayak Sen', *The Hindu*, 19 April 2009. Reproduced with permission of Justice V.R. Krishna Iyer and the publisher.

**Madhavi Tata**, 'A Really Dark Corner', *Outlook*, 26 April 2010. Reproduced with permission of the publisher.

**M. S. Swaminathan**, 'Our Freedom was Born with Hunger, We're Still Not Free', *The Times of India*, 15 August 2010. Reproduced with permission of the author.

**M. S. Swaminathan**, 'Grow Up', *Hindustan Times*, 5 June 2010. Reproduced with permission of the author and publisher.

**Nandini Sundar,** 'Bastar, Maoism and Salwa Judum', *Economic and Political Weekly*, vol. 41, no. 29, 22 July 2006, pp. 3187–92. Reproduced with permission of the author.

**Nitin Sethi**, 'As Forests Need Growth, Tribals Given the Go-By', *The Times of India*, 5 June 2010. Reproduced with permission of the publisher.

**Nitish Kumar,** 'Force Alone Can't Rout the Maoists', *Outlook*, 26 April 2010. Reproduced with permission of the publisher.

**Nirmalangshu Mukherji,** 'Arms over People: Maoists in Bastar', *Outlook*, 19 May 2010. Reproduced with permission of the author and publisher.

**P. Chidambaram**, 'Halt the Violence! Give Me 72 Hours', *Tehelka*, 21 November 2009. Reproduced with permission of the publisher.

**Prakash Jha**, 'The Nation Should Adopt the Maoists' Area', *DNA*, 3 June 2010. Reproduced with permission of the publisher.

**Swaminathan S. Anklesaria Aiyar,** 'No Military Solutions for Maoism', *The Economic Times,* 23 May 2010. Reproduced with permission of the author and publisher.

**Swapan Dasgupta,** 'Force Should Be Met with Force', *The Times of India,* 23 May 2010. Reproduced with permission of the author.

**Tusha Mittal,** 'Life in the "Liberated Zone": Inside Abujmarh The Mythic Citadel', *Tehelka,* 12 May 2012. Reproduced with permission of the publisher.

**Vinod Mehta,** 'Through an Egyptian Mirror', *Outlook,* 21 February 2010. Reproduced with permission of the publisher.

# Introduction

*Santosh Paul*

✪

The tribals of peninsular India are the unacknowledged victims of six decades of democratic development. In this period they have continued to be exploited and dispossessed by the wider economy and polity. (At the same time, the process of dispossession has been punctuated by rebellions and disorder.) Their relative and oftentimes absolute deprivation is the more striking when compared with that of other disadvantaged groups such as Dalits and Muslims. While Dalits and Muslims have had some impact in shaping the national discourse on democracy and governance, the tribals remain not just marginal but invisible.

Ramachandra Guha[1]

The whole history of my people is one of continuous exploitation and dispossession by the non-aboriginals of India punctuated by rebellions and disorder, and yet I take Pandit Jawaharlal Nehru at his word. I take you all at your word that now we are going to start a new chapter, a new chapter of independent India where there is equality of opportunity, where no one would be neglected.

Jaipal Singh[2]

On 18 March 1967 in the village of Naxalbari, West Bengal, a farmers' organisation called Siliguri Kisan Sabha led by a tribal leader Jangal Santhal declared their intention of commencing an armed revolt to redistribute the land controlled by local landlords to end centuries of exploitation. Large parts of the village belonged to tea

---

[1] Ramachandra Guha, 'Adivasis, Naxalites and Indian Democracy', *Economic and Political Weekly*, vol. 42, no. 32, 11 August 2007, pp. 3305–12.

[2] Jaipal Singh, *Constituent Assembly Debates*, vol. 1, pp. 143–4, 19 December 1946, http://164.100.47.132/LssNew/constituent/vol1p9.html (accessed on 27 February 2012).

plantations exempt from land ceiling legislations. The population of Naxalbari subdivision predominantly consisted of tribals and landless labourers. Since then several persons were picked up by the police and detained, causing resentment. There was constant conflict between the landless peasantry trying to claim access to uncultivated areas and local *jotedars*[3] forcibly evicting tenants. On 23 May 1967, a sharecropper, Bibul Kishan, was beaten up by the henchmen of a local landlord while trying to enter and cultivate upon a piece of land. The next day, Inspector Sonam Wangadi led a team of policemen to make arrests to quell the disturbances. In a confrontation, Wangadi fell to a hail of arrows. Versions differ. Sabitri Rao is the wife of former Naxalite Punjab Rao who had this account of the events to tell:[4]

> One morning, a few of the men went to till the fields and didn't return. We suspected that they had disappeared for a drink. But we got worried and scared when they did not return even the next day. A few others went missing the day after too. The next morning, some of us hid behind the bushes and watched. As soon as the men would begin tilling, the police would appear and take them away, telling them that the jotdar who owned the land has ordered their arrests. The next morning, many of us gathered in the fields at Borojorujot and decided we won't allow the police to do whatever they pleased. In the confrontation that followed, inspector Sonam Wangdi was killed by arrows. No one still knows who shot that arrow.[5]

The next day, on 25 May 1967, the peasants held a meeting at Prasad Jote in Naxalbari to protest against the police action. The meeting came under fire from the police in which 11 people were killed, which included seven women and two children. The names

---

[3] *Jotedar* is another term used for Zamindar or landlord or land owner, mostly in West Bengal.

[4] Mouparna Bandyopadhyay, 'It happened in Naxalbari', *Financial Express*, 29 June 2009.

[5] Ibid.

of those killed in the police firing are etched on a memorial at this spot. The revolt in Naxalbari was not the first of the revolts in tribal areas. In the 19th century, there was the revolt of Kol and Bhunj Tribes; in 1855 it was the Santhals; in 1911 it was in Bastar; in 1920 it was in Gudem–Rampe; 1945 saw the revolt of the Warli Tribes; and in 1966, there was once again a revolt in Bastar. The Naxalbari revolt was not the last but the beginning of extreme left-wing movements which would not only survive for over six decades, but would in the 21st century pose the single largest threat to the state, according to the Prime Minister of India Manmohan Singh.[6]

The events in Naxalbari not only triggered a wave of violence by extreme left-wing groups but also radicalised sections of students and the urban middle class. The Naxalite movement spread to the Presidency College, Kolkata; Jadavpur University; and also the prestigious St. Stephen's College. The Naxalbari Revolt was a cause for disenchantment with the politics of the Communist Party of India (Marxist). The CPI(M)'s leadership acquiesced in the government's decision to use police machinery against the rebels. The subsequent decision of the CPI(M) to dissolve the Darjeeling and Siliguri units and expel 19 members for Naxalite sympathies was viewed by the radical elements within the party as an ideological betrayal. The dissident left factions of CPI(M) formed the All India Co-ordination Committee of Communist Revolutionaries (AICCCR). There were defections from the CPI (M) in Andhra Pradesh, West Bengal, Kerala, Uttar Pradesh, Punjab, and Tamil Nadu.

The Naxalities gained sympathy amongst the landless peasants and sections of the youth in several states. They conducted raids on the homes of landlords, murder, arson and even attacks on police stations. Kanu Sanyal formed the new Communist Party (Marxist–Leninist) to 'liberate the rural areas through revolutionary

---

[6] Simon Robinson, 'India's Secret War', *Time*, 29 May 2008, http://www.time.com/time/magazine/article/0,9171,1810169,00.html#ixzz1lfmF50dx (accessed on 7 February 2012).

armed agrarian revolution and encircle the cities, and finally, to liberate the cities and thus complete the revolution throughout the country'.[7] The Communist leaders in Asia like Mao had found the conventional communist philosophy problematic. There was no proletariat or working class as conceived by Marx in Asian countries. The Asian economies had a huge subsistence peasantry and landless farmers. Maoists placed reliance on the revolution from the countryside. This pragmatic response from Mao was the source of the military success of the People's Liberation Army against Chiang Kai Shek's US-supported Kuomintang. The military success of the guerrilla tactics and the resistance of the rural masses surrounding the cities captured the imagination of Maoists from different parts of the world. Though the philosophy of Maoism has lost much of its significance in the country of its origin after China adopted hyper capitalism, it continues to inspire left-wing movements in its neighbouring countries.

The movement carried on till the middle of 1970s till it was substantially contained. Its offshoots kept surfacing in different parts of the country. The movement resulted in affirmative action by the state like the 'Operation Barga' of 1978 introduced by the CPI(M) government in Bengal which awarded tenancy rights to share croppers who tilled the land — 1.7 million cultivating tenants could get both a fair share of the crop as well as freedom from arbitrary evictions.

Naxalbari today is an idyllic village in West Bengal with a population of 25,000 and does not show any indications of its revolutionary past. However, the present-day Maoist movement in India is the continuation of the extreme left-wing movement of the late 1960s which commenced in Naxalbari. Mao's quoted line — 'political power flows out of the barrel of the gun'[8] — is still the movement's credo. By the year 2009, almost 170 districts

[7] Alex Peter Schmid and A. J. Jongman, *Political Terrorism: A New Guide to Actors, Authors, Concepts, Data Bases, Theories and Literature* (New Brunswick, NJ: Transaction Publishers, 2005), p. 571.

[8] Mao Zedong, 'Problems of War and Strategy (November 6, 1938)', in *Selected Works of Mao Tse-tung*, vol. II (Peking: Foreign Languages Press, 1967), p. 224.

in India in the 'Red Corridor' have come under the substantial administrative control of the Maoists. The source of Maoist violence in the 1960s and 1970s can be partly attributed to the dismal failure of the land reforms movement in India. But the sudden surge of Maoist activity in the Red Corridor in recent years is attributed to the large-scale loss of land by tribals, and marginalised sections dependant on land, to mining, resource extraction activities, dam building, development of Special Economic Zones (SEZs) and industrial townships, and demarcations for wildlife parks and sanctuaries.

After Dr Manmohan Singh took office in 2004, India has been witnessing an accelerated level of economic growth and investor confidence. In 2005, the Indian economy was growing at the rate of 9 per cent and economists believe that India could maintain a growth rate of 8 per cent right through to 2020. It is an admitted position that this growth has unfortunately not percolated to the grassroots level. A substantial section of the society in the rural areas has not received any tangible benefits from this economic surge. India ranks 134th on the Human Development Index with 41.6 per cent of India's population living on less than US$ 1.25 Purchasing Power Parity (PPP) per day.[9] It is ironic that while the Indian economy is on an unprecedented surge, the 2010 Human Development Report had some very shocking revelations:

Eight Indian states, with poverty as acute as the 26 poorest African countries, are home to 421 million multidimensionally poor people, more than the 410 million people living in those African countries combined.[10]

The liberalisation of the Indian economy and its opening up has speeded up the demand for the lands on which our tribes and

[9] United Nations Development Programme (UNDP), *Human Development Report 2011: Sustainability and Equity: A Better Future for All* (Basingtoke: Palgrave Macmillan, 2011), pp. 126, 144.
[10] United Nations Development Programme (UNDP), *Human Development Report 2010: The Real Wealth of Nations: Pathways to Human Development* (Basingstoke: Palgrave Macmillan, 2010), p. 98.

marginalised groups live. Mining and creation of Economic Zones have led to swallowing up of lands belonging to these groups. It is not by accident that the Maoist activities are concentrated in the Red Corridor which runs across the states of Andhra Pradesh, Odisha (formerly Orissa), Chhattisgarh, Bihar, Jharkhand, Uttar Pradesh, and West Bengal. It is this region which has 70 per cent of India's coal reserves, 80 per cent of iron ore, 60 per cent of bauxite, and most of India's chromite reserves.[11] This has led not only to the displacement of the large sections of populations living in those areas but also rendered them defenceless in a modern economy. Their only option is to languish on the fringes of the economy as unskilled labour in abject penury. Despite the constitutional guarantees of providing adequate safeguards to the backward and tribal areas and their people, the performance of the state on this front has been dismal. The literacy rate of Adivasis is 23.8 per cent and that of Dalits is 30.1 per cent; 62.5 per cent of Adivasi children and 49.4 per cent of Dalit children drop out before matriculation and 49.5 per cent of Adivasis and 41.5 per cent of Dalits live below the poverty line.

The noted anthropologist, Verrier Elwin, who headed the Committee on Special Multipurpose Tribal Blocks, had recorded the condition of the tribal population in the 1950s, which continues to be the same till date:

We have driven [the tribals] into the hills because we wanted their land and now we blame them for cultivating it in the only way we left to them. We have robbed them of their arts by sending them the cheap and tawdry products of a commercial economy. We have even taken away their food by stopping their hunting or by introducing new taboos which deprive them of the valuable protein elements in meat and fish. We sell them spirits which are far more injurious than the home-made beers and wines which are nourishing and familiar to them, and use the proceeds to uplift them with ideals. We look down on them and rob them of their

[11] Nitin Sethi, 'As Forests Feed Growth, Tribals Given the Go-By', *The Times of India*, 5 June 2010 (Chapter 18, this volume).

self-confidence, and take away their freedom by laws which they do not understand.[12]

The people who have been displaced from their lands have not taken this assault lying down. While some of the movements have taken place within the parameters of a democratic discourse, in several other places the resistance, unfortunately, has followed the path of violence. For instance, the Tata Motors' Nano car project in Singur ended in a complete fiasco after stiff resistance to the West Bengal state government's land acquisition programme for the project. The West Bengal government had sought to acquire 1,000 acres of prime agricultural land which would have displaced 13,000 peasants in Singur. This became an emotive election issue and resulted in Mamata Banerjee dislodging the well-entrenched CPI(M) in the West Bengal state elections in May 2011. One of the first decisions of the Mamata Banerjee cabinet was the return of 400 acres to the Singur farmers.

However, in stark contrast, the events in Lalgarh in West Midnapur took a violent turn. On 2 November 2008, the Chief Minister of West Bengal Buddhadeb Bhattacharya and Central Ministers Ram Vilas Paswan and Jitin Prasada were hit in a landmine attack by Maoists while returning from a foundation stone ceremony of a steel plant at Shalboni. The ministers escaped unscathed while six policemen were grievously injured. The West Bengal police immediately commenced operations in the Lalgarh area to flush out the Maoists. In November 2008, three high school boys from Bashbar village returning to their homes on foot were picked up by the police as suspected Maoists. The enraged villagers surrounded the Lalgarh police station and blockaded it. The support came from surrounding adivasi villages. The adivasis dug up roads and blocked them with felled trees. This prevented the deployment of police and paramilitary forces. The People's

---

[12] Committee on Special Multipurpose Tribal Blocks, *Report of the Committee on Special Multipurpose Tribal Blocks* (New Delhi: Ministry of Home Affairs, Government of India, 1960), pp. 20, 192.

Committee against Police Atrocities was set up, which demanded that the police stop illegally arresting people, especially women, and that the cases against the arrested children be dropped. Five companies of the Central Reserve Police Force and two companies of the Commando Battalion for Resolute Action (COBRA) arrived on 17 February 2009. The police assault began on the morning of 18 June which was met with human shields of about 2,000 villagers. For 12 days, police and paramilitary battalions battled with villagers and adivasis. The operation left several dead and 35,000 villagers fled to other places for safety and due to fear of police reprisals. The conflict zone has widened and is punctuated by death tolls that do not befit a constitutional democracy.

At the heart of this Maoist conflict is the battle for land between those who are dependent on land and those economic organisations and forces which require this very land for what is euphemistically called 'developmental' activities. It is ironic that while India is breaking out of the shackles of the 'Hindu Rate of Growth', it is now faced with the greatest challenge to its economic and political order, through the Maoist movement.

Maoism, both as an ideology and also as a political force in its new avatar, has got its foothold in over 182 districts in 10 states and is threatening democratic governance. There are two dominant and diametrically opposite viewpoints, along with the various shades of grey, on Maoism prevailing in India. The popular view in urban centres is that espoused by the Prime Minister Manmohan Singh and the Home Minister P. Chidambaram who perceive the Maoist movement as a violent law and order situation. On the other end of the spectrum are fierce defenders of the Maoist movement like Arundhati Roy who see the movement as a last ditch struggle by those millions who have been abandoned by the state in the development process and who have no hope in hell in the current economic scheme of the political structure. In between these two extremes lies the perception that Maoism is the outcome of a lopsided development policy which abandoned large segments of the population from receiving any tangible benefits. Sonia Gandhi's message to the party workers is an indicator of this view point when she articulated, 'While we must address acts of terror decisively and forcefully, we have to address the root causes of Naxalism. The rise of Naxalism is a reflection of the need for our development initiatives to reach the grass roots, especially in our most backward tribal districts'.[13] These middle-of-the-road views coalesce to advocate an inclusive development policy rather than rely exclusively upon a police–military option.

However, to not treat Maoism as a law and order problem has its own consequences. First, the scale of violence and the killings which happen with striking regularity would be difficult to ignore. The violence often does not end with of the police or the armed constabulary as the sufferers. The victims of Maoism are often the very people the movement seeks to protect. Besides, the Maoist ideology refuses to adhere to any form of democratic process and seeks to establish doctrinaire party authoritarianism. Time and again, history has shown that these political movements have brought about far greater oppression than the systems they seek to displace. The statement of the Prime Minister is high on hyperbole when he refers to the ragtag armies of landless peasantry and tribals as the single largest threat to the state. But, nevertheless it is a serious law and order problem given the scale of violence they have so far unleashed. To treat the Maoist problem through the lens of the police and paramilitary would not only be an error of judgement but would be absolutely foolish. Sixty five years of democratic governance in India is no mean achievement, and to squander it all in meaningless violence is the least desirable of the alternatives. There is another aspect of Maoists being co-opted within the democratic process which has so far eluded the thinking of the establishment in India. The classic illustration is of the Maoist movement in Nepal, spearheaded by the People's Liberation Army under the leadership of Prachanda, joining the mainstream parliamentary democracy in 2002 after 10 years of insurgency.

---

[13] Sonia Gandhi, 'Letter to the Congresspersons', *Congress Sandesh*, May 2010.

## The Alaska Permanent Fund Solution

It is unfortunate that governments working under a Constitution dedicated to the upliftment of the marginalised sections of the society, besides mouthing the rhetoric of inclusive development, are unable to bring in concrete developmental measures. There are effective models available, like the Alaska Permanent Fund. The mineral rich state of Alaska, after discovering that the revenues from mineral extraction were being squandered by the state with no tangible benefits to the Alaskans, set up the Permanent Alaska Fund. In 1975 the voters in Alaska approved a constitutional amendment to establish a dedicated fund — the Alaska Permanent Fund. The amendment mandated that 25 per cent of all mineral lease rentals, royalties, royalty sales proceeds, federal mineral revenue-sharing payments and bonuses received by the state were to be invested in the 'Fund'. The Fund invested in a diversified portfolio of public and private assets. The Fund, which started with an initial investment of US$ 734,000 in 1977, has grown to more than US$ 41.105 billion today. Its investment in US bonds is US$ 6.172 billion, in US stocks US$ 6.409 billion, US$ 12.626 billion in global and non-US stocks, and US$ 4.173 billion in real estate. The projected earning is US$ 4–5 billion annually and individual annual dividends are expected to be US$ 3,000–4,000 in the coming years. In the year 2005, every Alaskan inhabitant received US$ 845.76 and in the year 2008 they received US$ 2,069. From 1982 through 2009, the dividend programme paid out about US$ 17.5 billion to Alaskans through the annual distribution of dividend cheques.

The Alaska Permanent Fund is not the only Sovereign Wealth Fund in the world. There are 20 larger funds managed by various countries giving new meaning and dimension to equitable opportunity for human capital development. The list of countries with the largest sovereign funds is given in Figure 1.

## Rethink in India

There has been a rethinking in India too. After widespread disturbances and violence in the districts of Greater Noida by

**Figure 1:** Largest Sovereign-Wealth Funds

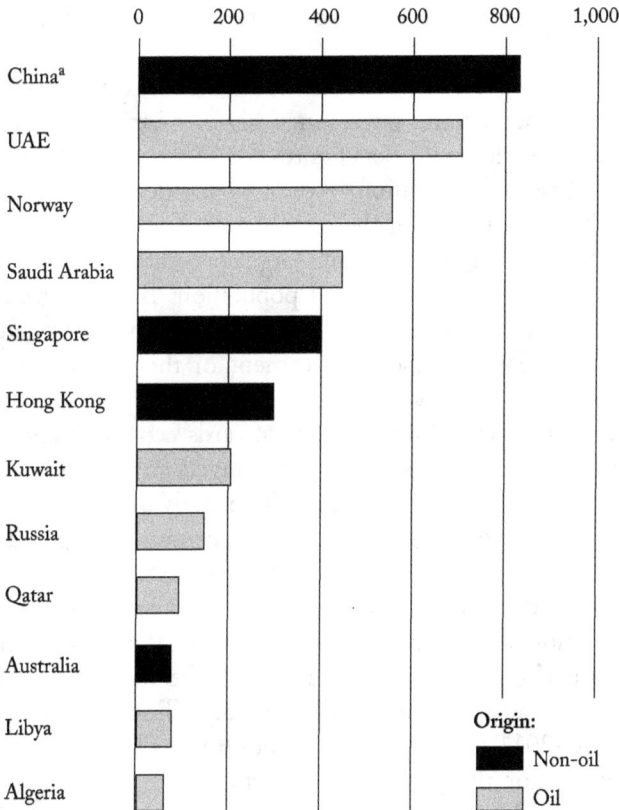

Source: Sovereign Wealth Fund Institute. Cited in *The Economist*, 'Largest sovereign-wealth funds', 10 March 2011, http://www.economist.com/node/18335007 (accessed on 19 March 2012).

Note:   a Based on estimates.

agitating farmers over the coercive land acquisition in 2011, the Uttar Pradesh government headed by Chief Minister Mayawati sought to bring in a new policy. Under this policy, 70 per cent of the farmers have to consent to the acquisition. It was also providing for a 33-year annuity of ₹ 23,000 per acre of land acquired. The most attractive proposition was the provision that 16 per cent of the developed land has to be returned to the farmer. This would ensure that the land-displaced do not feel cheated after seeing prices soar after development. This in essence is the beauty of democracy: the ability to provide innovative solutions to new and emerging problems.

There is adequate evidence and economic data suggesting that 60 years of democratic governance has not brought about any substantial development benefits to vast segments of the society. There is also a justification, especially in the mineral belts of India, that exploitation of the natural resources has only resulted in enriching mining interests and large corporations with nothing tangible percolating to the local population. Bauxite, gold, and now, platinum finds in India's tribal belts only accentuate the continuing misery of the displacement of the population from their lands.

The government's commitment towards economic and social empowerment of the socially disadvantaged groups and marginalised sections of society is suspect. The study of financial allocations to these groups shows that the sceptics may perhaps be right in perceiving that governments have virtually no intention to improve their lot and is keener on resource extraction and appropriation of their lands. Studies show that the actual economic package is abysmally poor. For instance, the funds allocated for the welfare and development of Scheduled Tribes (STs) for the year 2010–2011 was a pittance amounting to ₹ 3,206.50 crore. The outlay for the grants under Article 275(1) was a meagre ₹ 1,046 crore. The funds allocated for development of forest villages for the same year was a dismal ₹ 60.50 crore. The scheme of Top Class Education for ST Students provided for financial assistance for 625 students annually. The economic survey does not disclose what exactly the achievement of the Scheme for Strengthening of Education among ST Girls in Low Literacy Districts was a bare perusal of the financial commitment for the schemes for the welfare of Scheduled Castes (SCs) and STs shows a pathetic disregard to doing anything substantial for this section of people that is paying the highest price in this economy.

The battle against Maoists moved from intensive military and police action to the bizarre. The state of Chhattisgarh began arming thousands of illiterate and barely literate youth from the tribal tracts with little or no training and with even lesser clarity on the chain of command to battle with the Maoists. Besides, the union government and the state government had no answer as to how they would be disarmed. The Supreme Court's verdict by Justice Sudarshan Reddy and Justice Surinder Singh Nijjar on 7 July 2011 striking down this arrangement as unconstitutional is worth a careful study. The arming of such private militias like Salwa Judum and Koya Commandoes was held to be unconstitutional and governments are injuncted from appointing and supporting such militias. While the judgement was settling a constitutional issue, it also made an impassioned plea to the governments of the day and of the future to adhere to their constitutional obligations to secure a more equitable allocation of resources and stop violence on those whose resources and lands are being forcibly taken away.

Any battle for the minds of the people against the Maoist movement and for restoration of democratic governance in Maoist-controlled areas would have to adhere to what Bertrand Russell had to say about the fight against communism: 'Communism is a doctrine bred of poverty, hatred and strife. Its spread can only be arrested by diminishing the area of poverty and hatred'.[14] If only the governments paid as much attention to ensuring that a fair share of the proceeds is effectively deployed for the uplifting of the populations being forcibly displaced as they do to resource extraction, there could be a legitimate and democratic solution to this problem. If the People's Republic of China could pull 400 million out of poverty there is no reason why the Indian democracy cannot do the same with effective models of Sovereign Wealth Funds being deployed around the world.

᳭

[14] Bertrand Russell, 'Why I am not a Communist', in Robert E. Egner and Lester E. Denonn (eds), *Bertrand Russell: The Basic Writings of Bertrand Russell* (London: Routledge, 2010), p. 459.

# PART I

INTRODUCTION TO MAOISM

# 1

# What Maoism has Contributed

*Samir Amin**

✪

The Second International's Marxism, proletarian- and European-centred, shared with the dominant ideology of that period a linear view of history — a view according to which all societies had to first pass through a stage of capitalist development (a stage whose seeds were being planted by colonialism which, by that very fact, was 'historically positive') before being able to aspire to socialism. The idea that the 'development' of some (the dominating centres) and the 'underdevelopment' of others (the dominated peripheries) were as inseparable as the two faces of a single coin — both being immanent outcomes of capitalism's worldwide expansion — was completely alien to it.

But the polarisation inherent to capitalist globalisation — a major fact because of its worldwide social and political importance — challenges whatever vision we may have of how to surpass capitalism. This polarisation is at the origin of the possibility for large portions of the working classes and, above all, of the middle classes of the dominant countries (whose development is itself favoured by the position of the centres in the world system) to go over to social-colonialism. At the same time it transforms the peripheries into 'storm zones' (according to the Chinese expression) in natural and permanent rebellion against the world capitalist order. Certainly, rebellion is not synonymous

* This essay was previously published as 'What Maoism has Contributed', *Monthly Review*, September 2006.

to revolution — only to the possibility of the latter. Meanwhile, reasons to reject the capitalist model in the centre of the system are not lacking either, as 1968, among other things, has shown. To be sure, the formulation of the challenge advanced at a certain time by the Chinese Communist Party — 'the countryside encircles the cities'[1] — is by that very fact too extreme to be useful. A global strategy for transition beyond capitalism towards global socialism has to define the interrelationship between struggles in the centres and the peripheries of the system.

At first, Lenin distanced himself somewhat from the dominant theory of the Second International and successfully led the revolution in the 'weak link' (Russia), always believing that this revolution would be followed by a wave of socialist revolutions in Europe. But this did not happen; Lenin then moved towards a view that gave more importance to the transformation of Eastern rebellions into revolutions. But it was up to the Chinese Communist Party and Mao to systematise that new perspective.

The Russian Revolution had been led by a party well rooted in the working class and the radical intelligentsia. Its alliance with the peasantry in uniform (first represented by the Socialist Revolutionary Party) ensued naturally. The consequent radical agrarian reform finally fulfilled the old dream of the Russian peasants — to become landowners. But this historic compromise carried within itself the seeds of its own limits: the 'market' was, by its own nature, fated, as always, to produce a growing differentiation within the peasantry (the well-known phenomenon of 'kulakization').

The Chinese Revolution from its origin (or at least from the 1930s) unfolded from other bases guaranteeing a solid alliance with the poor and middle peasantry. Meanwhile its national

---

[1] Mao Zedong, 'A Single Spark Can Start a Prairie Fire', in *Selected Works of Mao Tse-tung*, vol. I (Peking: Foreign Languages Press, 1967), pp. 117–28. During the Chinese Revolutionary War, the Chinese Communist Party, led by Mao Zedong, established some revolutionary bases in rural areas, to start a guerrilla war with the Kuomintang based on the strategy of 'encircling the cities from rural areas'.

dimension — the war of resistance against Japanese aggression — likewise allowed the front led by the Communists to recruit broadly among the bourgeois classes disappointed by the weaknesses and betrayals of the Kuomintang. The Chinese revolution thus produced a new situation differing from that of post-revolutionary Russia. The radical peasant revolution suppressed the very idea of private property in farmland, and replaced it with a guarantee to all peasants of equal access to farmland. To this very day that decisive advantage, shared by no other country besides Vietnam, constitutes the major obstacle to a devastating expansion of agrarian capitalism. The current discussions in China largely centre on this question.[2] But in other respects the going-over of many bourgeois nationalists to the Communist Party would necessarily exert an ideological influence favourable to the support of the deviations of those whom Mao termed partisans of the capitalist path ('capitalist-roaders').[3]

The post-revolutionary regime in China does not merely have to its credit many more-than-significant political, cultural, material and economic accomplishments (industrialisation of the country, radicalisation of its modern political culture, etc.). Maoist China also solved the 'peasant problem' that was at the heart of the tragic decline of the Central Empire over two decisive centuries (1750–1950).

What is more, Maoist China reached these results while avoiding the most tragic deviations of the Soviet Union: collectivisation was not imposed by murderous violence as was the case with Stalinism; oppositions within the party did not give rise to the

---

[2] Samir Amin, *Pour un Monde Multipolaire* (Paris: Syllepse, 2005). See also Amin, Samir, 'Théorie et pratique du projet chinois de socialisme de marché', *Alternatives Sud*, vol. 8, no. 1, 2001, pp. 53–89.

[3] A capitalist-roader is a person or group who displays a clear disposition to submit to pressure from bourgeois powers and consequently tries to push the revolution on to a capitalist path. See Union Research Institute, *Documents of Chinese Communist Party Central Committee, Sept. 1956–Apr. 1969*, vol. 1 (Hong Kong: Union Research Institute, 1971), p. 825.

establishment of a terror (Deng [Xiaoping] was put aside, he returned).[4] The aim of an unparalleled relative equality in income distribution, both between the peasants and the workers and within each of those classes and between both and the ruling strata, was pursued — of course with highs and lows — tenaciously, and was formalised by choices of development strategy contrasting to those of the USSR [Union of Soviet Socialist Republics] (these choices were formulated in the 'ten great relationships'[5] at the start of the 1960s). It is these successes that account for the later developmental successes of post-Maoist China since 1980. The contrast with India, precisely because India had no revolution, thus has the greatest significance not only in accounting for their different trajectories during the decades from 1950 to 1980 but also for those characterising diverse probable (and/or possible) perspectives for the future. These successes explain why post-Maoist China, committing its development thenceforward to its 'opening' within the new capitalist globalisation, was able to avoid destructive shocks similar to those that followed the collapse of the USSR.

Nonetheless, Maoism's successes did not settle 'definitively' (in an 'irreversible' fashion) whether China's long-term perspectives would work out in a way favourable to socialism. This was, first of all, because the development strategy of the 1950–1980 period had exhausted its potential so that, among other things, an opening (even though a controlled one) was indispensable[6] — an opening which involved, as what ensued showed, the risk of reinforcing tendencies evolving towards capitalism. But it was also because China's Maoist system combined contradictory tendencies — towards both the strengthening and weakening of socialist choices.

Aware of this contradiction, Mao tried to bend the stick in favour of socialism by means of a 'Cultural Revolution' (from 1966

---

[4] Samir Amin, *L'avenir du maoïsme* (Paris: Éditions de Minuit, 1981), p. 57.

[5] Mao Zedong, 'On the Ten Great Relationships (April 25, 1956)', in *Selected Works of Mao Tse-tung*, vol. V (Peking: Foreign Languages Press, 1977).

[6] Amin, *L'avenir du maoïsme*, pp. 59–60.

to 1974). [On 5 August 1966, Mao Tse-tung, during the eighth Central Committee of the Communist Party of China, published 'Bombard the Headquarters' — a short document attacking] the bourgeois aspirations of the political class holding the dominant positions. Mao thought that, in order to carry out his course correction, he could base himself on the 'Youth' (which, in part, broadly inspired the 1968 events in Europe — consider Jean-Luc Godard's movie *La Chinoise*).[7] The course of events showed the error of this judgement. Once the Cultural Revolution had been left behind, the partisans of the capitalist path were encouraged to go over to the offensive.

The combat between the long and difficult socialist path and the capitalist choice now in operation is certainly not 'definitively outlived'. As elsewhere in the world, the conflict between the pursuit of capitalist unfolding and the socialist perspective constitutes the true civilisational conflict of our epoch. But in this conflict Chinese people hold several major assets inherited from the Revolution and from Maoism. These assets are at work in various domains of social life; they show up forcefully, for instance, in the peasantry's defence of state property in farmland and of the guarantee that all should have access to farmland.

Maoism has contributed in decisive fashion to ascertaining exactly the stakes in and the challenge represented by globalised capitalist/imperialist expansion. It has allowed us to place in the centre of our analysis of this challenge the centre/peripheries contrast integral to the expansion — imperialist and polarising by its very nature — of 'really existing' capitalism; and from this to learn all the lessons that this implies for socialist combat, both in the dominating centres and the dominated peripheries. These conclusions have been summed up in a fine 'Chinese-style' formula: ['countries want independence, nations want liberation, and the people want revolution'][8]. States — that is, the ruling classes (of

---

[7] *La Chinoise*, dir. Jean-Luc Godard, 1967.

[8] 'Joint Communique of the United States of America and the People's Republic of China (Shanghai Communique)', United States of America and the People's Republic of China, 28 February 1972.

all countries in the world whenever they are something other than lackeys: transmission belts for external forces) — try to expand their room for manoeuvre in the (capitalist) world system and to lift themselves from the position of passive objects (fated to submit to unilateral adjustment whenever demanded by a dominant imperialism) to that of active subjects participating in the formation of the world order. Nations — that is, historical blocs of potentially progressive classes — want liberation, meaning 'development' and 'modernisation'. People — that is, the dominated and exploited popular classes — aspire to socialism. This formula allows an understanding of the real world in all its complexity, and consequently, the formulation of effective strategies for action. Its place is in a perspective of a long — very long — global transition from capitalism to socialism. As such it breaks with the 'short transition' conception of the Third International.

&

# 2

# Rumour of Maoism

*Aditya Nigam**

✪

In his classic *Elementary Aspects of Peasant Insurgency in Colonial India*,[1] Ranajit Guha outlines a certain methodological imperative for the historian who wanted to 'get in touch with the consciousness of [peasant] insurgency'[2] when access to it is barred by the discourse of counter-insurgency that structures official records. How does one look beyond this discourse of the state that frames the archives in order to gain access to the voice of the rebels? Guha's solution was relatively simple — counter-insurgency, he argued, derives directly from insurgency and is so determined by the latter that 'it can hardly afford a discourse that is not fully and compulsively involved with the rebel and his activities'.[3]

Unlike British Marxist historian Eric J. Hobsbawm who had tried to track the story of 'social bandits' through a somewhat problematic reading of folklore,[4] Guha warned that 'folklore relating to peasant militancy can be elitist too',[5] for many singers and balladeers belonged to upper-caste families who had fallen on hard times and were, therefore, often suspicious of the revolt

---

* This essay was previously published as 'The Rumour of Maoism', *Seminar*, vol. 607, March 2010, pp. 75–81.

[1] Ranajit Guha, *Elementary Aspects of Peasant Insurgency in Colonial India* (New Delhi: Oxford University Press, 1983).
[2] Ibid., p. 15.
[3] Ibid.
[4] See Eric J. Hobsbawm, *Bandits* (London: Abacus, 2001).
[5] Guha, *Elementary Aspects of Peasant Insurgency in Colonial India*, p. 15.

of the lower castes or tribals. Guha underlined that though the records of the colonial state and its police officials registered the voice of those hostile to the insurgents — including landlords and usurers — they could not avoid being shaped by the will of the insurgents. His conclusion therefore was that the presence of rebel consciousness could be read in the body of evidence produced by the discourse of counter-insurgency itself.

The burden of Guha's argument was that in order to decode the language of counter-insurgency, it was often enough to simply reverse the values in the terms used by the official discourse: thus *badmashes* simply meant peasant militants and not 'bad characters'; 'dacoit village' would indicate an entire village involved in the resistance and 'contagion' would most likely refer to the solidarity generated by the uprising.

Those were happier days from the historian's point of view. For the peasant and tribal insurgencies that Guha was discussing were organic struggles which drew their leadership from amidst the peasants or tribal communities themselves. Whether it was Sidhu Kanoo, Birsa Munda or Titu Mir, the leadership of the movements and their 'ideologies' derived directly from the world of the tribals. The context of colonial India was also, in a significant sense, quite clearly polarised and the possibility of written records being produced from a multiplicity of sources was simply out of the question. It may, therefore, be possible to follow Guha's suggestion and merely reverse the values in order to get a sense of that other discourse.

In contrast, the methodological challenge for a scholar of contemporary India seems insurmountable. And if any future historian were to explore the Maoist movement of our times, say a hundred years later, she is likely to be completely misled if she decided to follow in Guha's footsteps. For not only would she or he be confronted with the official discourse of counter-insurgency, there would also be a 'Maoist discourse' to contend with — which is almost certainly not the voice of the 'insurgent peasant' (or the adivasi).

What this future historian will find in the archives, apart from the standard genre of documents produced by the state and its officials, will be a whole range of writings that claim to speak in the voice of the peasant/adivasi, produced by the state-in-waiting: the Maoist vanguard and their intellectual spokespersons. Among these will be actual party journals, pamphlets and statements, but they will also include a large body of writings produced by academics, journalists, human rights activists and other supporters of the movement.

For our historian-scholar, it will be relatively easy to deal with the documents and reports produced by the state and its officials. The real challenge lies in finding ways of decoding the mass of materials that are produced by the partisans of the movement. For one of the myths being endlessly reiterated in this genre of writings is that of virtually complete identity between the poor adivasi or peasant and the insurgents — a subsumption of the adivasi voice into the voice of the Maoist vanguard.

Unlike early colonial India, 21st century India is a world saturated by the media — it is indeed a world of media explosion; a world where the media is no longer captive to either the state or corporate elites. We live in an era where public discourses are framed by a multiplicity of voices. And yet, it might well be impossible for our future historian to find even one unfiltered voice of the adivasi — unfiltered, that is, through elite discourse.

The adivasis cannot represent themselves; they must be represented, it would seem. They must be represented either by the agents of the state — the Salwa Judum and Mahendra Karma for example — or by the revolutionaries. Unlike Karma who is at least himself an adivasi, the voice of the revolutionary is almost always that of a Brahman/upper caste Ganapathy or Koteswara Rao or their intellectual spokespersons.

So we have a Maoist-aligned intelligentsia vicariously playing out their revolutionary fantasies through the lives of adivasis, while the people actually dying in battle are almost all adivasis. Take the following killed in West Bengal in recent months: Rajaram Mandi, Lakhinder Mandi and Gopinath Soren on the side of the Maoists and Sadhan Mahato, Tapan Mahato, Barendranath Mahato and Gurucharan Mahato on the CPI(M) side. It will be hard to find a single Bhattacharya, Banerjee, Mukherjee, Basu or such like among the dead.

On the face of it, the list of the dead would seem to suggest that the Maoist story is correct and that the entire battle is being fought by and among the adivasis. But as a matter of fact, we do not even know whether the peasant or the adivasi in question is really the 'insurgent' we are looking for. I say this in a deliberately provocative vein because a point being repeatedly made by the Maoist-aligned intelligentsia is that to deny that the peasants or adivasis themselves are rising in arms, is to deny 'them' agency.

There is a definitional fiat at work here: you are by definition not an agent if you are not a Maoist. Claims like these abound in almost all writings of intellectuals sympathetic to the Maoists. And the only time we hear an actual adivasi voice (filtered, no doubt) is when an Arati Murmu, one of the endlessly harassed people of Lalgarh, assaulted by the police, says: 'Whenever there is a Maoist attack the police raid our villages and torture our women and children. For how long will we suffer this oppression by the police? All of us are Maoists, let the police arrest us. Today we have come out'.[6]

Statements like these have been endlessly retailed by the Maoist-aligned intellectuals in support of their argument that all adivasis are Maoists, as though the meaning of Arati Murmu's statement is quite so transparent. It is possible that she is actively involved in the Maoist movement, but it is also possible that she is making this statement in exasperation. If Arati Murmu is who she says she is, an ordinary adivasi woman whose fellow-villagers have repeatedly been bearing the brunt of police repression and harassment, then the statement can be read more as an expression of defiance of the police and not necessarily as a true and valid claim that all villagers are now Maoists.

It is indeed true that many adivasis in Lalgarh, Chhattisgarh and many other parts of the country have become Maoists in the

---

[6] Cited in Partho Sarathi Ray, 'Background of the Movement', *Sanhati*, 13 November 2008, http://sanhati.com/front-page/1083/#1 (accessed on 24 January 2010).

face of continued police harassment.[7] However, to conclude from this that [it is] the only way adivasis become or can become agents is to completely misrepresent the situation.

A related question is that of the 'organicity' of the Maoists' relationship to the adivasis. One of the ways in which Maoist-aligned intellectuals have been countering the charge of appropriating the voice of the adivasis is by claiming that the Maoists are the adivasis, that they are not an external factor in adivasi life — at least in areas of their influence.

Take for example, the following [Amit Bhattacharyya's] argument which takes historians Sumit Sarkar and Tanika Sarkar to task for criticising the Maoists.[8] According to the author [Bhattacharyya], they argue that the movement in Jangal Mahal had been going 'quite well until the Maoists entered the scene from outside and derailed the movement . . . [and] it is the violent activities of the Maoists that brought joint forces into the scene'.[9]

The author [Bhattacharyya] counters this position by asserting that '[T]he reality . . . is that the Maoists did not fall from the sky; the Maoist Communist Centre and the CPI (ML) People's War had been active there from the 1980s and 1990s and fought over day to day issues by the people's side and suffered persecution, molestation and incarceration for years together'.[10]

This apparently is 'proof' enough of the Maoists' deep roots among the adivasis, for the author then proceeds:

Their social roots lie in the soil of Jangal Mahal, however disturbing this may sound to these historians and sections of "learned

[7] See Aditya Nigam, 'A Million Mutinies Within', *Tehelka*, vol. 6, no. 26, 4 July 2009.

[8] Sumit Sarkar and Tanika Sarkar, 'Notes on a Dying People', *Economic and Political Weekly*, vol. 44, no. 26 & 27, 27 June 2009, pp. 10–14.

[9] Amit Bhattacharyya, 'Is Lalgarh Showing the Way?', *Economic and Political Weekly*, vol. 45, no. 2, 9–15 January 2010, pp. 17–21. For a similar claim, also see Saroj Giri, 'The Dangers Are Great, the Possibilities Immense: The Ongoing Political Movement in India', *Monthly Review*, 8 November 2009, http://monthlyreview.org/091106giri.php (accessed on 27 January 2010).

[10] Bhattacharyya, 'Is Lalgarh Showing the Way?', p. 20. CPI (ML) refers to the Communist Party of India (Marxist–Leninist).

personalities". *Thus the statement* that the Maoists are external to
the movement, that they have entered the scene all on a sudden
and taken control of it, *does not have any factual basis* at all.[11]

I have emphasised the phrases 'thus the statement' and 'does not
have any factual basis' in order to underline the structure of the
argument. The only 'facts' that Bhattacharyya refers to is that the
MCC and PWG have been active in the area since the 1980s and
1990s and from this it is supposed to follow that they have 'deep
roots' among the local populace. By that reckoning the RSS[12] and
Vishwa Hindu Parishad also must have 'deep roots' among the
adivasis (often in the same areas!). Let us leave aside the minor
possibility that different kinds of political forces can be active in
an area without managing to get any significant support from the
local population.

The writer [Bhattacharyya] then goes on to charge intellectuals
like the Sarkars with 'portraying the masses in a way that these
"ignorant" people are devoid of any initiative of their own, that
they are unthinking, unfeeling robots, which can only follow, but
cannot lead'.[13]

There are a number of issues here that are worthy of consid-
eration. First, the author's own rendering of the Sarkars' position
indicates that according to them, a movement was already on, and
in pretty good health before the Maoists took it over. How is this
a 'denial of agency' to the adivasis? It would not have been possible
for them to hold that position if they had been inclined to 'portray
the masses' as 'ignorant', 'devoid of initiative' and 'robots' as
Bhattacharyya alleges. It is also worth mentioning that the Sarkars'
account is based on the evidence of an active sympathiser of the
Lalgarh movement (an activist of the Lalgarh Andolan Sanhati
Mancha) who was by no means hostile to the Maoists. My point
is that for Maoist-aligned intellectuals, adivasi agency can be
recognised only as long as they are the foot soldiers of the Maoists.

---

[11] Ibid.; emphasis added.
[12] RSS refers to the Rashtriya Swayamsevak Sangh.
[13] Bhattacharyya, 'Is Lalgarh Showing the Way?', p. 20.

Second, the question of agency as it is routinely posed in a number of such writings assumes a simple and unproblematic relationship between the adivasi who becomes Maoist and the Maoist vanguard, i.e., the CPI (Maoist). The fact is that this is precisely where matters are considerably more complex and interesting. Those who pick up the gun and ally themselves with the Maoists are, indeed, not mere unthinking robots or 'ignorant' fools — they are agents in more complicated ways than simplistic Maoist-inspired accounts would allow us to see.

In the first place, to merely reassert a commonplace of much historical and political research of recent decades, most people (adivasis and peasants, as opposed to middle class intellectuals) who 'become Maoists' do not do so because they agree with their politics, their 'ideology' or their programme. They do so because 'Maoism' performs some function in a very immediate sense in their lives.

Take the story of Jagadish Mahato — one of the abiding legends of the rise of the Naxalite movement in the Bhojpur region in Bihar. A school teacher by profession, Jagadish Mahato was born into a poor peasant family in the now well-known village of Ekwari. He began his sojourn in politics in the context of the most vicious and unimaginable economic, social and sexual oppression of the local dalit people by upper caste landlords. Till 1968, he was an Ambedkarite of sorts and also published a short-lived newspaper by the name of 'Harijanistan'. He and his friends also organised demonstrations to raise the demand for Harijanistan but to no avail.

Peaceful struggle against the armed might of the landlords turned out to be utterly ineffective. Then he heard about the 'Naxalites' and their activities in Kolkata, in Siliguri and Medinipur. He and Rameshwar Ahir sought them out and established contact with the CPI (ML).[14] Thus began the drama of one of the

---

[14] Abhay Kumar Dubey, *Kranti ka Atma Sangharsh* (New Delhi: Vinay Prakashan, 1994), pp. 179–81.

most important segments of the Naxalite movement outside West Bengal. 'Naxalism' became the weapon in a battlefield of caste–class conflict. Jagadish Mahato died soon thereafter but the CPI (ML) Liberation struck roots in that region.

There are innumerable stories of similar kind in the history of social and political movements. The 'movement' first appears as a rumour in a situation of ongoing battle. To return to our earlier example, Jagadish Mahato could hardly have been an Ambedkarite in the sense we know Ambedkarism today, for the very name Harijanistan gives away the fact that his own self-identity was still being defined within an inherited Gandhian vocabulary.

Ambedkar too was little more than a rumour — the rumour of a leader of the 'depressed classes' about whom, possibly many legends were in circulation. And Jagadish Mahato did not have to wait for the 'real' Ambedkar or the Naxalites to materialise before he became an agent. He sought out the Naxalites and Charu Mazumdar. Both Ambedkar and Naxalism played, in his life, the role that he assigned them. The partnership can then carry on or not, depending upon a variety of factors. Mahato died too soon and we do not know what would have happened to his relationship with the CPI (ML). It is possible that he might have refashioned himself completely in order to become a party leader, but that is another story.

It is also well worth bearing in mind that agency is not always about noble struggle. If vanguards are instrumental in 'using' people for their purposes, ordinary people who choose to join them can be no less instrumental. Thus for instance, Bela Bhatia's field work revealed how, '[t]here have been instances where individuals have misused such power [as comes from wielding a gun] for private gain'. 'Attraction for armed power', she found, 'may lead unprincipled individuals to join the movement'. Some of them, she went on to observe, 'formed gangs after running away with the party arms and turned against the party itself (e.g. Jagnandan Yadav group in Bihar)'.[15]

---

[15] Bela Bhatia, 'On Armed Resistance', *Economic and Political Weekly*, vol. 41, no. 29, 22 July 2006, p. 3181.

It has been argued that exclusive focus on 'armed struggle' for 'capture of state power' 'involves intense paranoid secrecy and a normalization of a wartime mentality'.[16] It is worth considering what happens when such a situation combines with the ways in which wielding of technologically sophisticated arms shapes subjectivity as suggested by Bhatia's account. It is also worth considering how it can radically alter the dynamic of ongoing caste/class struggles. Take, for instance, the following report, once again from Jharkhand:

> The Maoists have not been immune to that fundamental and all-pervasive characteristic of Indian society — caste. Tussles over sharing money, as well as inter-caste clashes between Yadavs and Ganjus, a dalit community, have led to the formation of splinter groups like Tritiya Sammelan Prastuti Committee (TPC) and the Jharkhand Prastuti Committee (JPC). This has come as delightful news to the local administration which often supports one group against the other, and seeks to extract information by providing protection.[17]

Thus to make the argument that whoever joins the Maoists becomes an agent is certainly true if we bear in mind that it is not the agency of a Maoist revolution that is in question here but rather, agency in its precise social-theoretic sense — as belonging to a person who thinks and takes decisions and acts according to them in whatever way possible. S/he is, in that sense, always already an agent — even if decisions are always implicated in a web of power relations.

It is also clear from many independent accounts that from the late 1980s, resentment has been brewing against the Maoists in Chhattisgarh.[18] There is independent corroboration from different

[16] Nivedita Menon, 'Radical Resistance and Political Violence Today', *Economic and Political Weekly*, vol. 44, no. 50, 12 December 2009, p. 17.

[17] Prashant Jha, 'Complicating the "Naxalite" Debate', *Kafila*, 22 October 2009, http://kafila.org/2009/10/22/complicating-the-naxalite-debate/ (accessed on 24 January 2010).

[18] Human Rights Forum, *Death, Displacement & Deprivation: The War in Dantewada: A Report* (Hyderabad: Human Rights Forum, 2006).

quarters that the rise of the Salwa Judum as a state-sponsored counter-insurgency was preceded by a rising discontent against Maoist activities in May–June 2005.

Versions differ as to the reasons for the resentment. In one version, villagers decided to resist the Maoists who had come to take a young girl away from her family as a recruit — this forcible taking of one member from every tribal family being a standard practice of the Maoists. (What this does to the question of agency is best left to the reader to ponder.) Another version points to the Maoist-enforced boycott of trade in *tendu* leaves[19] against the backdrop of a drought, as the main precipitating factor behind the resentment.[20]

These are complicated questions but it is possible to sift through various contending accounts to get a sense of what is actually going on as far as the relationship between the adivasis/peasants and the Maoists is concerned. In this one sense, our historian is much better placed than Ranajit Guha. And here in these accounts of resentment against the Maoists, we get a glimpse of yet another dimension of adivasi agency, especially in Chhattisgarh but also in some other parts of the Maoist area of influence.

The most recent instance of the complex dynamic that the adivasi–Maoist relations embodies, comes from the Jangal Mahal area — precisely the area about which Bhattacharyya (cited earlier) makes his claims against Sumit Sarkar and Tanika Sarkar. This is the story of Gurucharan Kisku alias Marshal, from all accounts an important tribal leader of the Maoists. Kisku reportedly joined the MCC as far back as in 1988 and had arms training in handling all manner of sophisticated arms, including laying and detonating mines.[21] It is clear from Kisku's statements that his main grouse

---

[19] Temburni leaves or leaves of *Dyospyros melanoxylon* (an ebony tree with date-like fruit) in which tobacco is rolled to make *beedis*.

[20] Maureen Nandini Mitra, 'Red Alert in Chhattisgarh', *Down to Earth*, 31 October 2006, p. 23.

[21] Ravik Bhattacharya, 'Kishenji aide quits, says Maoists anti-tribal', *Indian Express*, 8 February 2010, p. 5.

centres on the 'tribal question':

> I decided to quit the party when I realized that it does nothing for the adivasis. In fact, the party is using them as instruments . . . Kishenji is an outsider who does not know anything about tribals here . . . Tribals are a social entity with distinct customs, religion and language. The party is destroying this tribal system and way of life in Jangal Mahal and other areas.[22]

It is possible that Kisku is particularly bitter at this moment of his break-up with a party and movement he has been involved with for two decades, and this articulation of his complaints could be an exaggerated overstatement. What is undeniable, however, is that in order to express his angst, he draws on an existing discourse among the adivasi populace where certain adivasi cultural practices are seen to be under threat from the Maoists.

Of course, this does not mean that 'Maoism' has no social support among the adivasis and peasants and is simply a fantasy of the revolutionary intelligentsia. Maoism exists and indeed, its area of influence has been expanding. It is impossible to reduce the growth of this 'Maoism', which arises out of an unstable compact between the political party — the CPI (Maoist) — and the ordinary peasants or adivasis, to any single factor. There are a number of different factors and indeed, different histories, that lie behind the phenomenon. At a superficial level, this difference can be located in the very different histories of the different components that went into the making of the party in its present form, namely the CPI (ML), People's War (better known as the People's War Group [PWG]), the CPI (ML) Party Unity and the Maoist Communist Centre — all of whom had different styles and different kinds of social base.

The history of the PWG goes back to the post-Emergency mass upsurge of the poor peasantry of Karimnagar district and other parts of Telengana in Andhra Pradesh. The primary issues were those of land, wages and vicious forms of caste oppression.

---

[22] Bhattacharya, 'Kishenji aide quits, says Maoists anti-tribal', p. 5.

'The organizational centre' of this struggle, writes K. Balagopal, 'was the agricultural labourers union or Raythu Coolie Sangham (generally known as the Sangham), and not the underground armed squads, known as dalams'.[23] The struggle was mainly of the unarmed poor, though the Naxalites did kill a few particularly vicious landlords.

Sympathetic critics have noted that this mode of operation continued till well into the 1980s — in the struggles in Adilabad against food shortages where common villagers would loot granaries and shops and redistribute food.[24] By 1985, however, as the state's retaliation, mostly on behalf of the rural rich, began, PWG strategy itself underwent a transformation. Gradually, mass struggles receded to the background and increasingly, their place was taken over by the *dalams*. However, it is not correct to say that this shift was entirely in response to state retaliation. It was increasingly becoming a short cut, for as the Naxalite legend spread, it struck fear among sections of the landlords — another form in which Naxalism then, as Maoism now, existed as rumour. Often then, mere putting up of the posters demanding a rise in wages, for example, could lead to a rise in wages. The rumour did its work.

The armed intervention of the Naxalites on behalf of the poor provided a counter, a backdrop against which the mass struggles were fought as the movement spread in other parts of Telengana. The arms of the Naxalites fulfilled a social function here that must be clearly recognised: they were a foil to the armed might of the upper/dominant caste landlords and local arms of the state that functioned, always in the interests of the former.

As distinct from the land and wage struggles of this period, the more recent growth of the Maoists, in say Northern Karnataka, was among tribals who were at the point of displacement with the formation of the Kudremukh National Park. Though many

---

[23] K. Balagopal, 'The Limits of Violence', *Himal*, vol. 20, no. 12, December 2007, p. 44.

[24] Ibid.

other organisations and movements have also been agitating in the area, holding road blockades, 'storming the forests', organising human chains and *satyagrahas*,[25] the attraction for the Maoists at least among a section of the poorest seems to have been quite evident.[26]

Here the conflict was not with the immediate oppressor, namely the landlord. Rather, the perceived threat was from a distant and impersonal force — the state and its officials — and the impending displacement that stared the adivasis in the face. Violence at least had the potential to make news and attract attention to their situation, where *satyagrahas*, nonviolent actions and human chains have been made completely ineffective and delegitimised by the state and the media.

In places like Lalgarh or in some other parts of Jharkhand too, the prospects of Maoist violence have often seemed liberating in the face of the most vicious nexus of forest contractors, local police and business interests. Elsewhere, I have written about how the state's repression of all legitimate democratic struggles has made the Maoist option look so attractive that it has ended up eliminating all intermediate spaces of mass politics.[27]

In the Dandakaranya region, which includes Gadchiroli and the districts of Dantewada, Bastar and Kanker — the current 'war zones' — there is yet another kind of state and state-sponsored violence that is destroying adivasi life.[28] Little surprise that the influence of the Maoists has phenomenally increased over the years. Here the most recent conflicts have been around the renewed drive by the state to industrialise and throw open the mineral-

---

[25] Mahatma Gandhi conceived of *satyagraha*, loosely translated as 'Soul Force', as a means of striving for truth and social justice through love, suffering, and conversion of the oppressor.

[26] See Muzaffar Assadi, 'Forest Encroachments, Left Adventurism and Hindutva', *Economic and Political Weekly*, vol. 39, no. 9, February 28 2004, pp. 882–85.

[27] Aditya Nigam, 'Democracy, State and Capital: The "Unthought" of 20th Century Marxism', *Economic and Political Weekly*, vol. 44, no. 51, 19 December 2009, pp. 35–39.

[28] Nandini Sundar, 'Bastar, Maoism and Salwa Judum', *Economic and Political Weekly*, vol. 41, no. 29, 22 July 2006, pp. 3187–92 (Chapter 34, this volume).

rich forest areas to corporations. This clearly involves large-scale displacement of the tribal population from their traditional habitats. Important steel companies like Essar Steel and Tata Steel have been in the process of acquiring prime agricultural land in the area.

Independent reports have testified to the fact that the entire process of land acquisition was being conducted at gun point. *Gram sabha* [local self-government] meetings, ostensibly meant to discuss and give or withhold consent to land acquisition, were a farce: instead of meetings, individuals were being called in to a room and made to sign their consent — or so the villagers felt.[29] Held under heavy-armed guard, these meetings were a farce in another sense. Legally, no outsiders are allowed to attend gram sabha meetings but the interested parties, namely Essar Steel officials — in the case of the report cited above — were inside, overseeing the process. As a reporter put it, the same procedure was being followed in other places: Gram sabha 'meetings' were held under the shadow of Section 144, while all outspoken critics of the acquisition would be under arrest.

Such stories have been filtering in from researchers in the field for some years now and it was clear that in this new phase of neo-liberal industrialisation, a new kind of violence was being unleashed on people who were to be dispossessed in order to make room for mining and industry. In many such cases (for example, Kashipur, Kalinganagar, Singur, Nandigram, Goa, Pen *tehsil* in Maharashtra),[30] mass struggles have been ongoing for some time.

Even apart from these well-known, emblematic names, there have been innumerable mass struggles throughout the country which have resisted the frenetic drive towards industrialisation and mining through displacement, often successfully.

However, it is equally true that often, in the face of the darkest state violence, the prospect of counter-violence holds great attrac-

---

[29] See Mitra, 'Red Alert in Chhattisgarh', p. 27.
[30] *Tehsil* is an administrative entity that performs local governmental functions.

tion for many people. Maoism seemed to provide precisely such a possibility.

It is important to understand this attraction that sustains the movement. It has become something of a liberal platitude to say that it is lack of 'development' that breeds Maoism and that if the adivasis have enough to eat and some basic facilities of education and health, there would be no Maoism. On the other hand, if the above instances are any indication, it would appear that it is rather the frenzied drive towards development that is breeding Maoist politics.

But to see the entire issue merely in terms of 'development' or its lack is entirely misleading. For, in the last instance, what is at stake here is neither 'development' nor 'industrialisation'; it is justice and democracy. What is at stake here is precisely the fact that in the name of development and industrialisation, the common resources of the country are being handed over to private corporations by displacing those who have inhabited that land for centuries. It is also worth remembering that even in the mass rebellions of the early colonial period that Guha studied, violence emerged as a last resort — when everything from petitioning to meetings failed.

It is important to understand that, at one level, it is not Maoism that is really at issue here, as both the state and the Maoist-aligned intellectuals would have us believe. It is really Indian democracy that is at issue. I have argued elsewhere that a deep split structures the Indian polity — a split between 'sovereignty' and the rule of the extraordinary and the impulse of democracy.[31]

The rule of the extraordinary, as evidenced in the rule through laws like [the] AFSPA[32] or [the] UAPA/POTA/TADA[33] on

---

[31] See Nigam, 'Democracy, State and Capital'.

[32] Armed Forces (Special Powers) Act.

[33] UAPA is the Unlawful Activities (Prevention) Act, POTA is the Prevention of Terrorist Activities Act, and TADA is the Terrorist and Disruptive Activities (Prevention) Act.

the one hand, and the indiscriminate manner in which violence becomes the primary mode of dealing with social struggles and dissent on the other, now structures our politics. Thus, even while Indian democracy can become the vehicle for the political rise of the dalits and lower castes, the seduction of violence at its peripheries always remains powerful for that is precisely where democracy gives way to a complete lawlessness of the Law.

৵

# 3

# The Maoist Insurgency in India: End of the Road for Indian Stalinism?

## Jairus Banaji
### Interview by Spencer A. Leonard and Sunit Singh*

✪

Given the considerable international interest in the progress of Naxalism on the Indian subcontinent, particularly in the wake of the 2008 Maoist revolution in Nepal, [here is an] interview with Marxist and historian Jairus Banaji conducted on 28 June 2010.

*Spencer Leonard (SL)*: The immediate occasion for our interview on the Naxalites or Indian Maoists is Arundhati Roy's widely-read and controversial essay, 'Walking with the Comrades', published in the Indian magazine *Outlook*. There Roy speaks of 'the deadly war unfolding in the jungles of central India between the Naxalite guerillas and the Government of India', one that she expects 'will have serious consequences for us all'.[1] Is Roy's depiction of the current situation accurate? If so, how have events reached such a critical state? How, more generally, does Roy frame today's Naxalite struggle and do you agree with this framing? Does the 'main contradiction', as a Maoist might say, consist in the struggle

---

* This article was previously published as 'The Maoist Insurgency in India: End of the Road for Indian Stalinism?', *The Platypus Review*, no. 26, 6 August 2010, pp. 1–3.
[1] Arundhati Roy, 'Walking with the Comrades', *Outlook*, 29 March 2010.

between the Naxalite aborigines on the one side, and, on the other, what Roy refers to as the combination of 'Hindu fundamentalism and economic totalitarianism'?[2]

*Jairus Banaji (JB)*: There certainly is a Maoist insurgency raging in the tribal heartlands of central and eastern India, much of which is densely forested terrain. The tribal heartlands straddle different states in the country, so at least three or four major states are implicated in the insurgency, above all Chhattisgarh, which was hived off from Madhya Pradesh in 2000. To the extent that there has been a drive to open up the vast mineral resources of states like Chhattisgarh and Orissa to domestic and international capital, there is the connection Roy points to. As a definition of the 'conjuncture' that has dominated the conflict since the late 1990s, she is clearly right.

But the Naxal *presence* in these parts of India has little to do with the factors she talks about. Naxalism, or Indian Maoism, goes back to the late 1960s. What distinguishes it as a political current from other communists in India is the commitment to armed struggle and the violent overthrow of the state. It is not as if the perspectives of Naxalism flow from the circumstances one finds in the forested parts of India. The question is why, after its virtual extinction in the early 1970s, the movement was able to reassemble itself and reemerge as a less fragmented and more powerful force in the course of the 1990s. To account for that we have to look to different factors than those Roy identifies.

The Naxalites have always seen the so-called 'principal contradiction' as that between the peasantry or the 'broad mass of the people' on one side and 'feudalism' or 'semi-feudalism' on the other. They have never abandoned this position since it was evolved in the late 1960s. The revolution has always been seen by them as primarily agrarian, except that now 'agrarian' has come to mean 'tribal', since their base is on the whole confined to the tribal or adivasi communities.

---

[2] Roy, 'Walking with the Comrades'.

*Sunit Singh (SS)*: Please explain the confluence that led to the formation of the Communist Party of India (Maoist) in September 2004, which united the Naxalite splinters, the People's War Group, and the Maoist Communist Centre? What explains the dramatic revivification of Naxalism after its decimation in the early 1970s and how do we understand the CPI (Maoist) as a political force today? To what extent has today's Naxalism changed from its predecessor, the original CPI (Marxist–Leninist) (CPI [M–L])?

*JB*: The key fact about the Naxals in the late 1990s and 2000s is that they began to reverse decades of fragmentation through a series of successful mergers. The most important of these was the merger in 2004 between People's War, itself the result of the People's War Group (PWG) fusing with Party Unity in 1998, and the Maoist Communist Centre of India (MCCI). That 2004 merger, which resulted in the formation of the CPI (Maoist), reflected a confluence of two major streams of Maoism in India, since People's War was largely Andhra-based and the MCCI had its base almost entirely in Jharkhand — the southern part of Bihar which also became an independent state in 2000. To explain the successful reemergence of Naxal politics in the 1990s, we have to see the [PWG] as the decisive element of continuity between the rapturous Maoism of the 1960s–70s, dominated by the charismatic figure of Charu Mazumdar,[3] and the movement we see today. The PWG was formally established in 1980 after some crucial years of preparation that involved a unique emphasis on mass work, the launching of mass organisations like the Ryotu Coolie Sangham, which was like a union of agricultural workers, and a 'Go to the villages' campaign that sent middle-class youth into the Telangana countryside. Kondapalli Seetharamaiah, its founder, was able to attract the younger elements because he was seen as more militant [as], among other things, he refused to have anything to do with elections. Following a dramatic escalation of conflict in Andhra Pradesh from 1985, [the] PWG was

---

[3] Charu Mazumdar (1918–72) was the first General Secretary of the CPI (ML).

able to build a substantial military capability and a network of safe havens for its armed squads (*dalams*) across state borders, in Gadchiroli in Maharashtra, directly north of the [Andhra Pradesh] border, and in the undivided region of Bastar or southern Chhattisgarh to the north and east. Regis Debray in his *Critique of Arms* points out that no guerrilla movement can survive without rearguard bases, by which he means a swathe of territory which it can fall back on with relative security in times of intensified repression.[4] This is exactly what happened with the squads that had been trained and built up in Andhra [Pradesh], or more precisely in Telangana, the northern part of the state, in the 1970s and 1980s. The recent flare up of conflict in Chhattisgarh is largely bound up with the intensified repression of 2005 that drove even more fighters into the Bastar region.

*SL*: In 'Walking with the Comrades', Roy sidesteps the question of Naxalite politics in favour of siding with a marginalised group, in this case 'the tribals'. Thus she states that '[some] believe that the war in the forests is a war between the Government of India and the Maoists . . . [they] forget that tribal people in Central India have a history of resistance that predates Mao by centuries'.[5] But she also wants to have it the other way around. For instance, this is what she says of the Naxalite leader and theoretician who first founded the CPI (M–L): 'Charu Mazumdar was a visionary in much of what he wrote and said. The party he founded (and its many splinter groups) has kept the dream of revolution real and present in India'.[6] What do you make of this curious political ambivalence respecting the actual Maoism (and the Marxism) of the Maoists? How do you understand Roy's anti-Marxist, tribal revolutionary romance?

---

[4] Regis Debray, *The Revolution on Trial: A Critique of Arms*, vol. 1, trans. Rosemary Sheed (New York: Penguin Books, 1977); Regis Debray, *The Revolution on Trial: A Critique of Arms*, vol. 2, trans. Rosemary Sheed (New York: Penguin Books, 1978).

[5] Roy, 'Walking with the Comrades'.

[6] Ibid.

*JB*: The idea that the tribals and the CPI (Maoist) share the same objective is ludicrous! What the tribals have been fighting against is decades of oppression by moneylenders, traders, contractors, and officials of the forest department — in short, a long history of dispossession that has reduced them to a subhuman existence and exposed them to repeated violence. A large part of the blame for this lies with the unmitigated Malthusianism of the Indian state. By this I mean that the adivasis have been consigned to a slow death agony through decades of neglect and oppression that have left them vulnerable to political predators across the spectrum, including the Hindu Right. As Edward Duyker argued in *Tribal Guerrillas*, the Santals whom the Naxal groups drew into their ranks in the late 1960s 'fought for specific concessions from the established rulers, while the CPI (Marxist–Leninist) fought for a new structure of rule altogether'.[7] There is a big difference between those perspectives! The tribal aim is not to overthrow the Indian state but to succeed in securing unhindered access to resources that belong to them, but which the state has been denying them. The tribal struggle is for the right to life, to livelihood and dignity, including freedom from violence and from the racism that much of India exudes towards them. The massive alienation of tribal land that has gone on even after Independence was something the government could have stopped if it had the will to do so. Today the huge mineral resources of the tribal areas are up for grabs as state governments compete to attract investment from mining and steel giants. But whatever the CPI (Maoist) might think, the vast majority of the tribals in India have no conception of 'capturing state power', since the state itself is such an abstraction except in terms of harassment by forest officials, neglect by state governments, and violence from the police and paramilitary.

---

[7] Edward Duyker, *Tribal Guerrillas: The Santals of West Bengal and the Naxalite Movement* (Oxford: Oxford University Press, 1987), p.102.

*SL*: In online comments on Roy's article posted on Kafila.org,[8] you responded to the preoccupation with tribals and Naxalites with a series of rhetorical questions:

> [w]here does the rest of India fit in? What categories do we have for them? Or are we seriously supposed to believe that the extraordinary tide of insurrection will wash over the messy landscapes of urban India and over the millions of disorganised workers in our countryside without the emergence of a powerful social agency . . . that can contest the stranglehold of capitalism . . . without mass organisations, battles for democracy, struggles for the radicalisation of culture, etc.?[9]

To this you add, 'in [Roy's] vision of politics, there is no history of the Left that diverges from the romantic hagiographies of Naxalbari and its legacies'.[10] Thus you contend that Roy's thinking is impeded by a kind of amnesia. How precisely does Roy's lack of awareness of and confrontation with the history of the Left compromise her ability to think through what it would mean to stage an emancipatory politics today? How does awareness of the history of the Left in the sense you intend differ from simply knowing the Left's past? What are the consequences we face because of the Left's widespread failure to work through its own history, a failure of which Roy is but a recent and prominent instance?

*JB*: Roy lacks any grasp of the history of the Maoist movement in India, which is why she can make that silly statement about Charu Mazumdar being visionary, when the bulk of his own party leadership denounced his 'annihilation' line as pure adventurism and a whole series of splits fragmented the movement within a year or two. Mazumdar also played a disastrous role in splitting the movement in Andhra [Pradesh] through a purely factional

[8] http://kafila.org (accessed on 23 February 2012).
[9] Nivedita Menon, 'Response to Arundhati Roy: Jairus Banaji', Kafila.org, 22 March 2010.
[10] Ibid.

intervention. Roy's background is clearly not the Left or any part of it, including the Maoists. What she does reflect is the disquiet generated, beginning in the 1990s, by the opening up of India to the world economy and the drive to create a globally competitive capitalism regardless of the costs this would inflict on workers and the mass of the population.

The Narmada Bachao Andolan (NBA), the campaign to halt the project to build a hydro-electric dam on the river Narmada, was the best example of the kind of 'new social movements' that emerged in India in response to issues that the party left simply failed to take up. It was not led by any party, was related to a major single issue, and had roots very different from those of the organised Left. It involved large-scale mobilisation of the communities uprooted by the dam, but the NBA of course was eventually defeated in the sense that it failed to stop the dam from being built despite massive resistance. The defeat of the NBA generated a profound disillusionment with the state of Indian democracy, which is strongly reflected in Roy's work — a kind of 'democratic pessimism'. The most extreme expression of this is the idea that India has a 'fake democracy', whatever that is supposed to mean.

But, let's get back to Roy's bizarre reference to Charu Mazumdar as a 'visionary' who 'kept the dream of revolution real and present in India'.[11] The fact is that the 'annihilation' line had led to such disastrous results by the end of 1971 that the majority of his own Central Committee denounced him as a 'Trotskyite' and expelled him from the party! Indeed, the majority of a 21-member Central Committee had withdrawn support from him by November 1970, and Satya Narayan Singh, who was elected the new general secretary, described his line as 'individual terrorism'. Even when the All India Coordination Committee of Communist Revolutionaries (AICCCR) transformed itself into a party in April 1969, leading figures of the early Maoist movement in India were unhappy with the decision and many stayed out.

---

[11] Roy, 'Walking with the Comrades'.

*SS*: Elaborate, if you will, on the exact form of struggle that Charu Mazumdar is associated with. What was the 'annihilation line' exactly?

*JB*: Like all Maoists, Mazumdar believed that the key social force in the revolutionary movement in India would be the peasantry. He adhered to the strategy mapped out in the deliberations between the CPI leadership and Stalin at the end of 1950, one product of which was a document known as the 'Tactical Line', which spoke of a two-stage revolution starting with a People's Democratic State that would be ushered in by an armed revolution. Of course, by then Liu Shao-ch'i was already recommending the Chinese revolution as a model for all colonial and 'semi-colonial' countries in their fight for national independence and people's democracy. This would have to be an armed revolution based on the peasantry and 'led by' the working class. The reference to the working class was purely rhetorical, since the leading class force in the revolution was the peasantry and the leadership of the working class existed in the more metaphysical shape of the party. The distinctiveness of Mazumdar's politics was that he seriously believed it would be possible to arouse revolutionary fervour among the 'masses' by annihilating 'class enemies' such as the *jotedars* or larger landowners of Bengal, by forming small underground squads that would selectively target landlords, state officials, and other representatives of the exploiting class and state apparatus. Such shock attacks, he felt, would create a decisive breach and unleash a mass response. Mazumdar believed that the revolution in India could be completed in this manner by 1975! The idea was that the masses were simply bursting with revolutionary zeal and only needed a catalyst. As I said, the line generated considerable dissent, not least because it abandoned any notion of mass work.

*SS*: So, when the Mazumdar faction constituted itself as the CPI (M–L) in April of 1969, what followed? Were other factions loyal to Peking folded into the new party? What happened to Mazumdar's Maoist critics, those who argued that their M–L [Maoist–Leninist] comrades had substituted terrorism for mass organisations such as trade unions and *kisan sabhas* [peasant unions]?

*JB*: The Chinese Communist Party backed away from the Naxals pretty early when they realised that they were talking about different things. There was a distinct loss of enthusiasm from Peking, and Mazumdar faced increasing criticism. Parimal Dasgupta, a prominent union leader, advocated the building of mass organisations among workers, and criticised the neglect of urban work by Mazumdar's followers. He disapproved of the idea of a clandestine party organisation because it would mean abandoning any effort to build broader class-based organisations. Another leading figure, Asit Sen, split on similar grounds. T. Nagi Reddy, the leading communist in Andhra Pradesh, disagreed with squad actions that were isolated from any mass struggle and simply substituted for it. He wanted a period of preparation and mass work before the armed struggle, but the group around him was disaffiliated from the AICCCR, the body that transformed itself into the CPI (ML) in April 1969. Even people who were otherwise close to Mazumdar like Kanu Sanyal and [Vempatapu] Satyam, a leader of the Srikakulam Movement, disapproved of individual assassinations based on conspiratorial methods by small underground squads. As Manoranjan Mohanty shows in his book *Revolutionary Violence* (1976), a unified M–L was already in decline by the middle of 1970, roughly a year after the party was proclaimed.[12]

*SS*: How should we view the embrace of revolutionary violence as a tactic by the Naxalites, both in its moment of inception in the late 1960s and in the present day by groups such as the People's Liberation Guerrilla Army? Does this zealousness signal radicalism, or helplessness? Can it be seen as the outcome of the defeat of the Left in previous decades, the consequence of the abandonment of a politics seeking to abolish alienated labour or, indeed, the abandonment of any explicitly labour-based politics?

---

[12] Manoranjan Mohanty, *Revolutionary Violence: A Study of the Maoist Movement in India* (New Delhi: Sterling Publishers, 1977).

*JB*: When the CPI (ML) was formed in 1969, its key function was seen as 'rousing' the peasant masses to wage guerrilla war. Mazumdar believed that the killing of landlords would 'awaken' the exploited masses. This, classically, was what Debray calls a 'politics of fervor', a politics in which revolutionary enthusiasm substitutes for ideas rooted in mass struggle and for the class forces that conduct those struggles.[13] But there were tendencies in Andhra that rejected this line and even went so far as to argue that, if the armed struggle were waged as a vanguard war, the people would become passive spectators. One writer quotes Nagi Reddy as saying, 'Their [the people's] consciousness will never rise. Their self-confidence will suffer'.

Today we can see that this is a vanguard war trapped in an expanding culture of counterinsurgency, and the most the CPI (Maoist) can do is flee across state boundaries and regroup in adjacent districts. What they have not been able to do and cannot do, given the nature of their politics, is consolidate enduring mass support in their traditional strongholds. In Andhra [Pradesh], where the fight against the Naxals has been most successful, from the state's point of view, the backlash has been ferocious and beyond all legal bounds. The state there has institutionalised 'encounter' killings, India's term for extra-judicial executions, on a very large scale, and trained special counterinsurgency forces to hunt down the Maoists. In Chhattisgarh the state has sponsored (armed and funded) a private lynch mob called the Salwa Judum, or 'Purification Hunt' in Gondi, the local language, that has emptied hundreds of villages by forcing inhabitants into IDP [internally displaced persons] camps where they can be easily controlled. In Chhattisgarh both sides have recruited minors. Both states have seen staggering levels of violence, with a pall of fear hanging over entire villages in Telangana, and the atomisation of whole communities in Dantewada. We should remember that it was successive waves of repression in Andhra Pradesh that drove the PWG squads into regions like Bastar and southern Orissa in the first place.

---

[13] Debray, *Critique of Arms*.

One consequence of the massive escalation of conflict from the late 1980s was a substantial weapons upgrade, a major increase in lethality. The Naxals have used land mines on an extensive scale, using the wire-control method, and inflicted heavy losses on the paramilitary. The crucial result of this conflict dynamic is a wholesale militarisation of the movement, a major break with the pattern of the late 1970s when they built a considerable base through mass organisations, in Telangana especially. The civil liberties activist K. Balagopal, who saw the movement at close quarters, became progressively more disillusioned as the military perspective took over and reshaped the nature of the PWG. In 2006, a few years before he died, he described the CPI (Maoist) as a 'hit and run movement', underlining precisely these features.[14]

*SS*: What kinds of affinities do the Naxalites share with other militant New Left groups?

*JB*: I would hardly call them 'New Left'. I think the best comparison for the CPI (Maoist) is Sendero Luminoso in Peru. Abimael Guzmán's idea that the countryside would have to be thrown into chaos, churned up, to create a power vacuum, is a mirror image of the CPI (Maoist) strategy. Guzmán called it *Batir el campo* — 'hammer the countryside'. The idea was to generate terror among the population and demonstrate the inability of the state to guarantee the safety of its citizens. That is how Nelson Manrique has described the strategy.[15] In the end it meant the assassination of village heads and increasing violence against the peasantry (from the Senderistas) that brought about their rapid downfall. A key element of the *Batir el campo* strategy was the systematic destruction of infrastructure with the aim of isolating whole areas of countryside from the reach of the state. The idea was that, effectively, these would become 'liberated zones'.

---

[14] Vijay Simha, 'Public Intellectuals in the Chair 7: "All the News we get is Killing and Getting Killed"', *Tehelka*, 21 January 2006.

[15] Nelson Manrique, 'The War for the Central Sierra', in Steve J. Stern (ed.), *Shining and Other Paths: War and Society in Peru, 1980–1995* (Durham, NC: Duke University Press, 1998), pp. 193–223.

The CPI (Maoist) have been pursuing a very similar strategy. The role they played in sabotaging the movement in Lalgarh bears a striking resemblance to the Sendero's interdictions against all forms of autonomous peasant organisation. The drive of the CPI (Maoist) to isolate the areas under their control from the rest of the country, to impose an enforced isolation on the tribal communities, is similar to the way the Senderistas worked in Peru. This is the deeper meaning of forced election boycotts. During elections the threat of violence is palpable. Sabotaging high-tension wires, goods trains, railway stations, roads, and bridges is simply the physical analogue of the election boycott. Interlinked with this is the continual execution of 'informers', a kind of exemplary punishment that is clearly designed to bolster a culture of fear in the CPI (Maoist) 'base', which breeds the kind of resentment that creates more informers. Balagopal was a powerful critic of these practices that, I suspect, were largely a product of the new leadership that took over the PWG in the early 1990s, when Kondapalli Seetharamaiah was driven out of the party.

A movement like this will obviously tolerate no dissent. There have been repeated instances of the different armed struggle groups murdering each other's cadre, sometimes over the course of years and on quite a large scale. Indeed, at least one reason for the merger between the PWG and the MCCI was the turf war between them in the years before 2004, when on one estimate they killed literally hundreds of each other's supporters. Left parties like the CPI (Marxist) have also seen their party activists being murdered, as if this is what the People's Democratic Revolution needs and calls for! I should add that the CPI (Marxist) is hardly blameless, either, since they have their own vigilante groups or terror squads called the 'harmads'.

*SS*: It seems to me that the perspectives of the Maoists do not arise from the circumstances of those they claim to represent, but are rather static in and of themselves. Party documents and Maoist 'theorists' seem capable of little more than the recycling of desiccated fragments of ideology.

*JB*: Maoist theory has a timeless quality about it. It deals with abstractions, not with any living, changing reality. The abstractions stem from the debates and party documents of the late 1940s and early 1950s, when the agrarian line emerged as an orthodoxy for the Left in countries like India. The Chinese Revolution was an incorrigible template and everything about India had to be fitted to that. Within India itself this generated what were called the 'Andhra Theses'. As I said, the deliberations with Stalin generated a series of documents that all factions of the undivided Communist party accepted to one degree or another. The Tactical Line mapped out the outlines of a strategy that flowed straight into the Naxalism of the late 1960s. Some of the terminology was changed, such that 'People's Democracy' became 'New Democracy', but these shifts in rhetoric marked no crucial differences. So there is a sense whereby the Naxalite split from the CPI (Marxist) did not represent a total break with orthodoxy within the Indian movement. It was the CPI (Marxist) that was poised ambiguously between the USSR and China.

*SL*: Embedded in this refusal of reality, this insistence upon rehashing empty abstractions, there seems an unmistakable retreat from the very project of Marxism. Am I wrong to see an elective affinity between Roy's insistence that the tribal people's impetus to resist comes from outside of capitalism, on the one hand, and on the other, the rhetoric popularised by Charu Mazumdar, which identifies the peasantry as the primary revolutionary class? Roy and Mazumdar seem to share the idea that the old anti-feudal struggle was and remains viable. Both exhibit a lack of interest in the question: what dynamics within capitalism point beyond themselves? While I agree that Arundhati Roy lacks any grounding in the history of the Left, there does seem to be common ground between the Naxals' nihilism and her romantic anti-capitalism.

In earlier comments you argued that Roy's 'democratic pessimism', as you referred to it, has led her to argue that the ongoing Naxalite insurgency 'is the best you can hope for'. Similarly, with respect to Maoists, you have suggested that, at bottom, they view those whom they claim to represent as 'cannon fodder', so that 'it is not hope but false promises that will lie at the end of the revolutionary road, aside from the corpses of thousands'.[16] To begin to understand what has brought together these two political streams — the new social movements and late Stalinism — is it fair to say that both, as expressions of political defeat and despair, are equidistant from what you have called 'the vision of the Communist Manifesto',[17] in which Marx argues that the task of the Communists is, as you put it, 'not to prevent the expansion of capitalism but to fight it from the standpoint of a more advanced mode of production, one grounded in the ability of masses of workers to recover control of their lives and shape the nature and meaning of production'?[18]

*JB*: There are different strands here. One is Roy's tendency to see Maoism as the passive reflection of a tribal separatism that is rooted in decades if not centuries of oppression of the adivasis. The trouble with this is that it makes the Maoists purely epiphenomenal. It is a reading that has little to do with politics in any sense. More to the point, Maoism simply is not a continuation or extension of tribal separatism. It is a political tendency committed to the armed overthrow of a state that is both independent (not 'semi-colonial') and democratic in more than a formal sense. Millions of ordinary people in the country have immense faith in democracy, despite the devastation that capitalism has inflicted on their lives — and when I say capitalism here I include the state as an integral part of it. The other strand relates to the way the Left has reacted to 'globalisation' and the isolationist stances that have flowed from that. This is not peculiar to the M–L groups — it is the soft nationalism of the whole Left and stems from the inability to imagine a politics that is both anti-capitalist and inter-nationalist in more than purely rhetorical ways. The rhetoric of

---

[16] Menon, 'Response to Arundhati Roy'.
[17] Ibid.
[18] Ibid.

anti-globalisation, which opposes the reintegration of India back into the world economy, forms the lowest common denominator of the entire Left in this country. The Indian Left today cannot conceive revolutionary politics apart from national isolationism. Everything is reduced to defending national sovereignty against the forces of international capitalism. But modern capitalism is not an aggregation of national economies, however much the working class is divided by country and in numerous other ways. It is hard to see how the movement in any one country, even one as big as India, can overthrow capitalism as long as it survives in the rest of the world. Paradoxically, it is the smallest countries, like Cuba and probably Nepal after the Communist Party of Nepal (Maoist) takeover, that survive best in these conditions!

*SS*: In its 1970 program, the CPI (M–L) claimed that 'India is a semi-colonial and semi-feudal country . . . the Indian state is the state of the big landlords and comprador-bureaucrat capitalists . . . and its government is a lackey of US imperialism and Soviet social-imperialism'.[19] What are the limitations of such a vision of anti-imperialism and of what might be referred to as the 'semi-feudal' thesis of capitalist development in India?

*JB*: The Naxalites haven't substantially modified their positions except to the extent that they realise that the forces they are up against today have more to do with capitalism than feudalism. So, if you read any of the interviews that they give to various publications like [the] *Economic and Political Weekly*, there are more references to capitalism than there used to be back in the 1970s. Back then it mattered much more whether you defined the social formation as mainly 'capitalist' or mainly 'feudal'. Today, it doesn't seem to matter as much, since it is obvious to everyone that India is capitalist. Perhaps this wasn't so obvious 40 years ago.

Most Naxalite groups still accept the four-class bloc, and the 'national bourgeoisie' is part of that alliance. This position derives

---

[19] http://cpindiaml.wordpress.com/about/programme-of-the-c-p-im-l/ (accessed on 29 February 2012).

from the 'semi-colonialism' line, and its only practical function today is that it can help the Naxalites justify a whole nexus of relationships necessary for the party to fund itself, largely by means of the tax imposed on traders and contractors. For example, in Jharkhand it is said that the Naxalites demand (and are paid) 5 per cent of all large, government-funded projects in the rural areas. If 'national bourgeoisie' is supposed to refer to the smaller layers of capital, those are of course among the worst exploiters of labour, as the appalling conditions in small-scale industry and so much of the caste violence in the countryside show. As for 'semi-feudalism', the irony is that the Naxalites' survival in the late 1970s and 1980s depended precisely on creating a base of sorts among the dalits and adivasis, the vast majority of whom have always been wage labourers. Indeed, the bulk of the population in India comprises the wage labouring and salaried classes, and a political culture that does not start from there — that does not start from the right to livelihood, the right to organise, and the aspiration to control resources and production collectively — is not going to make the least bit of difference. To keep referring to the land-poor and landless as a 'peasantry' shows how much one's political thinking is defined by dogma as opposed to reason.

*SL*: Earlier you spoke of how the Naxals, like the Sendero Luminoso, created a kind of ghetto around themselves. Is this the endgame of the politics launched in the 1960s and 1970s, which itself represented an inadequate response to what had become an increasingly bureaucratic and opportunistic Stalinism in India? How can the left politics that now trails this long legacy of failures reconstitute itself? But what about the larger question of intersecting the Naxalites, since many of these groups have been attracting some of the brightest young minds in India and, in this respect as in others, they represent a major impediment to the reemergence of the Indian Left? How do we break the appeal of political nihilism?

*JB*: As I said, the vast mass of India's population [consists of] wage labourers. They work in very different sorts of conditions from each other. So it's not as though we are dealing with a homogenous or unified class. One way forward as far as I can see is through the unions. Unions have been a stable feature of Indian capitalism and always survived despite repeated attacks. As a small but significant example of the kind of left politics we should be concentrating on, the New Trade Union Initiative (NTUI), which was formed around 2005, is an attempt to organise a national federation of all independent unions in the country, regardless of which sector they belong to. This started as an initiative of the unions themselves and it has seen slow but steady expansion all over the country and includes, for example, the National Federation of Forest Workers and Forest Peoples. There is also a great deal of rethinking on the Left, both against the background of the public relations disasters of the CPI (Marxist) in Singur and Nandigram and of course the violent internecine conflicts within the party left. There is a whole layer of the Left in India that can be called 'non-party', which is for that reason both more dispersed and less visible perhaps. It includes numerous organisations active in areas like caste discrimination and atrocities, communal violence, civil liberties, women's liberation, child labour, homophobia, tribal rights (e.g., the Campaign for Survival and Dignity), the Right to Food Campaign, campaigns against nuclear weapons and nuclear power, and many others. Dozens of Right to Information activists have been murdered, and there are numerous movements against displacement throughout the country. All of this reflects a different political culture from that of the left parties, more specialised and professional, also more autonomous, and the true agents of the churning of democracy that India is currently witnessing.

*SL*: How do you imagine the potential political expression of that? Does this take a party political form? How does it intersect parliamentary politics?

*JB*: If India could establish a workers' party on the Latin American model, then much of this non-party left would gravitate to that as its national political expression. But the culture of such a workers' party would have to be radically different from the sterile orthodoxies of the old left parties. It would have to be a massive catalyst of democratisation both within the Left itself and in society at large, encouraging cultures of debate, dissent, and self-activity, and contesting capitalism in ways that make the struggle accessible to the vast mass of the population. The fact is that the bulk of the labour force still remains unorganised into unions and a workers' party could only emerge in some organic relation to the organisation of those workers.

*SL*: What you are arguing then is that the Naxalites constitute a major impediment to the reinvention of the Left?

*JB*: Absolutely! That would be an understatement. The militarised Maoism of the last two decades is a politics rooted in violence and fear. Those in positions of leadership refuse to do any 'hard thinking' in Mao's sense. You cannot build a radical democracy, a new culture of the Left, on such foundations. The recent beheading of a CPI (Marxist) trade-union leader who refused to heed the *bandh* (strike) call of the CPI (Maoist) is a spectacular example of how profoundly authoritarian the Naxal movement has become under the pressure of its overwhelming militarism. When actions like that damage their credibility, they are explained away as 'mistakes'. But these continual 'mistakes' fall into a disturbing pattern. As a friend of mine [Nivedita Menon] wrote in [the] *Economic and Political Weekly*, 'the CPI (Maoist) is as little concerned about the lives of non-combatants as is the state'.[20]

ॐ

---

[20] Nivedita Menon, 'Radical Resistance and Political Violence Today', *Economic and Political Weekly*, vol. 44, no. 50, 12 December 2009, pp. 16–20.

# PART II

---

## REALITY AND EXPERIENCES

# 4

# The State at the Doorstep

## Smita Gupta*

✪

Can there be development in the time of Naxalism? Leaders like Digvijay Singh of the Congress and Bihar chief minister Nitish Kumar are of the view that the political executive must not play the role of the police and should instead address the problems of the people and ensure that they are not denied justice nor in any way exploited. The Bihar CM [Chief Minister] has been pumping resources for public works, education and health in the Naxal-hit Jehanabad district of the state. *Outlook* travelled through the district to make an independent assessment. Our reporters also visited two other districts — Lalgarh in West Bengal and Malkangiri in Orissa — two other Maoist hotspots. One stark contrast, in both places there's little in the name of development or governance on the ground.

◉

Under an unforgiving sun, old-timers in the village of Sikaria, a half-hour drive from Jehanabad town, talk about a time when they were scared to sleep at night. A time when this Kurmi-dominated village was a nerve-centre of left-wing extremism and the threat of retaliatory assaults by Bhumihar[1] landlords from the surrounding areas always hung in the air. Indeed, as recently as in November 2005,

---

* This article was previously published as 'The State at the Doorstep', *Outlook*, 26 April 2010.
[1] Bhumihar is a Brahmin Hindu community.

Maoists mounted a daring attack on the jail in Jehanabad town, escaping with 375 of their jailed colleagues.

But today, it's hard to believe those stories as you watch teen-aged girls from neighbouring areas cycle in for sewing classes. The Bihar government's 'Aapki Sarkar, Aapke Dwar' programme has provided every possible facility in the village — from a public health centre to a Madhya Bihar Gramin Bank to a computer centre and facilities to provide subsidised farm inputs as well as purchase of farm produce, even a veterinary centre. It has even made Sikaria an attractive destination for private enterprise. Last month, Anil Kumar Singh, a school teacher, decided to sink all his savings and start an English-medium private school here even though there's a government school not too far away. And in keeping with the new mood, the school has been named 'Ahimsa Vidyalaya' by its proud owner. Indeed, Sikaria has become symbolic of the changes sweeping through what were once 'the killing fields of central Bihar'. The bloody clashes that left hundreds dead in the districts of Jehanabad, Gaya, Arwal, Nawada and Aurangabad now seem a thing of a distant past.

How did all this happen? There are, of course, several reasons, but a major one is that when the JD(U)–BJP[2] combine came to power in 2005 — after 15 years of RJD [Rashtriya Janata Dal] rule — Nitish [Kumar], CM at last, decided to turn his attention to governance, to dovetail development with restoring law and order in the state. Senior civil servant H. C. Sirohi, who was home secretary then, recalls, 'I was sitting talking to the CM late into the night at the state guesthouse, shortly after he was sworn in. It was almost 2 am. I asked him, "What have you promised the people?" He said I have promised them nothing except that I will bring governance to their doorstep. And that was how the idea for the 'Aapki Sarkar, Aapke Dwar' programme was born'. On 5 January 2006, he set out for Sikaria in Jehanabad to launch it.

Indeed, development has become key to the Bihar government's policy of tackling Maoist violence, which has now virtually disappeared from central Bihar. All extreme left-wing activity

[2] Janata Dal (United)– Bharatiya Janata Party combine.

has been pushed to the borders, to the districts edging the hilly, forested tracts of Jharkhand in the south and Nepal in the north. In the budget [for the year 2010], deputy CM and Finance Minister Sushil Kumar Modi says money has been set aside to saturate 67 panchayats in 24 blocks of the seven districts most affected by Maoist activity with development work. 'We are also creating a network of roads in central Bihar. We have set aside ₹ 258 crore to lay 593 km of roads', he says.

But even with all this, the Bihar government is acutely aware that development by itself cannot counter Maoist violence. Bihar DGP Neelmani told *Outlook*, 'We are under no illusions . . . the armed Maoist squads have to be neutralised'. A special State Task Force like Andhra's Greyhounds has been created for the purpose.

That said, the key word for the state police now is 'selective action' to ensure that rights violations are minimised. 'We try and act only when we have specific inputs about armed assemblage. We have succeeded in arresting top leaders through selective action. We can't alienate the civil society as only they can provide us with intelligence', says additional DGP [Director General of Police] P. K. Thakur. In 2009, 34 top Maoist leaders, including area commanders, were arrested. Another 18 had been nabbed till 12 April [2010]. Anti-Maoist operations have also become more humane and arrested Maoists are now treated as political prisoners. 'Earlier', says Modi, 'they would be tortured, legs chained in "danda bedi", so that they couldn't run. We ended this in 2005, sending out a very positive message'.

Of course, these aren't the only reasons for the Maoist decline in central Bihar. In the RJD years (1990–2005), then CM Laloo Prasad Yadav had turned a blind eye to what was happening, leaving the Bhumihar-led Ranvir Sena to battle the Maoists. The first signs of improvement came during the last years of Laloo's successor, Rabri Devi, but this was partly because after Bihar's division, Maoists saw Jharkhand as a more fertile ground for their activities, monetarily and logistically. The sea change came after the JD(U)–BJP came to power. The police and administration were given a free hand in arrests and action — against both the Ranvir Sena as well as the Maoists. Long-pending trials relating to the various massacres were also speeded up.

The caste factor also came into play: many members of the erstwhile People's War which dissolved and became part of the united
CPI (Maoist) in Bihar in 2004 were Kurmis.[3] With a Kurmi CM
now, there was another route to justice. Indeed, the fact that Sikaria
was chosen as the starting point for the 'Aapki Sarkar' programme
was deliberate, says a resident: 'It's essentially a Kurmi village, and
it sent out a message to the entire community'. Simultaneously,
since the Bhumihars had also backed the JD(U)–BJP combine,
they too decided to put the Ranvir Sena in cold storage.

Still, despite the positive trends, things are far from picture
perfect. It's said that the Maoists are merely 'inactive' for the
moment. In Imamganj in Arwal district, a local businessman
speaks in hushed whispers about them waiting in the aisles, hoping
Nitish will lose the next polls. A 'retired' Maoist area commander
who came out of jail a year ago confirms that his comrades are
just biding their time. How is it, we ask, that the Maoists are not
blocking the development? 'Of course, they are', he says, 'they are
charging huge levies from contractors engaged in public works'.
DGP Neelmani admits it's extremely difficult to cut off the money
supply to the Maoists. And it cuts both ways. 'If we can't give protection to those from whom they are extorting money, we can't
punish them also. We can't protect every businessman'.

But it isn't just the Maoists who are extracting their pound of
flesh. Across Jehanabad and Arwal districts, locals say while the
free hand to the administration to tackle law and order has brought
peace to the area, it's also increased corruption. 'More money is
being spent on development so there's more room for corruption',
a local teacher says, adding, 'it shows in the quality of some of the
development works too'. Indeed, the irony is that while a village
like Sikaria is booming today, the eight-kilometre stretch from
the village to Karauna is patchy and potholed. The challenge
before Nitish Kumar now is: he's brought peace but can he end
the corruption, make his governance drive more meaningful?

৵

---

[3] Kurmi is a Hindu agricultural community.

# 5

# A Really Dark Corner

*Madhavi Tata**

✪

Malkangiri district, in Orissa, is back of the beyond. It borders both
Andhra Pradesh and the Dandakaranya region of Chhattisgarh.
Of its six lakh population, 80 per cent belong to the Bonda, Bidai,
Gadwa, Poraja, Kumbhar, Kamaar, Kondh and Karia tribes, and
live on the margins — no roads, no electricity, no hospitals, no
drinking water supply, and a very poor public distribution system.
No wonder this hilly, forested region has been a Maoist hotbed for
decades. The police and the special forces call this forbidding area
the AOB (Andhra–Orissa border) with the sense of a place they'd
rather not be in. The locals have never seen any government working
for them; and therefore, the Maoists are both their government and
their police. A senior police officer says at least 30,000 tribals of the
district openly support the Maoists; the rest do so tacitly.

The hardship is all too evident in villages like Guntawada. Many
young men, like Kanakaraju and Indrakarama, work as casual
labourers at APGenco's [Andhra Pradesh Power Generation Corporation Limited] Upper Sileru power project. When they come
home, they bring kerosene the supervisor hands out and use it to
light lamps. His generosity means the world to them: the village
has never had electricity.

In village after village in this district, this dark irony repeats
itself. Inaccessibility and deprivation are the norm.

---

* This article was previously published as 'A Really Dark Corner', *Outlook*, 26
April 2010.

In Kankaraipoda village, Lobo Khilo, Undartai Khilo and Dhalai Khara complain that few among them have ration cards. They grow some paddy but mostly work as labourers with private contractors, who never pay on time. 'Malaria is a constant companion in summer and we lose many workdays', says Lobo. 'The nearest hospital is in Chitrakonda, about 15 km away. When we fall ill, it is better to stay put than walk that far'.

A crumbling two-room house serves as an *anganwadi* and school in a village of Korukonda block. *Sabhiye padhantu, sabhiye badhantu* (Let's all study, let's all grow), it says on the wall. But this Oriya-medium school with classes till Std V has only one teacher. His teaching methods are as erratic as his schedule. Not a single child can elaborate on what has been taught in school. Any question, and they lapse into their tribal speech.

In village no. 9 of Korukonda block (many villages are known by just numbers), Boloma Khilo nurses a newborn boy as her daughter Rosmita, aged three, clings to her. Anganwadi workers supply a kilo of ragi–jowar powder per month for the child, but that has stopped of late. In Bhongur resettlement colony, Ordiba Khara says he gets rice and kerosene on a ration card, but the sugar is taken away. 'They ask us why you need sugar when you don't drink tea?' he says.

In the 1960s, the Balimela dam was built in this remote region, further cutting off the area from parts bordering what is now Chhattisgarh. It is here the Maoists have found a natural fortress. The 150-odd villages here, home to some 25,000 adivasis, are accessible only by boat. Officials avoid these '*narako* [hellish] islands'. 'Obviously, the government doesn't want to do anything for the tribals', says Videshi Goud, coordinator of the Malkangiri Adivasi Sangh. 'Nor does it want to give them their rights'.

Passing through Doraguda village, one notices a huge poster put up by the Adivasi Mahila Viplava Sangham near a small memorial to a 'martyred' Maoist. Intelligence officials say that in 2009–10, the maximum Maoist recruitments took place in Malkangiri. Most of those who joined up were Bondas.

Vineet Brijlal, SP [Superintendent of Police], Visakhapatnam, who earlier served with the Greyhound special troops in Malkangiri, says there must be 300–400 armed cadres in this Maoist bastion.

Some 200, he says, could be called 'semi-underground' cadres — those who lead normal lives till called upon to 'do duty' or fight. The support network, of course, runs into thousands. It's not as if there's nothing being done. In Badpada block, for instance, there is unusual activity: Joyaram Khara, a sarpanch, is supervising the laying of electricity lines in Pabliguda village. The tribals are ecstatic. Land *pattas* are also being prepared by officials. Next on the villagers' wish list is ration cards for all. Khara says only eight of the 108 sarpanches in the district do any work. Evidently, he counts himself among them.

Even so, he says, there's only so much the sarpanches can do, given Malkangiri's invisibility to the Orissa government. 'Chief minister Naveen Patnaik last visited the district in 2008, to inaugurate a bridge', Khara says. 'I've never seen an MP [Member of Parliament], MLA [Member of the Legislative Assembly] or minister touring this area. Projects under NREGA [National Rural Employment Guarantee Act] are implemented poorly, if at all'.

Funds allocated for the region remain on paper, says Simhadri Jhansi, state president of the Rythu Coolie Sangham, an NGO working for tribal rights. 'The reason tribals here tend to be sympathetic to the Maoists is because there is no governance here', he says.

The backwardness of Malkangiri and the constant alienation of the tribals from government serve the Maoists well. It brings them considerable support. No wonder they were able to ambush and kill 33 well-trained Greyhound troops on the Sileru river near Balimela in June 2009. The remoter parts of the district, where the Maoists operate, are heavily mined. Policemen steer clear of combing operations — it's too dangerous, and best left to trained troops like the Greyhounds. But even they can't do much without local intelligence, which the hostility of the tribals to government officials and police denies them. 'Most of the villagers are Maoist supporters. People see the Maoists regularly, so it is them they trust', says a top police officer. 'We can't risk lives by sending our force into these villages'.

ॐ

# 6

# Life in the 'Liberated Zone': Inside Abujmarh the Mythic Citadel

*Tusha Mittal**

✪

*Abujmarh was portrayed as the military HQ of the deadly Maoist insurgency. After an arduous week-long trip, Tusha Mittal discovered a totally different picture.*

On the morning of 15 March, a messenger arrived on the run in Jatwar, a remote village on a stony mountain slope in Chhattisgarh, with news of marching troops. A black radio, a 12-bore double-barrelled gun, a whistle, a blue plastic sheet — all his material possessions by his side — 21-year-old Nilesh was asleep under a thatched roof. A Maadia tribal, he had joined the Maoist Jan Militia three years earlier. He describes it as a 'people's squad to protect the village'.

The morning of 15 March was his first call to battle. The news was that 3,000 armed men were headed his way. On cue, Nilesh slung his rifle over his shoulder — a family hand-down from his grandfather who had used it to shoot birds — put whistle to mouth, and began the evacuation of all 30 huts in Jatwar.

As Nilesh led the villagers to a safer spot in the jungle, the sounds of firing began. This would be soon followed by the sound of mortars and grenades. The leaf cover of Jatwar's thatched roofs would be snuffed out by the propellers of an IAF helicopter. There

---

*This article was previously published as 'Life in the "Liberated Zone": Inside Abujmarh The Mythic Citadel', *Tehelka*, 12 May 2012.

**Plate 6.1:** Surviving against All Odds — Aidma Kaher was Threatened by SPOs Involved in Operation Hakka to Keep Mum or Else...

*Source*: All photographs in the chapter are by Tarun Sehrawat.

would be bloodstains by a tree where a CRPF jawan tried to hide, dodging bullets from across the river. By afternoon, Jatwar would become the epicentre of Operation Hakka: Abujmarh would have been breached by the Indian State.

In a world precision-mapped to an inch by Google and GPS [Global Positioning System], in a world where men have scaled the highest peak and dived in personalised submarines to its depths, it is difficult to imagine a place that has any mystery for the contemporary imagination. But until barely a few weeks ago, Abujmarh — the almost mythic citadel of the banned CPI (Maoist) in India — was such a place.

For decades, no one from 'mainstream' India had ever been inside the forbidden grove: 6,000 sq. km of forest, sudden streams and surging mountains. In that time, Abujmarh — which means 'the unknown hills' in Gondi — had swelled in people's minds into a place imbued with both fascination and dread. Be it the State, paramilitary forces, social activists or even seasoned jour-nalists doing the conflict beat, everyone was accustomed to point in its general direction and speak of it in whispered tones. No one knew what to expect there. It was India's only fully 'liberated

**Plate 6.2:** Splendid Isolation — A Hut in Kodenar Village Deep Inside Abujmarh

zone'. A place where the 'writ' of the State had ceased to exist altogether and the reign of the Maoists had begun.

So deep was the fear of the unknown that when the Indian forces stormed Abujmarh on 15 March in an assault codenamed Operation Hakka, they went in with sophisticated weapons like Swedish Carl Gustav rocket launchers and under-barrel grenade launchers. For several months before, the forces had sent drones to fly over the mountains and bring back satellite images. The dark patches in the hills that the machines brought back, they took to be armed fortifications and trenches: a citadel worthy of India's 'greatest internal security threat'.

It is a measure of both the complexity and the pathos of the Maoist-tribal crisis in India — and the inadequate narrative that

**Plate 6.3:** Basic Necessities — A Tribal Woman Goes About Her Daily Chore

has built up around it — that when Operation Hakka actually got off the ground, and the troops entered the great unknown, what they found in Abujmarh was not the military HQ [headquarters] of a deadly and well-organised insurgency but scraggly villages and forlorn clusters of leaf and bamboo huts. Their biggest recovery seems to have been an inkjet printer. 'We had 13 encounters with vardiwale Naxal', says Narayanpur SP [Superintendent of Police] Mayank Srivastav. In one, 'a Naxal running away with a laptop' was possibly injured. 'We could not get the laptop but we got the printer'.

Both *The Indian Express* and *Hindustan Times*, which reported the forces' official account of entering Abujmarh some weeks ago, mentioned this contrast between expectation and reality. But it is not the irony of their misplaced idea of Abujmarh that seemed to have caught the forces' attention. It is the psychological victory of having entered it.

'Our most significant achievement is that we have reached a stage where we can deploy 3,000 troops and prepare them so well that they can return unharmed', says T. G. Longkumer, Bastar IG [Inspector General]. 'There was a time when we lost 76 jawans in an encounter. We have grown since then. We are more secure now. We felt ready for such a challenge. There was always a view that the forces can't enter this area. It was very important to dispel it. We wanted to break the myth of Abujmarh'.

But if the old bogey of an impenetrable military fortress is replaced only by a monochromatic idea of frail and helpless villages, the myth of Abujmarh will not have been broken: it will only have been replaced.

The ambiguous story of the Maoist insurgency and India's tribal crisis cannot be understood properly unless Abujmarh is really breached the way it needs to be: with layered understanding. For the truth is, Abujmarh is as much a physical place as a state of mind, a shifting line, a struggle for 'area domination' between contesting stories.

As Dada, a Maoist area commander in Abujmarh, says to *Tehelka*, 'We do not have a fixed military base. We carry everything on our shoulders. Wherever the party goes, that becomes our stronghold'.

Where then is Abujmarh really?

*Jan Yudh.* People's War. A piece of white paper nailed to the bark of a tree brings our bikes to a screeching halt. 'Ordinary villagers of the people's war zone, teachers, children, elders and others', the paper says, 'this is an appeal from the CPI (Maoist) party of India. We are informing you that in the mountains, streams, villages and fields of Marh, in various places near the roads, explosive tunnels, mines and booby traps have been laid. Big holes with spikes have been dug across Marh. Travel cautiously. Do not venture into the jungles. Any resulting fatalities will not be our responsibility. The Indian Army, CRPF [Central Reserve Police Force] and Cobra Force is ready to enter our Marh. That is why we have been compelled to do all this. This notice is being given to you from 15 April 2012'.

It is 16 April now. Exactly a month since Operation Hakka and Day 1 of our own journey into Abujmarh. *Tehelka* photographer Tarun Sehrawat and I avoid each other's eye. The question of backtracking cannot be voiced. We have no idea what lies ahead. We have packed our bags with 12 bottles of Bisleri, some Maggi noodles and biscuits. As we left Narayanpur town the night before, a local contact stuffed half a bottle of Blender's Pride whiskey into our hands: 'It will numb the pain', he said.

This morning, we had set off early from Kondagaon town, snucked undetected past the CRPF camp at Kukrajor, the last policed checkpoint in the area, and kept riding in the general direction of the hills. We wonder now if this tree bark, with the paper warning fluttering in the wind, is where Abujmarh begins.

We ride on. The road slowly peters out into mud paths, criss-crossed by streams. The slopes become steeper, the sal forest thicker. We keep climbing. Hours pass. There are no mines, no explosives, no booby traps. We start to wonder: was the notice merely a psychological tactic? (*Kuch cheez dikhane ke liye hote hai*, Rajesh, our Maoist guide, would laugh later into the journey ['Some things are only for show'].)

As yet though, we have no guides. We are riding through a landscape of fragile, threadbare beauty. Everywhere, the palate is red mud and stony brown. The lime green forests have a tropical feel but never seem to acquire any real density. The most colourful things are Maadia graves — shreds of torn sarees swaying from tress to mark a life once lived. The village huts are all made of leaves and thin bamboo reed.

Suddenly we arrive at what seems to be the Abujmarh equivalent of India Gate. An iron and steel archway boldly declares: *Bharatiya Sena Vapas Jao, Bastar vasi bahari nahi hai. Jung mat lado* (Indian Army go back. Bastar residents are not outsiders. Don't fight a war with us). On the other side of the gateway, a call to arms: *Bastar ke yuvao, sarkar ke najais jang ke khilaph jan yudh mein shamil ho jao* (Youth of Bastar, unite against the illegal war waged by the government).

After this, we occasionally pass clusters of stepped red monuments crowned by a hammer and sickle: Maoist homage to martyrs. Suddenly our bike sputters and stops. We stop at a village en route for help. An old man speaks in whispers. 'I wanted a forest patta but the party has warned us against taking any help from the government', he says. 'Many men have disappeared from this village. There is no count of the number of people the party has killed'.

The man's account is a jolt. We had expected our first interaction in the party's own stronghold, the crucible of the revolution, to ring with fulsome praise for the Jantam Sarkar. Had their dream vision soured already or were we not in Abujmarh yet?

We continue on the endless red dirt track. As dusk falls, we start to worry. No one is waiting for us. We have no point of contact. We had expected to be stopped at Maoist checkpoints by Maoist sentries. Instead, we are just strangers riding into the darkness, hoping the party will find us. There is no way we can reach the interior villages unless the party sends escorts. No villager is willing to volunteer taking outsiders into Marh without their permission. In the distance, on the mountaintops, a fire line appears. Villagers are clearing the forest to plant the monsoon crop.

Finally, we are compelled to stop. It is too dark to go on. But by sheer accident, it seems we have arrived somewhere. The men in the village we stop at have radios and country-made weapons. The radio is sure sign of party membership in these parts. These men are part of the Sangam — the party's mass front at the village level. We send word.

A short while later, we are met by the local Maoist Gram Adhyaksh — the Maoist equivalent of a sarpanch. A frail scrawny man, he asks us to write a letter explaining our intent and asks to check our bags. We had evaded the CRPF's search. It is strange to submit to this. I ask for a woman cadre to do the search. There are none around, so an old man is deputed instead. Turns out, the only thing that interests him is our medicine. He has a wracking cough. The Adhyaksh too is a hunchback and suffers from crippling pain. He cannot risk going to town for treatment and wants medicines too.

The Gram Sarkar Adhyaksh is a key piece of the Maoist hierarchy and strategy. Twenty seven gram sarkars make up one area. Each area has a committee with seven heads overseeing seven departments: Economic, Military and Security, Justice and Law, Farming, Health, Public Relations, and Culture. An area committee can have both uniformed and non-uniformed party members. Non-uniformed members are considered part time. They can switch between home and field and have a domestic life. Uniformed members have no permanent home and are always in the field, and on the move. They can either be part of the People's Government or the military wing, People's Liberation Guerrilla Army (PLGA). There is an ongoing debate in the party whether the Sarkar and PLGA should dress differently. The party decides who will work full time or part time. 'We can't have everyone in the party dress in uniform or villagers will think all the decisions are being taken by an entity other than the Janta', says an area committee member. 'Part-timers interact more with the "janta" and therefore have more influence on the public'. Anyone who pays [₹] 5 annually to the party fund qualifies as the 'janta'.

*Paanch rupay do aur umeedvari pakki*, he describes. When questioned on what benefits the ₹ 5 brings to villagers, he says after a pause, 'While there is no externally visible benefit, it gives them so much power that they can voice their opinion anywhere'. This 'janta' are the citizens of the Maoist State; it is in their name that the Maoists run the Jantam Sarkar. These are people who vote in the Jan Adalat and form its mass front.

For the Indian State, one of the key challenges of confronting the Maoist insurgency is to distinguish between ordinary tribal and ideologue. In Abujmarh, it is almost impossible to do so.

The presence of a Ramakrishna Mission in the village refracts that riddle further. This ashram is one of five such in Abujmarh. Clearly, Abujmarh has not been as impregnable as one imagined. We are told to spend the night there. As we step inside, we find kids in blue uniforms singing songs that tell of a united nation: *Hind desh ke nivasi, sabhi jan ek hai. Rang, roop, vesh, bhasha chahe anek hai.* There is a Maoist memorial visible through the window. The chorus of the kids' voices transcends the idea and reality of Abujmarh. The distinction of where the village ends and party begins gets infinitely more complicated.

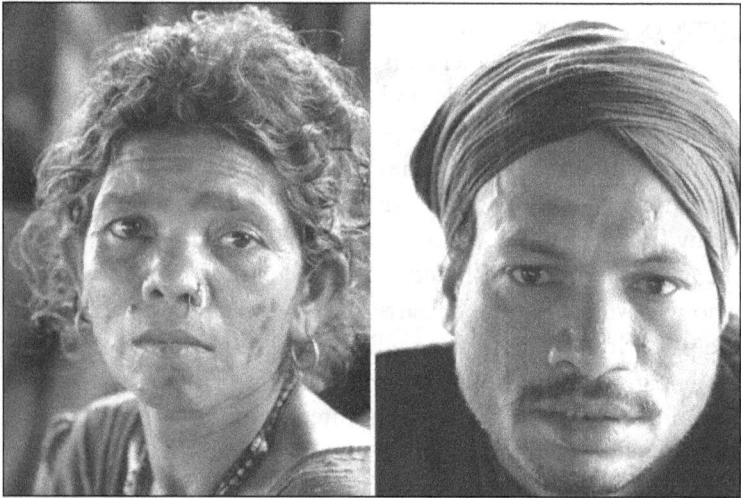

**Plate 6.4:** Living in Fear — Aite Gota's Husband was Killed by the State Forces; Sunil Vadde, a Farmer in Gambhir

Over the next six days and nights, Sehrawat and I trek 40 strenuous kilometres on foot to four villages — Toke, Kacchapal, Kodenar and Jatwar, deep inside Abujmarh. Each of these villages vividly demonstrates a sad trick of history: it is true that the Maoist insurgency raises just questions about the feudal and oppressive nature of the Indian State, but its own 'liberated zone' is no song to freedom itself. The very idea of dissent itself seems alien here. Tribals from these villages cannot venture into the towns. If they stay too long for business or even for medical help, they become suspect. The Maoist sarkar thinks they have become police informers. Returning becomes fraught with danger.

Sometimes, this cleft stick can take on tragic proportions. In 2007, villagers say Sajnu Vadde, a tuberculosis patient, left Marh for treatment in Narayanpur town. When he returned, he was tried in a Jan Adalat for attending a police meeting, found guilty and sentenced to death. Sonu, a young man in Kacchapal, who was shot by the forces in the leg during Operation Hakka, is limping around. The bullet is still in his body a month later. The party tried treating him but even a surgical cut two inches deep could not locate the bullet. But Sonu cannot risk going to the city.

Uncomfortably, stories like this abound. In 2000, Mangru, a sarpanch in Kacchapal, abruptly left his village. He is currently the chairperson of the Abujmarh Development Authority but he cannot return to Marh. Sonnu Gotta's story is even starker. Gotta and her husband had left Marh with a sick child. 'We ended up staying in Narayanpur for four months. After that, we were too scared to return', she says. 'We are still Maadias but we like it in the town. The Maoists have called us back, but here we use our minds and make our own decisions. Farming was such a tough life. It's so much easier to be paid to be a sarpanch here'. Gotta fought on a BJP ticket and won. It is from this pool that Special Police Officers have been recruited. There are at least 12 from Abujmarh. In a violation of Supreme Court orders, villagers confirmed that many guided the forces in during Operation Hakka.

But all of this comes later. On Day 2, we just wait endlessly to hear from the party. The men go for a swim in a nearby pond. I go to the anganwadi instead. Sukanya Salam, 22, the government anganwadi worker here, wears a sari and talks Hindi but is a Maadia from Gadpa village. I ask her what Abujmarh means to her. 'It's that area where people don't know anything, don't know how to talk Hindi or live cleanly. That area is Abujmarh', she says. But isn't she from Abujmarh too, I ask. 'My village is by the road', she says, 'we had a government school. But in the interiors, they don't know how to live'. To her, the Maadia customs seem foreign, a thing of the past. Adivasis in Marh just live together, she says. Once they have a few babies, if they are rich enough to afford it, they get married. The ceremony involves sitting together and pouring milk over cloth draped around the two. She wouldn't like to get married that way. *Mujhe poora tel chadhane hai* (I want to do the whole oil and ritualistic fire thing).

Finally, at 4 pm, word comes. We have been given permission to move interior. The Adhyaksh offers us three guides. They urge that we leave right away. We have to leave our bike behind. We fill our bottles. From here on, there are only goat paths through mountain and stream. And no more hand pumps.

The trek to Toke — the first village to be surrounded by Cobra battalions — is very hostile. As evening falls, we walk with torches along steep slopes in single file, two guides in front, one at the rear. The night is moonless but brilliant with a million stars. Suddenly, one side of the track gives way to a steep ravine. Sometimes, it is impossible to spot a flat stone to balance on. After my first fall, I reach for a bamboo stick and don't let go for the rest of the road ahead. The silence and glow of fireflies is broken only by our guides laughing at us. They race ahead as if this were a shining tar road.

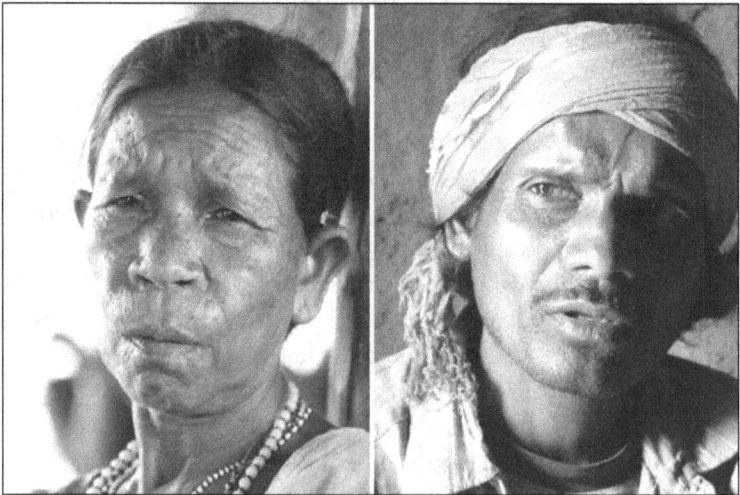

**Plate 6.5:** Horror Stories — Mase Pave's House was Ransacked by the Forces; Aidma Vadde's Son was Beaten up

At one point, two more men with guns join our convoy. They are our fortification against wild bears.

After over four hours of walking, we reach Toke. It is pitch dark but we finally feel as if we have entered Abujmarh. Perhaps, this has something to do with the disappearing roads, with the idea that a journey into Marh must test one's endurance.

Our first sensory experience of Toke is the sight of children in uniform peering at us from behind the mud walls of a two-room school. Some are sorting rice in pools of blue torchlight. Here again is a government-run ashram deep inside Abujmarh. We begin to question the hyperbole back home of the unbreached bastion. In a moment, there is a roll call followed by the slow recitation of the Gayantri Mantra. A chicken is slaughtered for us. The school has a solar lamp. We eat by its light, then drag our cane beds outside and sleep under the open sky. It's the last night we will have a bed to sleep on.

At dawn, I wake to a Maoist memorial amid empty fields. Suddenly, I have a feeling of being watched. I look to my right and find armed men, standing alert, looking on. Had they been guarding us all night? Attempts to speak with them fail. There are instructions from the party not to give any interviews. We're told the 'Raman Singh equivalent' of the Jantam Sarkar would like to speak with us directly. Until that happens, no one else has clearance to give an interview.

In the morning light, Toke, a village of 37 huts, is again a disorienting mix of the unusual and the ordinary. A group of Adivasis huddle in a circle to drink Sulphi, an alcoholic extract from the Sulphi tree. Others sit around weaving bamboo baskets. Two Jan Militia members sporting .303 rifles saunter into the school and carry away sacks of PDS [Public Distribution System] grain. But there seems to be no tension over this. Children in government school uniforms mill around. It is difficult to tell where the *Dilli ka sarkar* segues into the *Jan sarkar*. The masterji at Toke wears jeans, a watch and is surprisingly urban. He is from Narayanpur town. He didn't ask for Toke. The Indian government deputed him there.

As we talk, our guide Rajesh finally opens up too. He is a thin, cheery 23-year-old, with a slight moustache. He studied at a public school in Narayanpur town till Class VIII. Then his father, who had been part of the PLGA squad for 20 years, pulled him into the party.

'I came home for holidays once and my father didn't let me return', says Rajesh. 'I was disappointed but my father refused to budge. I didn't know much about *rajneeti* (politics) then. Now I understand my father's decision. Now I know how Adivasis live and suffer. I'm glad to be working for them'.

Rajesh is a teacher as well in one of the party's seven functioning schools in Abujmarh. Rajesh teaches math through a Gondi song; his history lessons focus on indigenous rebellions like the Bhumkal tribal revolt of 1910; then there are classes on *rajneeti* and Hindi. The party is experimenting with English, but the teachers are unable to go beyond the alphabet. Rajesh's favourite movie is *Sherdil*. In an epiphanic moment, we realise he means the Mel Gibson-starrer *Braveheart*. He has watched it at a Maoist camp.

There are other things he has done in Maoist camps: he has been part of a Jan Adalat that sentenced three women from Kawalnar village to death. They were accused of trying to bring a contingent of 500 forces into Abujmarh and carrying poison. The poison was

**Plate 6.6:** The Long Walk — Villagers from Hikonaar and Godelmarka Cross the Abujmarh Jungle

tested on a hen: it died. 'If we let such people live, our lives would become more dangerous than it already is', says a Maoist cadre. In the journey ahead, it will be difficult to reconcile this Rajesh, who beams with pride at the spot where the PLGA squad shot a CRPF jawan in Jatwar last month, with the jaunty Rajesh who sings *Pardesi pardesi, jaana nahin* as we walk through the jungle; offers me his blanket on a cold night and teases us about drinking water from streams where buffaloes are bathing. But the unflinching talk of summary deaths through jan adalats is routine for him and the other guides who join us later. It is just one face of Maoist governance.

A little later, as we gather the villagers at the Ghotul — a sort of village community centre — and ask about Operation Hakka, the flip narratives of oppression begin.

How the paramilitary forces beat Aite Gota's husband to death; how Keya Dhurva's house was burnt; how Goya Dhurva's chickens were stolen and cooked; how 40 kg of free rice that had cost a three-day walk to Kukrajhor base camp and a ₹ 200 tractor ride was seized; how others' cooking utensils were smashed, money was robbed, *imli* [tamarind] trees burnt and bhumkal grain razed to ashes.

As the testimonies finally begin to wind down, we prepare to leave. It is very hot outside. There is no potable water. We boil water from a nearby stream and mix some coffee powder into it. It does not take the thirst away. I barely have the energy to write notes. The next village Kodenar is a 10-km walk in the afternoon sun.

Over the next four days, this pattern would repeat itself. Long arduous walks. No water to drink. Plain boiled rice to eat. Fatigue. And nights under the open sky, lying on mats next to pigs and barking dogs. Through Kodenar, to Jatwar and then back to Kachhapal, the patterns and testimonies played themselves out with a familiar beat.

In Jatwar, we finally meet Nilesh, the boy who rang the alarm about Operation Hakka on the morning of 15 March. Barely 5 ft tall, dressed in a blue vest and brown pants, he blushes in the crisp jungle sun. Despite his enrolment in the Jan Militia, Nilesh does not think of himself as a Maoist. 'They are the sarkar, I'm just ordinary *janta*', he says.

That self perception — that distinction between taking to arms as an ideologue and taking to arms as self-defence against intrusion into one's home and land — is very key to understanding not just the nature of Abujmarh but the fundamental nature of the Maoist-tribal crisis in India.

It is the distinction that will define what approach the Indian State will finally take to allay the Naxal crisis.

*Tehelka* has been reporting the Maoist crisis extensively from the ground ever since the Salwa Judum began to escalate tension in Chhattisgarh. Writing from the conflict zones of Odisha, Chhattisgarh and Bengal, we have critiqued the Indian State; documented human rights violations; denounced the unjust takeover of tribal land and national resources and vociferously defended the right to dissent. We have also written of the plight of CRPF jawans, pushed into a deadly guerrilla war with inadequate preparation and battle-worthiness.

But Abujmarh is proof — if proof were needed — that the Maoists have a lot to answer for as well. They may have catalysed attention to many right and just causes — and it is difficult for even their most bitter critics to grant them that — but clearly, in their own strongholds, they are replicating exactly that which they say they are combating. Ordinary life is lived on their watch. Their political expansion is a greater cause than the immediate needs of those they speak for. This is most evident when a party member reveals that they are debating whether to allow Ramakrishna Mission to continue functioning in Abujmarh. 'They were not there at the time of our greatest need', he says. The point of contention is PDS ration shops that earlier operated through the Ashram, but were gradually moved out as the conflict escalated in 2009. While the party holds Ramakrishna Mission responsible, CRPF sources confirmed to *Tehelka* that it was a strategic government decision to move ration shops near CRPF camps so Naxals do not 'steal ration meant for villagers'. This has led to Maadias having to walk many extra days across mountains to access subsidised rice.

To add a new layer of force and terror to this would be an unmitigated disaster. There is talk of expanding the paramilitary strength in the region and setting up of an army training camp on the border of Abujmarh. The day before we entered Marh, Army Chief Gen. V. K. Singh visited Chhattisgarh. Unconfirmed reports suggest the state government has agreed to hand over land to the army, located in Abujmarh's Ghamandi panchayat — exactly where the forces went in for Operation Hakka.

'Operation Hakka was a recce for future operations', says IG Longkumer. 'We wanted to see locations where we can set up our posts and camps in the future'. At present, Bastar district has 104 police stations, 56 CRPF camps and 30 BSF camps. 'Look at Manipur. It has more than a lakh deployment. We are four times the size of Manipur and have half the number of troops', Longkumer adds. 'We need much more deployment. To address this area, we have to stay there. The takeaway from this operation is that the forces are willing to go inside Abujmarh and stay there'.

**Plate 6.7:** Lessons in Conflict — Students at the Government Ashram School in Mohundi

The point is, having dominated the area, what is it the Indian State would like to do there? Is the wreck of Manipur the model?

Narayanpur SP Srivastav has a much more cautioning voice: 'We want to show the people that the government's arms will reach wherever Indian citizens are. I was saddened to see the life the villagers are being forced to lead. I salute the villagers. It is true that on one side, the Naxals coerce them, and on the other, even when the police goes in, we can't tell who is a villager and who is a Naxal. Posted in these areas, I have felt confusion and bafflement. We are a country in a transition phase, that is why we have such a gap between the mainstream and the fringes. It is as if everything is fluid. The Naxal strategy is to look for grouses, and there is no dearth of grouses in this country. It is high time this is resolved. Our goal is to give the government the security to do what it should be able to do'.

As we come out of the jungles of Abujmarh, we hear the shocking news: Collector Alex Menon has been kidnapped by the Maoists, his two guards killed in cold blood. Among their list of demands is the release of innocent tribals languishing in jails. Can't the Indian government act on this itself without a ransom note?

For all its mythic reputation, villagers say that until 15 years ago, local *thana* police were seen at the fringes of Abujmarh. A village called Kokameta possibly had a police station and a government high school. It is only in the past decade that the party's influence has spread. In areas we visited, people recall that in 2001, the Maoists first installed their own village head in a village called Iraqbhatti in Kachhapal panchayat. Three years later, they called their first meeting in the area. Villagers were mandated to attend. In effect, the Maoists' area dominance of the Abujmarh story is only 10 years old. The Indian State had a 50 year head start. Why did it fail?

In the final count then, Abujmarh is not an impregnable fortress. Nor is it merely an innocent landscape of flimsy huts and primeval people. It is most essentially a rebuke for Indian democracy. The real tragedy of the Maoist crisis is that it has been reduced to a competition of equally false stories. Stranded in the middle is

an ancient people. Their fight is not about who will control Red
Fort in some distant future. Their fight is about the patch of land
they stand on and the dignity of the self-owned reed hut behind
them. It is our last evening inside Abujmarh. In the distance, a
Bhumkal — village cooperative — lies razed, destroyed in Operation Hakka, quintals of rice turned to black ash. Their backs to
it, our guides sit inside the village Ghotul. The young starry-eyed
comrade and an old, somewhat sceptical, party member, break
into song. 'Rise up, poor masses, let us walk together. Destroy the
imperialists and fight for our rights. For generations, the fight has
been on. The last fight will be won by the Red Flag'. As the song
continues, torchlight flickers over an old inscription on a wooden
pillar: 'Comrades, this is our *mandir*'.†

ॐ

---

†During their trip to Abujmarh, the Maoists' unbreached citadel, for this
story, Tarun Sehrawat, the photojournalist, contracted a fatal combination of
cerebral malaria, typhoid and jaundice, and Tusha Mittal suffered from an uni-
dentified high fever and severe stomach infection owing to the lack of clean
drinking water for miles, absence of healthcare centres and protection from
insects. *Falciparum* malaria — the dreaded strain that afflicted Sehrawat — is
rampant in Chhattisgarh's tribal regions. Though it kills people here in epidemic
droves, the phenomenon goes largely unreported. Severe malnutrition, jaundice
and typhoid are also routine here. While Tusha fortunately recovered, despite
the most specialized medical care, Tarun succumbed to his illnesses and a devastating brain haemorrhage on 15 June 2012.

# 7

# Here, Silence Speaks Volumes

*Supriya Sharma**

✪

The death of a loved one is always difficult to handle. More so a sudden and violent one. It can trigger anger, spark a search for agents and causes and leave the bereaved fixing blame and seeking revenge. If any of this was happening in Dantewada, it was hard to tell. This is a place often and aptly described as a 'war zone'. Last week, 15 civilians became 'collateral damage' of a Maoist attack here.

In a small clearing in the sal forest, less than half a km from where the carcass of the bus remained suspended in midair, a funeral pyre was lit. Madavi Kosa, a man in his fifties had perished in the blast — his body ripped apart. The entire village had come to mourn his death. Women raised their arms to hold their tilted heads at the back, in the tribal way of mourning. Meanwhile, Kosa's blind father wept, his wife sobbed and his brother and son stood by.

As the flames died down, we tried asking what the family and village felt about Kosa's death. Did they blame the Maoists for attacking the bus or the police for boarding it? Kosa's son and brother said nothing. The village sarpanch looked helplessly around and repeated, over and over, *Main kya keh sakta hai, main kuch keh nahi sakta* [what can I say, I can't say anything]. We

---

* This article was previously published as 'Here, Silence Speaks Volumes', *The Times of India*, 22 May 2010. The Times of India. © Bennett, Coleman & Co. Ltd., 2011. All Rights Reserved.

stood talking in the open, under the sal trees, surrounded by 20 men, among them perhaps Maoist supporters or police informers. Perhaps this inhibited the sarpanch.

But what kept Shanti Kashyap's family from speaking out? Shanti was a government nurse and by all accounts an exceptional woman and very special daughter. *Beti nahi beta thi* [she was my son, not my daughter], was how her mother, Somari Bai, summarised Shanti's contribution as sole breadearner of a fatherless family. She took up a village post and lived away from home, cycling to violence-affected villages deep in the interior as a health worker. All of this to pay for a life of dignity for her old mother and marry off her young sister. A short life of great sacrifice snuffed out.

Yet Shanti's family remains remarkably composed, sharing stories, showing her college pictures, offering a cold drink. They withdraw the moment they are asked who could be blamed for their loss. Shanti's sister Basanti starts to speak but her aunt interjects, 'You don't need to say anything, we don't need to get into this (politics).'

In a place where it is dangerous to express an opinion, is it fair to expect people to state their views? Yet, some people speak, and when they do, the sentiment defies easy categorisation or the obvious matrix of blame. Most say that the Maoists were wrong to target a bus packed with civilians. But they quickly add, often with even greater vehemence: 'The police had no business risking our lives by getting onto buses'. Some go even further, analysing the cycle of violence, looking at the point it all began. 'Why did they start Salwa Judum? Our lives worsened since then', says one woman, blaming the government for creating an anti-Maoist militia in 2005. A school teacher claims that at the time, people were resentful of Maoists and some joined the Judum, but it improved nothing. 'After living with violence for so long, it all gets blurred. It does not matter where it is coming from, all that matters is what will happen next'.

'Had this attack taken place anywhere, people would have been murderous with rage, but people here are too cowed down by the Maoists', says a police officer. He believes people support the Maoists out of fear, or simply because 'they are primitive and don't know any better'. The rule of thumb he relies upon: the further a settlement from 'the road and modernity', the greater the support.

To get to Goomiapal, one has to travel away from the towns and villages on the main roads, along dirt tracks. Two people were killed in this village on Sunday, just a day before the bus blast. They were innocent, claimed Maoist leader Ramanna in a statement. Their killing, and earlier ones, provoked them to target the bus carrying SPOs [special police officers], he said. But police insist the men were Maoists. 'One was an area committee member', says Amresh Mishra, SP of Dantewada. 'They were holding a meeting in the village.' An SPO, who was part of the operation, says: 'Old women ran and gave cover to the Maoists and helped them escape.'

Jimme Madiyami did run during the firing, but to save her life, she says. Her house caught fire when a bullet landed on its thatched roof. Only its mud walls remain, everything else is burnt black. 'Those men were innocent, they too were running as they were scared', says a villager. But were the Maoists holding a meeting in the village that day? 'No'. Do they come there at all? 'Never. The *andarwaale* never come here.'

*Andarwaale*, or people from inside, is what people here call the Maoists. As if the area is neatly divided into inside and outside. If Goomiapal is outside, and presumably, according to the police, the people here support the Maoists, then what about those who are inside?

'The Maoists live, sleep, eat with the people', says Manish Kunjam, CPI [Communist Party of India] leader. 'And so, they must think about the impact of this violence on adivasi society. They should consider using this opportunity to come for talks and place the people's agenda on the table. Where this fight will go, and will our society perish in it?'

ॐ

# 8

# Inside Maoistan

*Shafi Rahman**

✪

Dinesh Manji is a local libero hero. In volleyball, libero is a defensive player position and allowed only underarm passes. In a clay court off Orissa's Deomali mountains, Manji jumps and smashes every oncoming serve. I give a second to attune myself to the motion of the ball. The unruly libero is my first exposure to the liberated zones, where Maoists are changing the rules of the game and setting up Janathana Sarkars — People's Government — a Maoist Xanadu, a vital building block of the Maoist society based on ideological rhetoric. Janathana Sarkars collect 'taxes', decide on local disputes, fix prices of local products, run local amenities and provide basic healthcare. In the huge region of mineral-rich forests in eastern and central India from West Bengal through Jharkhand, Orissa and Chhattisgarh, these committees, mostly managed by local villagers, but with severe Maoist mentoring, control all things in life — even tippling habits to eternal supply of volleyballs. 'Instead of explaining to you what we intend to do if we assume power in the country, I can show you what we do in the areas we hold power over', says a Maoist leader, before sending me off on a bike of one of his cadres, my destination uncertain. Two hours into our journey, through narrowing road, often slipping down side-alleys, I ask him which village we are heading [to]. He smiles with a glint of mischief.

---

* This article was previously published as 'Inside Maoistan', *India Today*, 11 February 2010.

In fact he has no clue. Before I conclude my journey on motorable road, I was made to travel with two other bikers — the last one with a spider tattooed on his chest, which gave him an air of defiance. As abruptly as the hellish ride began, the journey ends four hours later. I was handed over to the last 'contact', Lakshman Manji's village is at one of the areas within the Maoist compass in Mahendragiri Mountains — foremost of the seven Kulagiris or principal mountains of India — in the district of Gajapati, 51 km to the south-west of Brahmapur. The river Mahendratanaya flows down the mountain in the east through Mandasa and joins the Bay of Bengal at Barua. Off Mandimara, Mahendratanaya flows like a guide along cracked mud road to Manji's village. [It] is easy to get lost in the path overgrown by shrubs and twists upwards in relentless climb. At his village, the muddy river drops its suspended silt and gains glass-like clarity.

The village, with over 29 tribal hamlets, recently changed its ways and got into collective farming. Manji is the village's representative in Janathana Sarkar and is the pointsman of Maoists in the village. With heavy-lidded eyes and a broad sweep of forehead, he is without the weathered looks of a war-zone commander. 'For the first time in ages, we have done collective farming last year. We have stopped approaching police over disputes and the committee decides over the disputes', says Manji.

The CPI (Maoist) is not a top-heavy outfit. It is led by general secretary Ganapathi and 13 other Politburo members with a clear division of tasks which includes 'military' operations, intelligence and budgeting. But it is Janathana Sarkars that have been helping them to focus more on overall armed offensive rather than on the nuts and bolts of administering their strongholds.

The 'liberated zones' are not gated districts within the districts. These are the areas were Maoists have loose military control but have made strong roots among the villagers by engaging them in their life and livelihood — albeit under the vigil of guns. Without actually pitching tents at these places, they run their writ here. Most of these committees are in the Dandakaranya Special Zone, the vast forest area situated between the borders of Andhra Pradesh, Chhattisgarh, Maharashtra and Orissa. Around 59 work teams with up to 70 members in each were set up last year to prepare land for millet, paddy and dal. In Bastar alone, around 1,436 acres of land were seized from landlords. Of this, 1,057 acres were distributed to 482 families and 310 acres was put under the control of the Janathana Sarkar and 65 acres were given to the militia. The mode of adivasi agriculture in all these divisions was primitive, rarely using cattle for agriculture. 'We are now using cattle to plough the fields. We were used to building tanks in areas were water collected naturally in earlier days and water was carried manually from these tanks. Now we are using canals to take water to these points', notes Manji, before confiding that I am the first journalist he ever met, but maintaining a spokesman-like gravity. At first glance, the villages don't look daunting. The slow pace of tribal life and absence of uniformed squads free them from any appearance of wary fear. I insist upon the villagers to tell me about Maoists but many comment in single sentences. 'Maoists are good people and they help villagers', is the refrain, a reminder of shared fear.

The Maoists gained control over the villagers over the years due to a variety of reasons. But the commonality here is straightforward: the Maoist sympathisers in the village are who couldn't, didn't, wouldn't — you pick the verb — fit in the various development plans of the state. 'If we are Maowadis, you are MoUwadis', he tells me, indicating that displacement due to large-scale land acquisitions resulted in the growth of Maoism in the region.

Government expenditure on health, education, child care, electricity, roads, water, etc. is lacklustre in 28 of the 33 LWE (left-wing extremism) districts in Jharkhand, Chhattisgarh, Orissa and Bihar. In percentage terms in Jharkhand, the expenditure for child care in the 10 worst affected districts is 15 while the state's average is 86; the seven LWE districts in Chhattisgarh spend 15 per cent on water while the state spends 83 on average. Malkangiri in Orissa has a literacy rate below 25 per cent but it spends under 4 per cent of funds under Sarva Siksha Abhiyan.

There are no restraints on exercise of naked power — both by the Maoists and the security forces. At Rai Panga, Kornoil Bodo Roito, a 27-year-old farm worker shows me marks of the bullet wound from a CRPF [Central Reserve Police Force] raid on his village in November 2008. 'When the CRPF came on their raid, the villagers went helter-skelter. At first I thought someone stabbed me on my neck. Then I realised that it was a bullet which brushed my neck', he says. He insists he never had any connection with Maoists. But Junus Roito, another villager, was less lucky and was shot down by the police in a cattle shed. Though his family insists that he is not a Maoist, a memorial was erected for him by Maoists. 'I approached the government for compensation after the killing. While the cattle owners got ₹ 20,000, I was given ₹ 50,000 as compensation for my dead son', says his father Rono Roito.

At times bronzed men with arms on their shoulders descend on the villages and preside over Jan Adalats held by these committees. I head to one of the 'Jan Adalats' of Hathimunda in Gajapati district where Prasanth Bhima gets a hasty punishment. He had roughed up his neighbour over a financial dispute. The villagers gathered around are asked to give the verdict. Manji lets him off with a minor punishment — 50 sit-ups. Bhima does it smiling sheepishly. The gathered crowd breaks into laughter. But it's not laughing matter every time. In many instances, the Maoists are just rights-abusing thugs. On 15 June, last year the Maoists beheaded one of their surrendered cadres at Murgaon at Gadchiroli. Beheading of Inspector Francis Induwar in Jharkhand is the latest in the line. But Jan Adalats are not an easy run. It has caused unease even within the Maoist party. Yugal Pal, who was till recently a member of powerful Special Area Committee of Jharkhand, Bihar and Northern Chhattisgarh, left the party saying that party is forcing its decision on villagers via 'Jan Adalats'.

But Maoists question the idea of leaving decision-making completely to the villagers. Recently in Andhra Pradesh, a village landlord was put on trial for raping a tribal girl. The villagers wanted the wife of the landlord to be raped in retaliation. 'In such a situation you can't leave it to the villagers. We have to intervene in such occasions', says a Maoist leader.

As one move away from Koraput — the town hosts the Hindustan Aeronautical Limited factory which makes spare parts for the MiG jets — the land gets greener and settlements get

sparser. Most of the tribal settlements here are beneath a colon-
nade of palm trees that offers eternal supply of toddy. Now liquor
contractors across Orissa, who often pep up the brew with ammo-
nium chloride, have been asked to stay away from selling the liquor
by Kranthikari Adivasi Mahila Sanghatan, a Maoist frontal organisation. Drunk with the intrigue, I ask local carpenter Prasant
Mantri about the new move. His hard face breaks into a boyish
smile as he speaks about [the] prohibition. 'This is our only past-
ime. How can we be stopped from drinking?' In Chhattisgarh, the
Mahila Sanghatan also took up the task of breaking the taboos.
They launched a campaign against the tribal belief that women
shouldn't be allowed in certain agricultural activities like sowing
seeds and reaping the harvest. The tribals are also being introduced to a new script for tribal languages, which has so far been
scriptless. Chloroquine, an anti-malaria medicine, is given in
packets replete with slogans — *Soshiko Athanko, Soshito Shruthi*
[terror for the oppressors, dear for the oppressed].

Near Hathimuda panchayat, the lone teacher at a primary
school lowers the volume of a blaster, badly tuned into a radio
station, to tell me about the school. 'Teachers refuse to come to
the school citing Maoist problem. Since then I have been deputed
by the party to take classes.' The curriculum here has a new addition, a script for tribal languages introduced by the Maoists and
developed by its leader Dasuram. One of the chapters in the text-
book explains early 19th century Parlkot rebellion by tribals and
had a cover-page slogan saying, *Aaj pade, aaj lade, janata ko aage le
jayen* [learn today, fight today, take the people forward].

But every financial activity in these vast tracts is helping the
Maoists to enhance their financial resources. Maoists run a huge
financial empire by extracting commission from contractors of
government projects, mining companies, and in sale of tobacco
leaves. In many Maoist-controlled southern districts of Orissa and
Andhra Pradesh, the fragrance of pine yields to the smell of *ganja*
[marijuana].

At the night camp, the kitchen bursts with busy chefs, preparing
glutinous *dal* [lentils], brinjal and rice. The *athithis* [guests] get
generous portions of *desi* [local] chicken. I notice two other guests

getting the benefit of chicken. Soon after the dinner, I side up to them and ask about their visit. 'We are officials from state revenue department. We are here to finalise sketch of the village to give *patta* [land deed] to the villagers', one of them says. The Maoists are allowing signposts of the state to come in, wherever it fits their plans. The NREG [National Rural Employment Guarantee] roads have been approved selectively, ensuring that they don't make easy passage for security forces into Maoist hideouts. Indira Awaas Yojana is widely allowed, but with a pinch of salt. 'Why is the Government keen on allowing the project only in Naxal areas? It is an effort to make the Government presence here', says a Maoist pamphlet. But ₹ 33,000 for constructing a home is alluring in this poverty stricken belt.

Sometimes dispensing 'justice' becomes the darkest comedy. S. Dominic, a priest in Latehar district, ignored a Maoist leader who walked into a song and prayer session led by him. With his ego hurt, the leader later picked up the priest from the street and made him dance on hot rocks under the blazing sun for four hours. When the locals objected, the Maoist leadership brought the commander to the village and he was made to dance for four hours on roasted sand.

On 27 December, Maoists set ablaze four passenger buses of the Orissa State Road Transport Corporation near Nalaghat in Gajapati district late in the night during its Orissa bandh. Though passengers were not harmed, the Maoist attackers had taken mobile phones from passengers to stop them from calling [the] police. After the operation, Maoists couldn't return the mobile phones to villagers while they were fleeing in a hurry. 'We are not petty thieves, we are revolutionaries. We never wanted to take it along with us', says a Maoist leader. I rub further salt into the wound: 'For the passengers, you may look like petty thieves.'

'We want media to help us return the phones. But nobody is ready be an intermediary', he complains.

And then there is a world of sleaze. Barely twelve hours after Maoists blew up two police stations and an outpost in Koraput district, a former divisional commander of the rebel outfit surrendered before the Orissa police in June last year. Ghasiram alias

Akash, a resident of Kharikapadar village in Rayagada district, joined the Maoist ranks seven years ago and rose to become the outfit's Ghumusar division commander a few years ago. 'Akash was twice demoted in the party and pulled out of its armed unit for his "womanising habits". He threatened to quit unless he was asked to return to the military unit', says Manji as he gives first bits of Akash's life. I probe further on escapades, but the Maoist leader refuses to open up. 'He believed in bigamy and refused to eat beef', he says reluctantly.

As the face-off stiffened, he surrendered to Orissa police. Now, the Maoists have brought out a circular saying that without Akash the party has become cleaner like 'gold without dust'.

The gaps in governance and a host of other state failures have helped the Maoists to make fresh inroads in many areas — Orissa's Narayanpatna, West Bengal's Lalgarh and mining towns in Jharkhand are the latest examples. The long shadow of Maoists is visible in Telangana, where they wish for a smaller state, which could bolster their chances as in Chhattisgarh and Jharkhand. In communal violence-hit Kandhamal district, many young Christians are leaning towards the Left extremists. Now there are many fresh recruiting areas. Uper Kandy, the last village in Similiguda near Andhra Pradesh border, has been bypassed by politics and signs of modernity till recently. As the vehicle approaches the village, the taxi driver throws his handkerchief over the miniature national flag on the dash board. 'The Maoists are moving into the area', he warns me. The 200-year-old [village] got a road connecting it to the city just recently. 'Now we are given notices to vacate [because] the Government wants to hand over the place to a mining company here. We are ready fight to any extent to keep our land', says Hanak Tading, a resident of the village.

Policing these vast tracts of land has become almost impossible with the lack of security force presence. Inspector in-charge at Adhaba police in Gajapati district, Devendra Mahapatra, is well-protected in his station with a cathedral-like gate and a platoon of CRPF stationed in the premises. As Maoists established grip over local dispute handling, the number of criminal cases filed in the station have come down from over 300 five years ago to 48 last year. Outside the station, he and his colleagues go around in civil dress to escape the Maoists' attention. 'After waiting for years, the station got a satellite phone recently. We are yet to fill up posts of two more sub-inspectors. We live in [a] nearby irrigation guest house and are always under threat of attacks', says Mahapatra. Though the CRPF makes routine route march[es] to nearby forests, the terrain makes the task tough.

It's not a bad prison, but it's hard to be stuck here in the anteroom of Maoism. Like many of his buddies, Prakash was trying to adjust to passive life as farmers to active life as a squad member patrolling mountains, with combat gear complete with Insas rifles and butt bags. As we rumble through the forests, he moves close enough to whisper in my ear to say that it is fatal to wander from the routine path. 'Mines are all around to trap the police', he confides. In rotating shifts, the soldiers spent 14 hours on duty, mostly on patrolling neigbourhoods.

The CRPF rarely surprise the Maoists. 'We get information the moment CRPF moves towards the forest. In many occasions, we don't put up a fight. We retreat deeper into the forests, forcing the CRPF to camp in one of the hills and go back after a day or two', he says. A combination of measures has helped Maoists to control the vast stretches of land — making their presence known by simply marching through villages, setting up [a] strong intelligence system among villagers and resisting all forms of civil administration with stray attacks.

'Most of the beaten paths are mined. We avoid these roads, move forward using GPS [Global Positioning System] in favour of a tougher journey by setting up new paths. The moment we enter into these forests, the Maoists light up torches and give signals to their counterparts around, making it easy for them to retreat', says H. K. Jasoria, Officer Commander at CRPF station in Gajapati district.

You don't need a crystal ball to recognise that the Government will face a list of tough tasks to clean up the menace. The Maoists are trying to outstrip the existing system with quick-fix solutions for people living on narrow margins of survival. While they are carrying out their plans with alarming ease, the state is on a retreat.

The Government is getting increasingly pre-occupied with military action and the Maoists are responding with fits of terror and competing with their own version of 'democracy', tearing down and constructing social and economic models.

In many instances, the Government is confused how to bring the people it once offended into its big-tent political system. In last February, police in Gajapati district decided to reach out to the villagers as a part of its 'public–police contact programme' by distributing volleyball kits in Kattama village. While the forces were on the way, an Improvised Explosive Device (IED), planted under a culvert, blew up before the bus could pass over it at Andharighati village in Mohana block. But the impact was such that it injured eight persons.

The police since then have abandoned the contact programme. Now, the Adhabha station sports a volleyball court and, of course, a lot of spare volleyballs. As I leave, policemen were preparing for a game of volleyball. I don't wait to see whether the libero here follows the underarm rules.

ॐ

# 9

# Address the Root Causes of Naxalism

*Sonia Gandhi**

✪

Dear Friends,

Parliament is in session once again and we have a full calendar ahead of us. We have many significant issues to discuss and debate. I hope that in this final Budget Session for 2010, we will not waste precious time but instead use the parliamentary process to address the issues that are most critical for our country. There are several important pieces of legislation that need to be debated and passed in this session. I am hopeful that the opposition will work with us to ensure that parliamentary proceedings in this session are productive, so we can make progress on the tasks of governance.

As we know, our country faces enormous challenges, and chief amongst them is the continuing poverty and lack of access still faced by the poor and dispossessed. While our government has been implementing policies that seek to fight poverty and empower the poor, much remains to be done. Since coming to power in 2004, the UPA [United Progressive Alliance] government has initiated several important social development programmes. The Mahatma Gandhi NREGA and the Right to Information Act are amongst our major achievements. In keeping with this spirit of substantial and meaningful empowerment of the poor, we are preparing to roll out the Right to Education Act. The Right to Education Act will ensure that education becomes a fundamental entitlement for every citizen of India. It will give the poor and marginalised access

---

* This article was previously published as 'Address the Root Causes of Naxalism', *Congress Sandesh*, May 2010.

to quality education, where they don't have it yet. We have to ensure that our youth are ready and equipped to participate in national development and benefit from the numerous opportunities that will be generated as a result of India's continuing economic growth. Our government is fully committed to implementing this Act in letter and spirit. It is our sincere hope that the States will come on board in ensuring full implementation of this seminal law and cooperate in ensuring that red tape and corruption does not dilute the intended results. The UPA government is currently engaged with the drafting of another bill that will strike at the very roots of poverty and deprivation in our country. This is the Right to Food Bill, the contours of which are currently being finalised. Access to food needs to be a fundamental right. Our country is also facing an enormous challenge from the Naxalites. We have recently lost 73 brave *jawans* [soldiers] of the CRPF in an attack in Chhattisgarh. Our thoughts go out to the grieving families of these men who have lost their lives. While we must address acts of terror decisively and forcefully, we have to address the root causes of Naxalism. The rise of Naxalism is a reflection of the need for our development initiatives to reach the grass roots, especially in our most backward tribal districts.

This is why our government is putting in place more targeted development schemes for our most backward districts. The Prime Minister Dr Manmohan Singh participated in several important international meetings. He was in the United States of America to discuss issues of Nuclear Disarmament. You will recall that Shri Rajiv Gandhi was one of the great advocates of universal nuclear disarmament. He raised the matter at the United Nations in June 1988 and since then India has consistently attempted to bring about an international consensus on this issue. The Prime Minister also had the opportunity to attend the IBSA [India, Brazil, South Africa] and BRICS [Brazil, Russia, India, China and South Africa] summit in Brasilia, where he interacted with the Heads of States of Brazil, South Africa, China and Russia. These are important regional groupings that reflect the growing importance of India and other emerging economies in the new world order. This month we celebrated the birth of Dr B. R. Ambedkar, leader and architect of our Constitution. Dr Ambedkar fought for equality of all Indians, especially for the rights of the underprivileged. The Congress Party, by launching a mass movement in Uttar Pradesh on the occasion of his birthday, pays tribute to him and resolves to continue to be inspired by thoughts and actions. Let us persevere to keep moving forward.

Jai Hind!

಄

# 10

# Nothing Very Civil About this War

## Shobhan Saxena*

✪

A day after a CRPF platoon was wiped out by Maoists in
Dantewada, the war arrived in Delhi. That was last month [April
2010]. Two groups of students — leftists opposing 'Operation Green
Hunt' and Congress–BJP supporters backing the offensive —
clashed on the JNU [Jawaharlal Nehru University] campus. Earlier,
a peace march to Dantewada by 50 eminent citizens, including
JNU chancellor Yash Pal and noted Gandhian Narayan Desai, was
'busted' by some Congress and BJP workers, who attacked the
'Maoist sympathisers'.

Bullets are flying in Bastar, but another conflict — between the
government and some civil society groups — is taking place in
Delhi. When the rebels blew up a bus in Chhattisgarh this week,
home minister P. Chidambaram launched an attack on civil society organisations that were 'getting in the way of the state's efforts
to contain the rebels'. The minister went on TV to say, 'It is almost
fashionable to be sympathetic to the Maoist cause'.

Human rights activists have been locking horns with the government on the Maoist issue for some time but the debate has
become so shrill it now seems almost as if the armed rebels are the
third party in the war between the state and civil society. Are the
battle lines so hard there is no room for debate anymore? Is
the space for civil society shrinking in India?

---

*This article was previously published as 'Nothing Very Civil About this War',
*The Times of India*, 22 May 2010. The Times of India. © Bennett, Coleman &
Co. Ltd., 2011. All Rights Reserved.

Supreme Court lawyer and human rights activist Prashant Bhushan says the government 'wants this space to shrink'. 'Chidambaram has been saying he has a "limited mandate" and he needs a "bigger mandate" to tackle the Maoist issue. What they are planning is genocide of the tribals by the use of Air Force, etc. and they don't want any criticism by the media and NGOs. That's why they are threatening civil society activists', he says.

Filmmaker Mahesh Bhatt, who has made a documentary on the tribals of Bastar, believes the government is applying the Bush Doctrine. 'They are following the policy of "if you are not with us, you are against us". This is dangerous for democracy. I would advise the politicians to stop war-mongering', he says. 'The government is trying to control dissent. I want to know where the democratic space in this country is.'

The debate has existed from the Naxalbari uprising of the late 1960s. But it's only recently that it has become so heated. Arundhati Roy's 36-page essay on Maoists, whom she called 'Gandhians with guns', may have acted as a trigger.[1] On 6 May, a few days after Roy's article appeared, the home ministry issued a statement saying that 'some Maoist leaders have been directly contacting certain NGOs and intellectuals to propagate their ideology and persuade them to take steps which would provide support to the CPI (Maoist) ideology'.

In an earlier statement the home minister had accused organisations such as the People's Union for Democratic Rights (PUDR) and People's Union for Civil Liberties (PUCL) of backing the Maoists' cause. 'The government is interested only in military action', says Kavita Srivastava of [the] PUCL. 'They have been saying that the Army will not join the operations but the Army is already there in the battlefield running 20 jungle warfare schools for paramilitary forces. It's issues like these that the government wants to hide, hence the attack on civil society.'

Activists may give the impression that the government has launched an all-out war on them, but politicians like Mani Shankar

---

[1] Arundhati Roy, 'Walking with the Comrades', *Outlook*, 29 March 2010.

Aiyar, who has been openly critical of the government's military approach, believe that there is plenty of space for debate. 'Compared to the kind of blind reliance on the gun that appeared to be building up in early April, I think there is much greater balance in the approach now, especially after the Prime Minister's National Panchayat Raj Day speech on April 24 in which he advocated the "two-pronged" strategy of security and development, and the Congress President following this up with her emphasis on participative development in Congress Sandesh', says the Rajya Sabha MP. 'It is a lacuna in our democracy that marginalised people need civil society activists to mediate between them and governmental authorities. Yet, the fact that a completely voiceless people are securing recognition is in itself encouraging.'

The BJP has a totally different take on this as it doesn't trust some civil society groups. 'Nobody is against a debate on the human rights issue, but we have to be careful about the NGOs who only raise this issue when Maoists are hit and keep quiet when the police and ordinary people are affected', says Nirmala Sitaraman, a BJP spokesperson. 'We also have to be careful of the politics that is being played by the Congress on this issue. The situation is really alarming.'

Indeed, the situation is alarming. But a clash between the state and civil society won't change the ground reality in the jungles of Dantewada.

ॐ

# 11

# The Path Rarely Taken

*Dola Mitra\**

✪

Officially, Lalgarh town has three schools — a primary, a secondary and a higher secondary school. It also boasts [of] one rural hospital and, according to the official in charge, an NREGA work project that has 'been implemented since the inception of the scheme'. But even a random check will reveal that the benefits are not reaching the people. Some people have received BPL [below poverty line] and APL [above poverty line] ration cards, but the guarantee of 100 days' work every year falls way below target.

'Hundred days?' asks Robi Bag, 50. 'I'd be happy to get even 10 days.'

To feed his wife and six children, Bag does what they've always done for generations — live off the forest, collecting twigs and leaves and selling them. In the old days, tribals could go into the forests without fear, he says, but now it involves risk. 'If the police catch us in the jungle, they beat us up', he says. On a good day, he manages to make ₹ 50.

Given the strange ways in which the administration works, his wife has been given an APL card while he has a BPL card. So he can buy rice for ₹ 2 per kilo and wheat for ₹ 5 per kilo. But his wife has to buy rice for ₹ 10 per kilo. In one card, his teenaged daughter has been recorded as being 50 years old.

---

* This article was previously published as 'The Path Rarely Taken', *Outlook*, 26 April 2010.

Sanjay Sinha, a farmer of Bhatmore village, says people in his village haven't been issued BPL cards. The primary school, like in many other villages in the area, always remains shut. Even the hospitals in Lalgarh remain closed. The reason cited by the authorities is that the indefinite strikes — called by the Maoists — have paralysed life.

N. S. Nigam, the district magistrate of Midnapore, agrees that development in the area is 'far from satisfactory'. But he argues that it is a Catch-22 situation: the concerted efforts at development and whatever little was done earlier, not just in Lalgarh but also areas bordering it, are sabotaged by the Maoists.

He says it's difficult to honour the 100 days' work guarantee offered under NREGA because development works just cannot be undertaken in what have become 'core Maoist areas' like Lalgarh, Pirakata, Goaltore, Pathardanga. 'Villagers are prevented from benefiting from the NREGA scheme', says Nigam.

He cites the example of Nader Bandh, an irrigation project. ₹ 32 lakh was sanctioned and work was started but later, the engineers refused to work as the environment was not conducive', he says. 'Five hundred acres would have come under irrigation. We initiated the project because the villagers asked for it. But we couldn't implement it.'

A few projects, however, have seen some success, even in 'core Maoist' areas, he says. These include rural electrification and immunisation, for which 40 doctors have been recruited. But with the hospitals closed, it's difficult to imagine the efforts yielding results. Nigam also claims the mid-day meal scheme is working and that, while many still don't go to school, it may bring in students.

However, in the villages bordering the forests — not completely in the control of the Maoists — there is some activity. Signboards have appeared over the last one year, announcing projects under NREGA. These include desiltation of ponds, works to recharge groundwater and harvest rainwater, and digging of trenches to keep elephants off crops. Hundreds of locals have gained employment.

But clearly, this is far from enough.

ॐ

# 12

# Through an Egyptian Mirror

*Vinod Mehta\**

✪

Could it happen here? The leaderless revolution in Egypt has caused some anxiety locally over whether the wretched of our earth could come out to challenge their rulers. Conventional and unconventional wisdom has it that the answer is an emphatic no. We have a vibrant democracy, regular elections, a free media, an alert judiciary — all these checks and balances, it is fondly assumed, provide a safety valve through which the above-mentioned wretched can ventilate their frustrations. It is a cosy and comforting thesis but it needs to be tested. Not just to shake us out of complacency, but to force us to ask some hard questions.

One could in fact argue that it is already happening here. The injustices the protesters at Tahrir Square are raging about — corruption, no jobs, rising prices, appalling governance — are rampant in our blessed land. The tribal population of India, over three times the size of Egypt's total population, lives daily with hardships ten times worse than those faced by the *aam aadmi* [common man] in Cairo. The per capita income in Egypt is four times the per capita income of adivasis in Dantewada. Moreover, under the influence of the Maoists, our destitute have taken up arms in a do-or-die struggle against the Indian state. Altogether, we are confronted with a situation infinitely more dangerous than the one

---

\* This article was previously published as 'Through an Egyptian Mirror', *Outlook*, 21 February 2010.

prevailing in Egypt. Indeed, in contrast to the carnival and celebratory atmosphere in Tahrir Square, our deprived and desolate are waging a grim and violent battle. India is already at war with its own people. If you asked a bow-and-arrow-wielding woman to throw down her weapon because she possessed a wonderful thing called 'democracy', I shudder to think what her response would be.

Shining India, fortunately, does not have to watch pitched clashes outside the street on which it lives. However, unless we wake up, that prospect is fast approaching. Supposing, 200,000 of our citizens march into Jantar Mantar demanding regime change or immediate redressal of their grievances, how will the Indian state respond?

ॐ

# 13

# Andhra's Maoist Dens Turn Havens of Development

## Srinivasa Rao*

✪

'Tribal Primary Health Centre, Kuturu; 24-hours working women welfare centre' — reads a board on a road side amidst deep jungles connecting Kunavaram and Chintoor blocks of Khammam district across the Sabari river.

There is a *pucca* [concrete] bus shelter as well on the road which leads to Kuturu tribal hamlet, about 2 km from the main road. And the path leading into the hamlet is also a black-top road.

'This was not the case a decade ago. This area was a stronghold of the Naxalites. Leave alone government officials, even common people used to be afraid of passing through this forest', recalls Satti Babu, a resident of V. R. Puram block near Kunavaram.

Now, these jungles are no more Maoist dens. There has been a rapid turnaround in the lives of people in these areas. One can witness tribal healthcare centres in almost every major panchayat, if not interior hamlets; every village has a well-laid road and bus connectivity; there are residential schools being run by the Andhra Pradesh tribal welfare department in the villages and junior and degree colleges at block headquarters like Kunavaram, Chintoor and V. R. Puram.

For every few kilometres on the road passing through jungles, one can find boards bearing statistics of the National Rural

* This article was previously published as 'Andhra's Maoist Dens Turn Havens of Development', *India Today*, 3 November 2009.

Employment Guarantee Scheme (NREGS) being implemented in the nearby villages.

At Edugurrallapadu, about 30 km from Chintoor, which is still considered a Maoist-influenced village because of its proximity to the Chhattisgarh forests, there is a big black board explaining the works taken up under various components of NREGS.

'Yes, there has been a rapid transformation in the lives and also thinking of local tribals in the last few years. The youth are no more inclined towards Maoists and have become career-oriented. They are looking towards towns and cities, rather than jungles. And there have been instances in the last couple of years that the youth resisted the entry of Maoists in their villages', points out J. Venkatesh, district coordinator of the NGO Internally Displaced Project.

Andhra Pradesh was, in fact, once the strongest citadel of the Naxalite movement, beginning with the agrarian uprising in Srikakulam in 1969. The movement, which reached its peak in the 1990s, started fizzling out gradually due to severe police repression, coupled with socio-economic policies initiated by the governments in the last 10 years.

The abortive talks with the state government proved the proverbial last nail in the coffin of the Maoist movement in Andhra, as the security forces supported by a strong intelligence network bumped off one leader after another, forcing all the top leaders to beat a retreat into the Chhattisgarh jungles.

Till a few years ago, Maoists used to frequently come to villages, hold people's courts and kill people in the name of informers. On the other hand, police forces used to raid villages and torture innocents in the name of Maoist sympathisers.

Subsequently, the government changed its strategy by targeting only Maoists leaders and sparing the common people, while implementing welfare and development schemes in a big way, as a result of which there has been a gradual decline in the Maoist activity in the Khammam–Chhattisgarh border areas.

'The police forces have strengthened their intelligence network so much that any movement of Maoists in the area would come to their notice immediately. As a result, the Maoists have retreated into the Chhattisgarh jungles and they hardly move in our areas anymore. As a result, the police repression, too, has come down considerably', Venkatesh said.

Yet, there is a lot to be done to ensure that the frustrated youth do not go back to Maoism, says V. B. Chandrasekhar of Girijan Seema Welfare Association. 'There is a lot of corruption involved in the implementation of government schemes and there is no proper mechanism to monitor it. If the benefits of the scheme do not reach the people properly, it leads to a lot of unrest. The situation, then, would come back to square one', he cautions.

Most importantly, the government has to rehabilitate tribals migrating from neighbouring Chhattisgarh. 'There should be a policy especially for migrating tribals. Otherwise, they might go back to the Maoists', Chandrasekhar said.

৵

# PART III

MINING AND ENVIRONMENT

# 14

# I Have Differed with Chidambaram on His Strategy, But We Remain Friends

*Digvijay Singh*
Interview by Saba Naqvi*

✪

Digvijay Singh is considered one of the most powerful general secretaries in the Congress. He's also the man charged with reviving the party's fortunes in Uttar Pradesh — the state critical for the 'evolution' of Rahul Gandhi as the future leader. The former Madhya Pradesh chief minister is a man who speaks his mind and is unafraid to take controversial positions for he has strong backing in the party organisation. He has famously taken contrarian positions on the Batla House encounter, even visited Azamgarh from where most of the 'terrorist' boys hailed, and most recently critiqued Home Minister P. Chidambaram's counter-Maoist strategy. Since then he has met Chidambaram, again shifting tracks and discussing the issue of Hindu militancy. That, he says, is the issue he would now like to keep the focus on. It's significant that the veteran Congressman has been connecting the dots and keeping an eye on scattered incidents of Hindu militancy for several years now. In late 2008, he had written to Prime Minister Manmohan Singh, listing several suspicious incidents linked to Hindu militants.

---

* This article was previously published as 'I Have Differed with Chidambaram on His Strategy, but We Remain Friends', *Outlook*, 24 May 2010.

He had then recommended that the home ministry set up a special cell to look into the activities of all RSS-linked organisations. He spoke to Saba Naqvi about controversies, his own ideological convictions and political projections. Excerpts:

◎

*Saba Naqvi (SN)*: You wrote a letter to the PM [Prime Minister] on 1 October 2008 about the problem of Hindu terrorism, much before Sadhvi Pragya was arrested by the Maharashtra ATS [Anti Terrorist Squad] and the issue came into the public domain. Do you think the government made a mistake in ignoring your advice?

*Digvijay Singh (DS)*: I have been saying for a long time that Hindu radicals and Muslim radicals are two faces of the same coin. It is these elements who have brought a divide between Hindus and Muslims and led us to a situation where we have acts of terrorism in the country. We all know that terrorist attacks flared up after the Babri Masjid demolition. This in turn led to the radicalisation of a section of Hindus. There is so much evidence of the RSS/ VHP [Vishva Hindu Parishad] combine operating through various militant organisations. There have been a number of instances where there's proof that they have given training in making and planting bombs. So the government has to look at both types of terrorism. Unfortunately, the media mostly goes with a one-sided story. Whenever there is a bomb blast, the same day the media comes out with the names of Muslim boys. They are picked up but the conviction rate is very poor. This kind of action only leads to mistrust and fear in the entire community.

*SN*: Was this the agenda in your meeting with the home minister (after the storm over the article criticising his policy in handling Maoists)?

*DS*: This is the main agenda I have taken up with him and, of course, the issue of Hindu radicals infiltrating our government, bureaucracy and armed forces.

*SN*: You have attacked the home minister's policies in tackling the Maoists and you have called him arrogant.

*DS*: If you see my article in its totality, you will realise that I have not actually attacked him but am defending him. Why is he unnecessarily taking the responsibility for the BJP? I still hold him in the highest respect. He is a friend. But I have always maintained that unless you win back the people living in these areas, you will not be able to deal with the Maoists. Look at the Andhra Pradesh model. There, after the 2004 elections, the government under YSR [Y. S. Rajasekhara Reddy] started peace talks with them. They had three rounds of talks which broke down on the central issue of whether they can carry arms or must surrender them. How could any responsible government allow any citizen of this country to carry illegal arms? So the talks broke down. But all the pro-poor measures that the Maoists had recommended, the Congress government of YSR implemented strongly. Secondly, the Congress party took up the issue at the political level also. APCC [Andhra Pradesh Congress Committee] President and MP, Dr Keshav Rao, went on a *padayatra* along with local Congressmen. For 14 days, they walked in Maoist-affected areas. It had a very positive impact, along with the pro-poor measures. And along with this, the government also picked up the hardcore Maoist leadership which had been propagating violence. Violence can never be condoned. I have differed with Chidambaram on his strategy but we remain friends. It is for the Centre to take a holistic view and plan a package. Law and order is for the state government to handle. The buck should stop with the chief minister, not the Union home minister. So I was actually defending the home minister.

*SN*: The Congress represents a dual face. There is Chidambaram on one side and there is you, a general secretary who articulates the most secular liberal views. Is this dualism deliberate?

*DS*: I don't think so. If you see the Congress resolutions and ideology — even before Independence — it has always opposed both Hindu and Muslim radicals at the same time.

*SN*: Do you think the Congress is fighting the Hindu radicals adequately?

*DS*: Well, you may question the degree to which they are fighting them. But one thing is certain; the Congress party can never compromise with Hindu radicals or Muslim fundamentalists. It has been toeing the middle-of-the-road line and I think this country needs that.

*SN*: In all these matters you are seen as speaking for a strong section of the Congress party while Mr Chidambaram is often praised by the BJP...

*DS*: I really can't comment on that. Probably, the BJP may sort of approve of certain things. The fact remains that Mr Chidambaram is a highly competent minister, very articulate, very hard working, very sincere. The only issue on which I really did not agree with him — and which was wrongly projected also — was that the government of India wants to control the Maoists through army, air force and drones, which I think was not correct.

*SN*: *Outlook* recently did a story about your phone being tapped along with that of others?

*DS*: I found out from my own sources. The NTRO [National Technical Research Organisation] had some problems among the top officials and one section leaked this against the other. They had bought some equipment which they were trying out and it so happened that I passed through that area and they must have picked that up. I don't think it matters . . . or someone was after me deliberately (smiles). As far as I am concerned, I don't mind my phone being tapped. I have nothing to hide.

*SN*: The Batla House issue and the encounter and the follow-up trip to Azamgarh was very controversial, very interesting. How do you see it now? It has also been said that your relations with Chidambaram soured when you took the boys' families to meet him and he was not supportive.

*DS*: I have always held that, and I still believe, the Batla House encounter was not real. At the same time, I also have the greatest regard for Mr Sharma, who laid down his life. But from the facts that came to light, according to me, this kind of encounter looks quite unlikely. I took up the issue with the PM, who gave it to the National Human Rights Commission. In its own wisdom, it inquired into it and came out with the view that the encounter was genuine. Then a PIL [public interest litigation] was filed in the high court asking for a judicial inquiry. It was turned down. The matter went to the Supreme Court, which also turned it down. I don't want to go into that. But the fact remains that because of the incident over 26 boys from Azamgarh and thereabouts was picked up on the basis of telephone conversations they had with the boys who were killed. I don't think that is evidence enough. Against some of these boys, more than 60 cases have been registered in six different cities in four states. And the way such cases move in our country, it will take years and years . . . their lives will be ruined. For example, this boy who has been found innocent in the Lajpat Nagar bombing spent 14 years in jail. In the Mecca Masjid case also, an innocent was charged . . . I think there's a need for a speedy trial of all these boys so that cases can be decided one way or the other. Second, for those who are absconding, we have asked for a reinvestigation.

*SN*: What happened when you took the families to the home minister?

*DS*: Well, he spoke to us. He had his own views on the issues and we are waiting to hear what he has to say about it. He said he'll get back to us.

*SN*: Was Sonia Gandhi upset with you over the timing of the article that attacked Chidambaram?

*DS*: I would not like to discuss that.

*SN*: How would you describe Rahul Gandhi's style of functioning?

*DS*: He's very thorough. Goes into details. Has an inquisitive mind. And he has great political sense.

*SN*: Is he PM material?

*DS*: He has the ability and the political sense to make a very fine prime minister.

*SN*: You are handling the most challenging project for the party, Uttar Pradesh, where the Congress did well in the 2009 Lok Sabha elections. It is also a state to which Rahul Gandhi is devoting much of his energies. But now that the UPA has come to some sort of understanding with Mayawati (to survive the cut motions), does it complicate your life? How do you call her *daulat ki beti* [daughter of wealth] if she is helping your government?

*DS*: There's no confusion here. The BSP [Bahujan Samaj Party] has given its support to the present government and they have not withdrawn it. So, as it stands today, they are supporting us. They have been given the mandate to run the UP [Uttar Pradesh] government for five years. They have to deliver. But the kind of corruption that has set in in Uttar Pradesh is unparalleled. The way money is being made, the way mining rights are being given away, the way contracts are being given away. They are giving contracts to build parks, walls, elephants and things which are quite unnecessary. Uttar Pradesh is a poor state. What it needs is more investment in infrastructure. Not a single power plant has come up in UP since the Congress government went in 1989. Industries are closing down. State power houses are being sold off. Mayawati has to deliver. All our government of India schemes is being squandered away. The PDS [Public Distribution System] has collapsed. So it is our primary duty as a political party to bring this to the notice of the people.

*SN*: Is this a test case for Rahul Gandhi? Is your UP campaign entirely built around him?

*DS*: No, Rahul Gandhi cannot be confined to one state. Of course, UP is his home state and he has a lot of interest in it. But as a national leader, he cannot be confined to one state.

*SN*: Is Rita Bahuguna on her way out as party chief in UP?

*DS*: No. She's working hard, doing a fine job.

*SN*: Sonia Gandhi is said to be quite adamant about pushing women's reservation through even at the cost of her government. Do you have any insight into how things will pan out?

*DS*: She has very strong convictions. For example, on the issue of the NREGA and Right to Information she never compromised. She has been strongly advocating the food security bill. Similarly, she feels very strongly about women's reservation.

*SN*: Do you think she will push it in the foreseeable future or closer to the next general election?

*DS*: Well, knowing Mrs Gandhi a little bit, I feel she has great political will and no one will be able to stop it.

*SN*: Political allies have lately been an embarrassment for the Congress?

*DS*: Every party has its own political agenda. But Dr Manmohan Singh has been quite clear that on the issue of corruption, there can't be any compromises. About Sharad Pawar and Praful Patel, their names have been brought into the IPL [Indian Premier League] scandal but are there any substantial charges? And as far as Shashi Tharoor is concerned, the poor fellow had to lose his job. The impression created was such that he had to resign. But I don't think there is any substantial evidence against him.

*SN*: You were a powerful CM once, now you are powerful in the Congress organisation but you choose not to be in the cabinet. What role do you see for yourself in the future?

*DS*: I am not going back to state politics. I enjoy being a general secretary in the AICC [All India Congress Committee] and also enjoy the confidence Sonia and Rahul Gandhi have reposed in me while giving me this most sensitive state, Uttar Pradesh. My biggest political challenge now is that the Congress should form the government in the state in 2012.

*SN*: You stand by the views expressed in your article. Do you also stand by the remark that Mr Chidambaram is arrogant?

*DS*: No, no. It's a private sort of comment I made. He's a friend. I'm sure he did not mind it.

ॐ

# 15

# No Back Door Entry to Private Firms for Mining

## B. K. Handique*

✪

The government today said it would not tolerate any 'back door' entries by industry for seeking mines, a move that could dampen corporate efforts of forging alliances with PSUs [public sector undertakings] for their mining projects. Asked about the industrial controversies relating to mining activities like that in Orissa, Mines Minister B. K. Handique said that mining lease was given to a state PSU and not the corporate giant Vedanta Resources.

'In the name of PSUs, no more back door entry will be allowed. Yes, they (private companies) have made back door entries', Handique told reporters on the sidelines of FIMI's [Federation of Indian Mineral Industries] 44th Annual General Meeting here.

Sources in the ministry said that the new mining bill will not allow such indirect route[s] adopted by private firms to pursue mining projects by joining hands with state mineral companies.

'We are not against joint ventures. But if the mining lease is given to PSUs it should be utilised by PSUs. In the new Act, we will plug the existing legislative loophole to ensure this', a senior Mines Ministry official said.

The Mines Ministry is working to bring in transparency in the sector through a new legislation which is likely to be presented in the winter session of [the] Parliament.

* This article was previously published as 'No Back Door Entry to Private Firms for Mining', *Hindustan Times*, 15 September 2010.

Many state PSUs have tied up with private firms forming projects including Orissa Mineral Corporation (OMC) and Mysore Mineral Limited (MML). While [the] OMC has inked [a] pact with [the] Vedanta Group firm, [the] MML has entered an agreement with JSW Steel Limited for mining. [The] Andhra Pradesh Mineral Development Corporation has also tied up with [the] JSW Group for bauxite mining at Araku region.

[The] OMC holds bauxite mining lease at [the] ecologically sensitive Niyamgiri hills in Orissa while [the] MML has got the rights to mine iron ore in Thimmappangudi Mine in Karnataka.

Meanwhile [the] apex miners' body FIMI had blamed state PSUs for taking advantage of private firms under the joint venture mining route.

Billionaire Anil Agarwal-led Vedanta Group was refused green clearances for its proposed mining project at Niyamgiri hills in Orissa for which it had tied up with [the] OMC.

Vedanta Resources' flagship firm Sterlite Industries had entered into a pact with [the] OMC in 2004 for bauxite mining to feed its aluminium project in Orissa.

'In 2004, it (mining lease for Niyamgiri) was given to [the] OMC, so through back door entry they have done it. Whichever route you take that must be correct. We have not given approval to Vedanta. We approved it for OMC', Handique said.

'Definitely I do agree, Environment Ministry should be staying it, otherwise there will be a disaster', Handique said.

಄

# 16

# Ironic? Story of the Great Indian Loot

## Shankar Raghuraman*

✪

Take a look at the accompanying map and you can't but notice the extent of overlap between India's thickly forested areas, the regions with the bulk of the country's most important mineral wealth and the territory over which Maoists are dominant. Is this just a coincidence? No, that would stretch credulity.

So what connects the Maoist menace with forests and mining? Clearly, forests give a guerrilla force its best chance of taking on the might of the state. But any guerrilla army needs more than just thick foliage. Insurgents thrive where the local population is sympathetic to them or at least not sympathetic towards the state.

That's where mining comes into the picture. There has been a long history of traditional forest dwellers being denied the right to live off the forest, a process that cannot but lead to alienation. Add to that a mining policy regime that has allowed massive scaling up of mining in the same areas for super profits, and it is not difficult to see why many tribals believe the state is hostile to their interests, but in tune with corporate interests.

Mining projects have repeatedly led to localised protests. In many cases, the administration has muttered darkly about agent provocateurs from outside fishing in troubled waters. In states like Orissa, Maoists have been accused of exploiting local resentment for their own ends.

* This article was previously published as 'Ironic? Story of the Great Indian Loot', *The Times of India*, 5 June 2010. The Times of India. © Bennett, Coleman & Co. Ltd., 2011. All Rights Reserved.

Source: Centre for Science and Environment.

To understand how mining policy has actually helped the Maoists, let's take the specific case of iron ore — crucial for Chhattisgarh and Orissa and not insignificant for Jharkhand, all states with a serious Maoist problem on their hands.

At the turn of the millennium in 2001–01, India exported iron ore worth a measly ₹ 358 crore. By 2008–09, that figure was up to ₹ 21,725 crore, a sixty-fold jump in just seven years. Driving this export of ore were several factors. One was the decanalisation of exports of ore with an iron content of 64 per cent or less in the late 1990s. The other was China's seemingly insatiable appetite for iron ore in the run-up to the 2008 Beijing Olympics. As a result, the international price of ore — with 63 per cent iron content — soared to $ 200 per tonne in March 2008, more than four times the price five years ago.

Indian ore exporters thus had a ready and profitable market. The icing on the cake was provided by the royalty rates charged by the government. The rates fixed in October 2004 varied from as little as ₹ 4 per tonne for low-grade ore to a maximum of ₹ 27 per tonne for the highest grades. There was also no export duty.

To see what this meant, check out what the Karnataka Lok Ayukta had to say on the allegations of illegal mining in the Bellary region of the state. Its report submitted in December 2008 pointed out that when the export price was hovering around ₹ 6,000 to ₹ 7,000 per tonne, the state government was getting between ₹ 16 and ₹ 27 by way of royalty. The extraction cost to the miner was, by the state's own admission, of the order of ₹ 150 per tonne. The Lok Ayukta noted that even if the transportation cost was estimated at ₹ 250 per tonne, the total cost for the exporter would be no more than ₹ 427 per tonne.

Since the export price of the ore even in a slump was never lower than ₹ 1,500 per tonne, that would leave a neat profit of ₹ 1,073 per tonne. Out of this, the state was getting at best ₹ 27.

So outraged was the Lok Ayukta by these calculations, that the report went on to advocate a complete ban not just on export of ore but also on its trading, saying it should be reserved only for captive mining by domestic steel producers.

A committee appointed by the planning commission in 2005 to examine the national mining policy, observed that 'the margins available in the mining sector have been very substantial and are widely expected to continue being so in the foreseeable future'. It recommended in December 2006 that royalty rates be reviewed. A subsequent study group suggested that the royalty be pegged at 10 per cent of the sale price of ore.

It took another two years before the ministry finally notified the new rates in August 2009. But there was a catch. The 'sale price', which was to form the basis for the ad valorem rates, would be determined by the Indian Bureau of Mines (IBM) on the basis of the average of sale prices reported by non-captive producers.

To see why this made a mockery of the 10 per cent rate, just look at the numbers for February 2010, the last month for which the IBM has put up the sale prices on its website. The all-India sale price average for lumps of 62–65 per cent iron content was ₹ 1,760 per tonne. The highest sale price for any state for this grade of ore was put at ₹ 1,949 per tonne.

Against this, the average international price prevailing in February for Indian ore of 63 per cent iron content bound for Chinese ports was $ 128 per tonne, which is closer to ₹ 6,000 per tonne. Even allowing for transportation costs, which can be significant, clearly there is a wide gap between the price at which the royalty rate is being applied and what the exporter is actually getting.

Why do these details of iron ore extraction and sale matter? Because the enormous margins involved — in exports as well as domestic sales — mean that the scope for sleaze and the temptation for illegal mining are huge.

And this is where the connection with Maoists lies. Not only has rapacious mining turned the tribal away from the state, it has reportedly provided a steady source of funding for the Maoists through extortion. In short, by promoting this variety of crony capitalism, the state has shot itself in the foot.

So, what's the way out? When TOI [*The Times of India*] recently asked a union minister whether it would be a good idea to auction mines to raise more revenues for the states, which could then put a chunk of it back into development work for the local community, the minister's response was, 'But why allow exports in the first place?'

That's the language of Left radicals, but when it comes from a minister, it's an indication of how serious the problem has become.

Since 2007, the government has imposed export duties on iron ore that have varied between 0 and 15 per cent, but are we in for a further tightening of the screws?

ॐ

# 17

# Cannot Deny Links between Forest Departments and Mining Lobbies

*Jairam Ramesh*
Interview by Shalini Singh*

✪

Jairam Ramesh, 56, has been India's environment and forest minister since May 2009. His ministry gives environmental clearances — mandatory for all mining activities. In November [2009], it rejected coal-mining proposals in Tadoba Andhari Tiger Reserve in Maharashtra. In April, activist groups along the Western Ghats wrote a letter to Sonia Gandhi praising the minister's efforts to protect India's forests.

*Shalini Singh (SS)*: The question that's on everyone's minds — is the earth really getting warmer?

*Jairam Ramesh (JR)*: Anecdotally it certainly seems to be true. Every time the temperature shoots up to over 42 degrees, and since all of us are amateur scientists we think it is . . . but is there incontrovertible evidence to show that the world is getting warmer? Well, responsible scientist like James Hansen of NASA is on record as having said that the earth is getting warmer. Rainfall patterns have certainly become irregular — every time I go to Cherapunji for example, people tell me it's raining much less

---

* This article was previously published as 'Cannot Deny Links between Forest Departments and Mining Lobbies', *Hindustan Times*, 15 May 2010. © HT Media Ltd.

than what it used to earlier. So yes, perhaps, the earth is getting warmer.

*SS:* Let's talk about mining. We've been seeing cases of rampant and illegal mining tumbling out — it has become a serious issue now. How has your ministry responded to it?

*JR*: Well, we have identified regions of our country where clearly mining has reached limits that may cross the carrying capacity of that region. Goa is a classic example, where we have put a moratorium on future mining. Western Ghats is another area where I've set up an expert panel under the chairmanship of Madhav Gadgil, one of our top ecologists, who is identifying the critical areas in the Western Ghats. Then we have put critical mining projects on hold, like the Vedanta project is still under examination. We are much more careful now. We've put a number of coal mining projects on hold. We've identified go areas and no-go areas and have actually rejected a number of coal mining openings in no-go areas particularly in Chhattisgarh. But we need to mine. Let us be very clear. Mining activity cannot come to a halt. But illegal mining must stop. We have taken very tough action. I've written to the chief minister of Karnataka for example where a lot of illegal mining has taken place, we've cancelled a number of mining leases also in Karnataka. Mining must go on, legal mining must go on. But even where there is legal mining and if it is in dense forest areas, then we have to have a second look as is in the case of coal. It's a ticklish issue. But unfortunately in our country, mining has not been done in an ecologically sustainable manner so far . . .

*SS:* Is there a sustainable way to mine?

*JR*: Well yeah, the Germans have done it, the Americans have also done it. Even in India, Neyveli Lignite is a good example of sustainable mining. Singareni is another one in Andhra Pradesh. If we are more sensitive we can come up with ways. But we have to be careful of mining in tribal areas particularly — where you have to look at issues like who's going to be the beneficiary of those mines . . .

*SS:* How do you read mining scams like the Reddy brothers in Karnataka, Madhu Koda in Jharkhand?

*JR*: I can't do anything about the scams. I can only enforce the acts, which are the Environment Protection Act, the Forest Conservation Act and the Wildlife Protection Act. Those are the only three instruments I have. I can't go after Madhu Kodas, if he has violated any of these acts, then I can take action.

*SS:* Ok, so how does the ministry look at the state forest departments who are in collusion with mining lobbies in their states?

*JR*: Well, I cannot deny the collusion. Whether it's Orissa, Jharkhand, Madhya Pradesh . . . any state, there is collusion. But then remember state governments are also under pressure to show results of investment. Chief ministers want to get private investment; they want to show their economies are doing well.

*SS:* In the case of Goa, recently there were two approved projects that your ministry overturned, and there is enough material to prove that the forest department of Goa is hand-in-glove with the mining lobby there. How does the ministry look at this?

*JR*: You take tough action . . .

*SS:* What kind of tough action?

*JR*: We've issued a moratorium on mining; we're rejecting projects . . . what more action do you want?

*SS:* What about action against such officials?

*JR*: There is a fine constitutional balance to be protected here. I can only bring it to the notice of the state government. They have to take action against its officials. If there are officers in the forest department, in our regional offices, then we can take action against them.

*SS:* What about forest departments denying the presence of tigers in certain areas because they don't want buffer zones that would affect mining? Again, taking an example from Goa.

*JR*: Yes, that and even Maharashtra has been very slow in declaring buffer zones around Tadoba. Traditionally, state governments have been reluctant to declare buffer zones because it would preclude mining activity. But I've also rejected a proposal of opening a coalmine in Tadoba buffer zone in Maharashtra. I think the signals that have gone from the ministry are strong. But the idea is not to stop mining activity or bring economic activity to a halt. The idea is to deal with illegalities in mining and ensure mining doesn't violate the three acts under the environment ministry.

*SS*: So how do you look at preventing illegal mining?

*JR*: We've taken action against Oubalapuram where there were allegations of illegalities. We've ordered a survey. [The] Supreme Court has also intervened. I've written to the chief minister of Karnataka where there are a lot of allegations of illegal mining. If they are violating the forest conservation act we can take action against them.

*SS*: Let's talk about the dams coming up in Arunachal Pradesh . . .

*JR*: See, on the same river you can have a series of projects and we know the project-wise assessment is not going to work, so we must look at the carrying capacity of the river. We have done this for the north Teesta, we have put a halt to five projects. Similarly we have made recommendations on abandoning projects on the Bhagirathi because you need a minimum environmental flow in these critical rivers. The idea is not to stop dam construction per se but the idea is to, say, look at balance between development and environment. And where these projects are essential, let's do them in an ecological sustainable manner.

*SS*: Forest clearances are required for mining. How does the ministry look at these? People on the ground in Goa have said that mining continues in places without relevant leases.

*JR*: That the state government has to take action. All I can say is if a project has got clearance under the Forest Clearance Act, it's not an illegal project. An illegal one is where they don't have permission. It'll start with the local authorities where the state governments have to play their role. I can't be a policeman all the time, only a facilitator. The laws are central; the legislation has to be local.

*SS*: How does one enforce them?

*JR*: The state government has to enforce them. The machinery is under them . . .

*SS*: In case there's violation, how does the ministry deal with it?

*JR*: We can certainly take action if there is violation. In the case of Vedanta, we sent a team, they gave a report, [and] we are examining that report. Where reports come to us of violations we don't have the machinery to check ourselves so we send teams. I have sent teams to Kerala, on Vedanta, Goa, Karnataka . . .

*SS*: How has the coastal regulation zone (CRZ) played out on India's coastline over the years?

*JR*: We have a CRZ 1991; we have had 25 amendments to it. We're now in the process of Draft CRZ 2010, which will clean up a lot of the CRZ 1991. We don't want to weaken CRZ 91. We're coming out with CRZ 2010, which will strengthen CRZ 1991 and recognise certain areas in India that need specialised treatment. For example, Goa, Kerala, Mumbai, Andamans, Lakshadweep. You may have an overarching CRZ but for each of these ecologically special areas, it'll require special treatment. The Draft will be put in public domain; I've already had five public consultations in Goa, Mumbai, Cochin, Puri and Chennai with the public and fishermen . . .

*SS*: The mining policy in India is not legally bound. But the government is in a position to regulate activities. How does the government look at the scams?

*JR*: I can't do anything about the scams, my mandate is limited. I have to ensure the laws are not violated. You're asking larger questions of the nexus of mining and politics, I can't get into that, I don't have the wherewithal . . .

*SS*: But the environment ministry plays a big role in clearing mining leases . . .

*JR*: The environment ministry's mandate is to ensure the three laws are complied with. We can't get into corruption act, money laundering etc., that's not our mandate. We have to see that our troika of acts is implemented in letter and spirit.

*SS*: What kind of development is the environment ministry looking at?

*JR*: There are three responses I will have to any project — one is yes, second is yes but, third is no. This can't be a 'yes yes' ministry, it can't be a 'no no' ministry, it has to be a nuanced ministry. The nuance is that today a bulk of the projects are in the 'yes' category, a good number in the 'yes but' category, a few in the 'no' category. The headlines only end up on the 'no' category, the media will focus on clashes between two ministries. The fact is that this ministry clears 95 per cent projects from an environmental point of view, over 85 per cent from the forest point of view . . .

*SS*: Then how do some projects get clearances faster than they should?

*JR*: Some projects have had push and pulls. Today the system is transparent, I have removed all conflict of interests; I have changed chairmen of environmental appraisal committees. Today all information on each pending project is on the website, we are making it as business-like as possible.

*SS*: How are you planning to crackdown on illegal mining projects?

*JR*: We will be more careful . . .

*SS*: How can violations by forest departments in states be dealt with?

*JR*: Not clearing projects without feasibility studies, we will take action if there are violations. Look at them more carefully. I have turned down many proposals recommended by forest advisory committees. We plan to do more studies. It all starts from the top; I have to send the right signals.

*SS*: What about sustainable economic development?

*JR*: There's no magic formula. All three have to form part of finding the balance, find the golden mean. You can't be theological, you need development, you need projects; they create employment.

*SS*: India is looking to increase its forest cover and yet there's rampant mining taking place. How do we reconcile these two?

*JR*: We have identified go and no-go areas especially in the case of coal mining in nine major coalfields. Almost 35 per cent of coal blocks are in no go areas, where there is high tree density and forest cover. We haven't done this for iron ore yet. Coal is serious because we have to double our coal production in the next 7–8 years. Incremental coal is going to come from forest areas — Orissa, Jharkhand, MP [Madhya Pradesh], Chhattisgarh . . .

*SS*: How will you look at illegal mining?
*JR*: Stop illegal mining. Courts. Only way to do it. Rule of law prevails.

ॐ

# 18

# As Forests Feed Growth, Tribals Given the Go-By

## Nitin Sethi*

✪

Naxals are not Gandhians with guns. But nor do adivasis go around dancing in the forests draped in exotic costumes and enjoy tranquil lives, as tourist brochures and Doordarshan would have us believe.

The truth is that over the past century, millions of tribals, who grew up and live in these forests, find themselves dispossessed of their forest land and its produce. Before their eyes, the adivasis have seen their means of livelihood being taken away. Simultaneously, mines have sprung up on their forest lands, earning thousands of crores every year for everyone else but them. In fact, the forests have fed India's growth story.

This isn't an exaggeration. The three tribal-dominated states of Orissa, Chhattisgarh and Jharkhand are the most productive mineral-bearing states in the country. They account for 70 per cent of India's coal reserves, 80 per cent of its high-grade iron ore, 60 per cent of its bauxite and almost 100 per cent of its chromite reserves. Of the top 50 mineral-producing districts in the country, almost half are tribal.

---

* This article was previously published as 'As Forests Feed Growth, Tribals Given the Go-By', *The Times of India*, 5 June 2010. The Times of India. © Bennett, Coleman & Co. Ltd., 2011. All Rights Reserved.

There are more startling statistics. The average forest cover in the 50 mineral producing districts is 28 per cent, much more than the national average. Chhattisgarh has the highest forest cover — around 43 per cent. Jharkhand has 30 per cent, Orissa 27 per cent and Madhya Pradesh 26 per cent. They continue to have this green cover despite years of rampant deforestation.

An estimated 1.64 lakh hectares of forest land has already been diverted for mining in the country. The tribals, who are the 'original' inhabitants here, don't own much of these rich forests. They once did. But when the forest laws were brought into force, first by the Raj and then by independent India, thousands were evicted and their property converted into state property. Most of the tribals ended up working on their own forestlands, in some cases, as bonded labour. To make matters worse, the Indian government named many of them encroachers and began a violent phase of forced evictions. The courts, which too wanted to protect forests but not necessarily the forest dwellers, often added to their misery.

Take the case of Orissa. 'More than 50 [per cent] of the all scheduled tribe landowners in Orissa are marginal landholders and another 20 [per cent] at least are landless', writes Kundan Kumar, an academic and tribal activist, citing the ['Agriculture Census 1995–96'].[1] Three-fourths of the scheduled lands are owned by the state governments with almost half of them declared as forest lands.

Of the 50 major mining districts, 60 per cent are among the 150 most backward districts of India. Four of these districts — two in Orissa and one each in Jharkhand and Chhattisgarh — are among the 25 most backward districts in the country, and 13 figure in the 50 most backward districts list.

For those who claim mining (and such 'development') would help find employment, here is a telling fact. The formal mining sector employs just 5.6 lakh people and this number is coming

[1] Kundan Kumar, 'Dispossessed and Displaced: A Brief Paper on Tribal Issues in Orissa', Discussion Paper, Vasundhara, Bhubaneswar, Orissa, 2004.

down. Between 1991 and 2004, the number of people employed in mining came down by 30 per cent, but the value of mineral production went up several times. Tribals have seen the value of mineral production rising since the liberalisation of the mining sector in 1993 from ₹ 25,000 crore in 1993–94 to ₹ 84,000 crore-plus in 2005–06.

These figures, of course, don't reflect the hundreds of crore worth of illegal mining that goes on in this region, virtually unchecked. Nor do they tell the story of the paltry royalty paid to the government by the mining industry that enjoys mind-boggling profits on exports.

Does this explain, even if partially, why Maoists find ready refuge among these tribals?

ॐ

# 19

# An Eco-Visionary Par Excellence

### Jairam Ramesh*

✪

The first United Nations Conference on the Human Environment began on 5 June 1972, and it is to commemorate this historic conclave that the day is marked as World Environment Day ever since 1973. Olaf Palme was the Swedish Prime Minister then and, therefore, was obliged to be present. The only other Head of State to attend was Indira Gandhi.

It was my friend Tariq Banuri at the UN [United Nations] who placed Gandhi's participation at the Stockholm summit in its larger setting. In a conversation, he said that four events have shaped the modern discourse on environment. The first was the publication of Rachel Carson's *Silent Spring* in 1962.[1] The second was the publication of Paul Ehrlich's *Population Bomb* in 1968.[2] The third was the release of *Limits to Growth* by the Club of Rome in early-1972,[3] and the fourth was Indira Gandhi's speech at Stockholm in which environmental issues were, for the first time, situated in their larger developmental context. Apparently, in recognition of her contribution in Stockholm, the first choice

* This article was previously published as 'An Eco-Visionary Par Excellence', *Hindustan Times*, 5 June 2010. © HT Media Ltd.

[1] Rachel Carson, *Silent Spring* (Boston: Houghton Mifflin, 1962).

[2] Paul R. Ehrlich, *Population Bomb* (New York: Ballantine Books, 1968).

[3] Donella H. Meadows, Dennis L. Meadows, Jorgen Randers and William W. Behrens III, *The Limits to Growth; A Report for the Club of Rome's Project on the Predicament of Mankind* (New York: Universe Books, 1972).

for locating the new United Nations Environment Programme (UNEP) was New Delhi but ultimately it was headquartered in Nairobi.

My own appreciation of Gandhi's contributions has been deepened over the last year. I knew of Silent Valley and how single-handedly she saved that rainforest. But the Valley was only one instance of her zeal. It is to her [that] we owe a slew of legislation[s]: the Wild Life Protection Act, 1972; Project Tiger, 1973; the Forest Conservation Act, 1980; and the Coastal Regulation Zone Notification, 1991. That her mind was on saving India's natural heritage is revealed by an extraordinary event — her writing to Kedar Pande, the then Chief Minister of Bihar, in July 1972 from Shimla conveying her displeasure on how forests were being felled in that state, even as she was negotiating the Shimla Pact with Zulfiqar Ali Bhutto.

To Gandhi, environmental preservation meant more than pollution control or saving endangered species. She had a much broader conception and that is why she set up the Delhi Urban Arts Commission. One of her directives in this regard given in 1982 is worth quoting in full: 'Maharashtra Government should be asked to ensure that on the Nhava and Elephanta islands no commercial or building activity of any description is allowed and positive steps are taken to green them and if necessary convert them into parks with birds, wildlife etc.'

Only a biography will unravel the well-springs of Gandhi's contributions in the field of environment. Perhaps this biography will draw our attention to the influence of her parents, particularly her mother who, in her own words, 'used to tell me of the links between all creatures'. Perhaps, her reading habits had something to do with it. Then perhaps, her fascination with Tagore's poetry and her stint at Shantiniketan itself moulded her thinking. Perhaps it could be her enduring love for the wondrous eco-system of Kashmir that she shared with her father that shaped her love for nature. Perhaps it was her friendship with people like Salim Ali that influenced her actions. Whatever it was, India owes her a debt of gratitude.

We are now being forced to make tough political choices in different sectors like power, mining and industry to make the inevitable trade-off between environment and development explicit. Almost three decades ago, Gandhi made one such choice in regard to Silent Valley and protected that biodiversity-rich region. This 5 June, we can do no better than to resolve to use her as a talisman as we strive to sustain high economic growth not at the cost of our environment and biodiversity in its myriad forms but while protecting and regenerating them.

༄

# PART IV

POSSIBLE SOLUTIONS

# 20

# Force Alone Can't Rout the Maoists

*Nitish Kumar**

✪

Bihar CM Nitish Kumar has publicly crossed swords with Union Home Minister P. Chidambaram on his anti-Maoist strategy. Excerpts from an interview:

◉

*Outlook (O)*: The Centre and states have not exactly seen eye to eye on the Maoist issue?

*Nitish Kumar (NK)*: The Centre must go beyond giving advice or sending central forces — they should provide intelligence and resources for development. We're doing what we can with our limited resources. We've been pleading for a saturation of quality development, for roads, schools, health centres. In a federal structure, there must be mutual respect between the two, with the Centre as facilitator.

Chidambaram has created the impression that some states are not cooperating with the Centre. A fuss was made because I didn't attend the Calcutta meeting (called by PC [Chidambaram]) earlier this year. We were in Delhi, it could've been held there. As CM, I have many responsibilities. I can't remain engaged in

---

* This article was previously published as 'Force Alone Can't Rout the Maoists', *Outlook*, 26 April 2010.

one job. Once overall policy is declared, states can coordinate on inter-state operations without supervision.

*O*: How should the Maoist problem be tackled?

*NK*: All disadvantaged sections must get their rightful share. They have to feel they are at an advantage by being part of the democratic process, which in turn will create the right atmosphere for police operations. The Maoists can't be finished off through force alone. When governments fail to deliver, all kinds of forces spring up. The political executive is different from the bureaucracy or the police. The CM can't be the head of the police force. He should give policy directions, not micro-manage police operations.

*O*: Do you agree with those who say the Maoists are criminals?

*NK*: I don't. Without ideological motivation at the higher levels, you can't have such a movement. The lower levels may be different though. All kinds of political views exist in a democracy. Maoists want power through violence. I disagree with that as I believe change through violence will be unstable.

*O*: One argument against development in Maoist-affected areas is that they destroy government-built facilities.

*NK*: If those in power settle on the course of inaction, the people will blow up their *kursi* [chair]. Every year, there are floods but do we stop repairing what's destroyed because there may be another flood? We must deal with problems as they arise, not stand back and do nothing. Democracy through inclusive growth can only happen after a long struggle.

৵

# 21

# Maoism: The Alaska Permanent Fund Solution

## Santosh Paul

✪

The first task of this Assembly is to free India through a new constitution to feed the starving people and cloth the naked masses and to give every Indian fullest opportunity to develop himself according to his capacity. . . . But at present the greatest and most important question in India is how to solve the problem of the poor and the starving. Wherever we turn, we are confronted with this problem. If we cannot solve this problem soon all our paper constitutions will become useless and purposeless.

Jawaharlal Nehru speaking on the Aims and Object resolution in the Constituent Assembly, 22 January 1947[1]

At first blush, the Alaska of Sarah Palin — the unsuccessful 2008 Republican US Vice Presidential candidate — and that of the terrain of the Maoists — in the forests belts of India — appear to be worlds apart. But there is a common thread that runs through these two worlds. Sarah Palin was born in 1964 when the State of Alaska was exploiting its gas and oil reserves. It was a time when the Alaskans were vexed with the problem of how they could directly benefit from the huge royalties and revenues being generated

---

[1] Jawaharlal Nehru, *Constituent Assembly of India Debates*, vol. 2, 22 January 1947, pp. 316–17, http://164.100.47.132/lssnew/constituent/vol2p3.html (accessed on 27 February 2012).

through mineral mining. The Maoist argument is a radical extension of that very same thought. They argue that mineral exploitation entails the land-dependent poor losing their lands and not getting a penny's worth from the sale of minerals.

Huge revenues were generated after successful oil explorations in the 1960s in the State of Alaska. The millions of dollars of revenue from the leasing of mines were quickly squandered by the politicians without any tangential benefits to the citizens of Alaska. Then came the Trans-Alaska Pipeline System built in the mid-1970s that pumped the high-priced oil into America. Alaskans realised the transient nature of their oil reserves and their mineral wealth. They desired that the revenues generated from the oil must benefit the present and future generation of Alaskans. In 1975, the voters in Alaska approved a Constitutional Amendment to establish a dedicated fund — the Alaska Permanent Fund. The amendment mandated that 25 per cent of all mineral lease rentals, royalties, royalty sales proceeds, federal mineral revenue-sharing payments and bonuses received by the State of Alaska were to be invested in the 'Fund'. Article IX, Section 15 of the Alaska Constitution contains the laws pertaining to the Alaska Permanent Fund:[2]

> At least twenty-five per cent of all mineral lease rentals, royalties, royalty sale proceeds, federal mineral revenue sharing payments and bonuses received by the State shall be placed in a permanent fund, the principal of which shall be used only for those income-producing investments specifically designated by law as eligible for permanent fund investments. All income from the permanent fund shall be deposited in the general fund unless otherwise provided by law (Effective 21 February 1977).[3]

Till 1980 there was considerable confusion as to what was to be done with the incomes of the funds. In 1980, the Legislature

---

[2] Gordon Scott Harrison and Alaska Legislative Affairs Agency, 'Article IX, Section 15 — Alaska Permanent Fund', in *Alaska's Constitution: A Citizen's Guide* (Juneau: Alaska Legislative Affairs Agency, 2003), p. 156.

[3] Ibid.

of Alaska decided to use the Fund as a trust and established a programme of individual dividends to be paid from the income of the Fund. They created an independent corporation to invest the revenues within legislatively specified parameters. The Legislature also identified three goals[4] for the Fund in 1980:

(a) Provide a means of conserving a portion of revenue from mineral resources to benefit all generations of Alaskans;
(b) Maintain safety of principal while maximizing total return; and
(c) Be used as a savings device managed to allow the maximum use of disposable income from the Fund for uses designated by law.[5]

Although the Permanent Fund began as a receptor for oil revenues, investment earnings is now the largest contributor to fund balance.

The Fund, which started with an initial investment of US$ 734,000 in 1977, has today grown to more than US$ 41.105 billion today.[6] Its investment in US Bonds is US$ 6.172 billion, in US stocks is US$ 6.409 billion, in global and non-US stocks US $ 12.626 billion, and in real estate US$ 4.173 billion.[7] The projected earning is US$ 4–5 billion annually and individual annual dividends are being projected at US$ 3,000–4,000 in the forthcoming years.

The website of the Alaska Permanent Fund declares that their mission is to 'administer the permanent fund dividend programme

---

[4] Cheryl Frasca, Eric Wohlforth and Commonwealth North, 'At A Crossroad: The Permanent Fund, Alaskans, and Alaska's Future', Commonwealth North Study Report, November 2007, http://www.housemajority.org/coms/hfsp/pdfs/CWN_PF_Study.pdf (accessed on 16 March 2012).

[5] Frasca et al., 'At A Crossroad: The Permanent Fund, Alaskans, and Alaska's Future', p. 8.

[6] Unaudited Balance Sheet of the Alaska Permanent Fund as on 16 November 2010. See http://www.apfc.org/home/Content/home/index.cfm (accessed on 25 February 2012).

[7] Ibid.

assuring that: all eligible Alaskans receive timely dividends'.[8] There cannot be a better assurance to a community than to ensure them their share in the proceeds of the minerals mined from their lands. In the year 2005, every Alaskan inhabitant received US$ 845.76 and in the year 2008 they received US$ 2,069. From 1982 through 2009, the dividend programme paid out about US$ 17.5 billion to Alaskans through the annual distribution of dividend cheques. This programme has been a significant contributor to the increase of Alaskans, especially those in rural Alaska. The more the mining, the greater is the prosperity of the Alaskans. The Alaska Permanent Fund is larger than the Gates Foundation (US$ 33 billion) and the Harvard endowment (US$ 34.9 billion),[9] yet smaller than the various sovereign funds of the world. Other governments around the world have created Sovereign Wealth Accounts, which are variations on the Permanent Fund theme. The countries and the estimate of the world's largest sovereign funds are given in Table 21.1.

This concept of 'citizen fund' or 'asset-based egalitarianism' is nothing new or novel. It is a concept that originated in Thomas Paine's 1797 work *Agrarian Justice* where he said '[m]en did not make the earth. It is the value of the improvements only, and not the earth itself, that is individual property. Every proprietor owes to the community a ground rent for the land which he holds'.[10] The Alaska Fund is a successful experiment worth emulating the world over. The fact that several countries have created and are administering Sovereign Wealth Funds is an indicator of the new methodology of equitable accountable governance.

In 1947, Jawaharlal Nehru had warned the Constituent Assembly that unless the problem of poverty was redressed 'all our paper constitutions will become useless and purposeless'.[11]

---

[8] http://www.pfd.state.ak.us/MissionState.aspx (accessed on 28 February 2012).

[9] Gates Foundation value, as of 31 March 2007, and Harvard Endowment value, as of 30 June 2007.

[10] Thomas Paine, *Agrarian Justice* (Philadelphia: Folwell for B.F. Bache, 1797).

[11] Nehru, *Constituent Assembly of India Debates*, vol. 2, pp. 316–17.

**Table 21.1:** Sovereign Wealth Fund Rankings: Largest Sovereign Wealth Funds by Assets under Management[a]

| Country | Fund name | Assets (in US$ billion) | Inception | Origin | Linaburg–Maduell transparency index |
|---|---|---|---|---|---|
| UAE — Abu Dhabi | Abu Dhabi Investment Authority | 627 | 1976 | Oil | 5 |
| Norway | Government Pension Fund – Global | 611 | 1990 | Oil | 10 |
| China | SAFE Investment Company | 567.9[c] | 1997 | Non-Commodity | 4 |
| Saudi Arabia | SAMA Foreign Holdings | 532.8 | n/a | Oil | 4 |
| China | China Investment Corporation | 439.6 | 2007 | Non-Commodity | 7 |
| Kuwait | Kuwait Investment Authority | 296 | 1953 | Oil | 6 |
| China — Hong Kong | Hong Kong Monetary Authority Investment Portfolio | 293.3 | 1993 | Non-Commodity | 8 |
| Singapore | Government of Singapore Investment Corporation | 247.5 | 1981 | Non-Commodity | 6 |
| Singapore | Temasek Holdings | 157.2 | 1974 | Non-Commodity | 10 |
| Russia | National Welfare Fund | 149.7[b] | 2008 | Oil | 5 |
| China | National Social Security Fund | 134.5 | 2000 | Non-Commodity | 5 |
| Qatar | Qatar Investment Authority | 85 | 2005 | Oil | 5 |
| Australia | Australian Future Fund | 73 | 2004 | Non-Commodity | 10 |
| UAE — Dubai | Investment Corporation of Dubai | 70 | 2006 | Oil | 4 |
| Libya | Libyan Investment Authority | 65 | 2006 | Oil | 1 |
| UAE — Abu Dhabi | International Petroleum Investment Company | 58 | 1984 | Oil | 9 |
| Algeria | Revenue Regulation Fund | 56.7 | 2000 | Oil | 1 |
| South Korea | Korea Investment Corporation | 43 | 2005 | Non-Commodity | 9 |

*Continued*

*Continued*

| Country | Fund name | Assets (in US$ billion) | Inception | Origin | Linaburg–Maduell transparency index |
|---|---|---|---|---|---|
| US — Alaska | Alaska Permanent Fund | 40.3 | 1976 | Oil | 10 |
| Kazakhstan | Kazakhstan National Fund | 38.6 | 2000 | Oil | 8 |
| Malaysia | Khazanah Nasional | 36.8 | 1993 | Non-Commodity | 5 |
| Azerbaijan | State Oil Fund | 30.2 | 1999 | Oil | 10 |
| Ireland | National Pensions Reserve Fund | 30 | 2001 | Non-Commodity | 10 |
| Brunei | Brunei Investment Agency | 30 | 1983 | Oil | 1 |
| France | Strategic Investment Fund | 28 | 2008 | Non-Commodity | n/a |
| UAE — Abu Dhabi | Mubadala Development Company | 27.1 | 2002 | Oil | 10 |
| US — Texas | Texas Permanent School Fund | 24.4 | 1854 | Oil and Other | n/a |
| Iran | Oil Stabilisation Fund | 23 | 1999 | Oil | 1 |

*Source:* 'Sovereign Wealth Fund Rankings', Sovereign Wealth Fund Institute, http://www.swfinstitute.org/fund-rankings/ (accessed on 16 March 2012).

*Note:* All figures quoted are from official sources. Where the institutions concerned do not issue statistics of their assets, other publicly available sources have been used. Some of these figures are best estimates as market values change on a day-to-day basis.

ᵃ Updated in March 2012.

ᵇ This includes the oil stabilisation fund of Russia.

ᶜ This number is a best guess estimation.

More than six decades after the working of the Indian Constitution Nehru's warning has become ever more relevant. The violence apart, about 30 different naxalites' groups are active in about 182 of India's administrative districts.

The heart of the problem is the inability of the democratic state to redress poverty. The substantial grievance fuelling the Maoist problem is that people dependent on land are displaced and the mineral wealth is exploited without any benefit to them. It is ironic, that some of 'the poorest people of this country live in the parts of India richest in mineral wealth'.[12] Maoist insurgency is to a large extent confined to the red corridor which runs across the states of Andhra Pradesh, Orissa, Chhattisgarh, Bihar, Jharkhand, Uttar Pradesh and West Bengal. It is this region which has 70 per cent of India's coal reserves, 80 per cent of iron ore, 60 per cent of bauxite, and most of India's chromite reserves.[13] The disaffection with the state by those dependent on the land, who find its mineral wealth exploited without any tangible benefits accruing to them, is forceful argument for the Maoists mounting insurgency against the State.

There are now data available showing that the resources of the country are being sold by a small segment of mining interests without compensating the state for its real worth. There is substance in the complaint. Justice Santosh Hegde, who was Karnataka's Lok Ayukta, was outraged to find that iron ore which was being exported was fetching prices ranging from ₹ 6,000 to ₹ 7,000 per tonne in the year 2006, while the Government merely got royalty ranging from ₹ 16 to ₹ 27.[14] This by any standard is an unacceptable situation.

India, the world's largest democracy, at the end of 60 years of working a constitutional democracy, has nothing to boast about

---

[12] All India Seminar on 'Judicial Reforms', Vigyan Bhawan, New Delhi, 31 July–1 August 2010.

[13] See Nitin Sethi, 'As Forests Feed Growth, Tribals Given the Go-By', *The Times of India*, 5 June 2010 (Chapter 18, this volume).

[14] Shankar Raghuraman, 'Ironic? Story of the Great Indian Loot', *The Times of India*, 5 June 2010 (Chapter 16, this volume).

on poverty alleviation. The unemployment rate for 2010–11,[15] according to the South Asian Association for Regional Cooperation (SAARC), was 9.8 per cent nationwide. Malnutrition remains common particularly among children — 40 per cent of children are underweight.[16] Based on the data for 2011, the United Nations Human Development Report has shown that India ranks at the 134th place on the Human Development Index with 41.6 per cent of India's population living on less than US\$ 1.25 Purchasing Power Parity (PPP) per day.[17] India has severe levels of child malnutrition — third highest in the world — and is home to the largest number of hungry people in the world.[18]

If this problem of equitable distribution of revenues from sale of its mineral wealth vexed a state in capitalist America, the grouse of the displaced poor in India appears legitimate. If the mines pull out all the bauxite from their part of the earth, will their lives be any different? This war of the Maoists, unlike the previous ones, is challenging democracy itself. A purposive legislative instrument and prudent executive action on the lines of the Alaska Permanent Fund and the other Sovereign Funds of the world will go a long way in bringing real development and restoring the faith in democratic governance. Concrete benefits in terms of dividends from revenues of mineral development to the displaced poor is perhaps the first step in the battle for winning over the masses towards democracy.

꙳

---

[15] South Asian Association for Regional Cooperation (SAARC), 'India Country Report 2010: Mid-Term Statistical Appraisal', SAARC Development Goals, Central Statistics Office, Ministry of Statistics and Programme Implementation, Government of India, 2010, http://mospi.nic.in/Mospi_New/upload/SAARC_Development_Goals_India_Country_Report_24mar11.pdf (accessed on 15 March 2012).

[16] Ibid.

[17] United Nations Development Programme (UNDP), *Human Development Report 2011: Sustainability and Equity: A Better Future for All* (Basingstoke: Palgrave Macmillan, 2011), pp. 126, 144.

[18] Ibid.

# 22

# The Nation Should Adopt the Maoists' Area

*Prakash Jha*
Interview by Venkatesan Vembu*

✪

Filmmaker Prakash Jha wears his politics on his sleeve, although he'll tell you that his primary *dharma* is to narrate well-packaged entertaining stories. In Hong Kong for the premiere of his latest film *Rajneeti* [2010][1] a few weeks ago, he attended a charity event hosted by Jade Group International to raise money for an NGO he runs in Bihar. Jha sat down with *DNA* and talked of his fascination with politics, the Maoist insurgency, and the need for 'all good people' to enter politics.

◉

*Venkatesan Vembu (VV)*: As a director of an intensely political film, how difficult was it for you to subject yourself to extra-administrative 'censor' authorities, particularly political parties?

*Prakash Jha (PJ)*: This is the society I'm making a film about; it's a society that still needs to find its roots. This is what our democracy is about: it's still developing, but at another level, it is thriving.

---

* This article was previously published as 'The Nation Should Adopt the Maoists' Area', *DNA*, 3 July 2010.
[1] *Rajneeti*, dir. Prakash Jha, 2010.

We haven't fully attained those levels of freedom, or a transparent system.

Other films too faced problems: *My Name Is Khan* [2010][2] faced trouble from Shiv Sainiks. These parties try to whip up sentiments, but it doesn't work. I try and detach myself from all that drama because this is a process we have to go through.

*VV*: You're not only an observer of politics; you contested two parliamentary elections in 2004 and 2009, and lost. Do you feel your understanding of politics is inadequate?

*PJ*: Firstly, I am not a politician. I contested elections only because I believe that people who can think right and who understand social dynamics should not be afraid of getting into politics. You need good people to come into politics, so long as they can make a difference in any way — by being a successful entrepreneur or even a film-maker. Politics and democracy have to be taken seriously and nurtured. But I have decided that I will not contest elections any more.

*VV*: Are you giving up because politics doesn't have the space for people like you?

*PJ*: I'm not giving up: I will contribute in other ways. I would like to go to campuses and universities and engage students and young people, and generally raise political awareness.

It's true that I wasn't elected, but I made a brave attempt, and very nearly won: that's a 'near-victory' I savour. In any case, there will be other, younger people. By the time of the next elections, I will be 62 years of age, and there are other things I want to do — like learn to play the piano and learn to fly!

Active political life requires a certain amount of dedication, focus and time. If I had won in 2004 or 2009, my film-making would have taken a back seat, and I would have devoted 26 hours a day to politics. But now, my film-making will continue.

---

[2] *My Name Is Khan*, dir. Karan Johar, 2010.

*VV*: You're involved with a charity, but doesn't the 'charity model' itself represent a failure of governance?

*PJ*: I don't look at this as charity, I think of it as my duty. Whether I'm a businessman, or an economist, or whoever, I have to support things beyond the public realm. That's because public investments alone are never going to be adequate: they may create the infrastructure for growth, but real growth has to come from the private sector. It's my way of taking responsibility.

*VV*: The biggest socio-economic-political issue in India today is perhaps the Maoist insurgency. Is that a theme you'll explore in a future film?

*PJ*: I've been studying it for a long time, but I need to get some real answers. It's not an issue that lends itself to easy solutions.

*VV*: But what do your political instincts as a social observer tell you?

*PJ*: When you have centuries of subjection, and when growth is not inclusive, you will face these social problems. I remember a passionate discussion that happened when the Mandal Commission recommendations on caste-based reservations were accepted in 1989. Students from upper castes were committing self-immolation, saying they were losing out on opportunities they deserved on merit. Backward class students said they were ready to fight on merit, provided the upper caste students would live in a *basti* [colony/settlement], take a broom and clean the streets. So, without equality of opportunity, what's the point of talking of merit? Just look at the extremes in our society. Mukesh Ambani builds a 20-floor house just for himself. What does he sleep on? What does he eat? What does he think when he gifts his wife a plane on her birthday?

*VV*: Are you suggesting that a high-visibility high-life is . . .

*PJ*: It's wrong! These stories go to the Maoist areas. There has to be some moderation. It's okay for you to have what you earn: I too want to live a comfortable life, and if you work hard, you need to eat well and sleep well. But, bloody hell, share it! Go there, create opportunities. Do something! *Kya leke aaye hain? Kya leke jayega, yaar?* (What have you brought with you, and what will you take with you?)

Today, if the nation adopts the whole Maoist area, the problem will go away. Those people there will feel that there's someone who cares. Instead, you send your police, then your army . . .

*VV*: You sound like Arundhati Roy!

*PJ*: Some of what she says is a little extreme, like justifying violence and so on. But some of what she says is right, just as some of what P. Chidambaram says too is right.

But my point is that it's time for not only the government but also for citizens to understand that this is a human problem, a calamity, and that we have to come together and contribute in whatever manner we can.

৵

# 23

# No Military Solutions for Maoism

*Swaminathan S. Anklesaria Aiyar**

✪

Having killed 76 paramilitary troops in April [2010], Maoists killed 30 more in a bus explosion in Dantewada district, Chhattisgarh. Some cabinet ministers want aerial bombing of Dantewada's jungles to kill Maoists. This will kill civilians and strengthen the Maoists. The problem is not military, and has no military solutions.

Home Minister Chidambaram says he wants the air force not for bombing but surveillance and logistics. This too is a quasi-military approach, short-sighted and doomed to [fail].

Maoists have flourished in several states but been routed in Andhra Pradesh. [Andhra Pradesh] achieved success not through military force but a well-trained and politically empowered police, plus intelligent politics. A similar model crushed Sikh terrorism in Punjab. It needs replication in all Maoist-hit states.

Initially, the then [Andhra Pradesh] Chief Minister Rajasekhara Reddy tried negotiating with the Maoists but found they were merely buying time. So he formulated a new strategy using the full administration, not the police alone.

First, the police got additional staff, superior training, arms, vehicles and communications, as in Punjab. Second, the government built an intensive network of roads in the jungles of the

* This article was previously published as 'No Military Solutions for Maoism', *The Economic Times*, 23 May 2010. The Times of India. © Bennett, Coleman & Co. Ltd., 2011. All Rights Reserved.

four worst-affected northern districts. Trying to control a jungle belt with a few roads is a death trap, as shown in Dantewada.

In [Andhra Pradesh], the new road network was used to set up not just new police stations but the full range of government offices and services. This included irrigation, schools and health clinics, and welfare services (cheap rice, employment schemes). Earlier, when Maoists ruled supreme, most government staff had run away, leaving a vacuum filled by the Naxalites. To reoccupy that vacuum, Reddy provided the full range of government services. This gave locals the confidence that the state government was here to fight to the finish. Only then could the police recruit informers, infiltrate Maoists groups, and winkle them out.

In the 1990s, MLAs dared not visit Maoist-hit constituencies for fear of death. But Reddy's strategy reduced Maoist incidents from 576 in 2005 to 62 in 2009, Maoist killings from 211 to 17, and police deaths from 25 to 0. [The] GDP [gross domestic product] improved — from 8 per cent to 32 per cent per year in Adilabad, Karimnagar, Warangal and Khammam, the worst-affected districts. This disproved activist claims that people were better off under Maoists.

Why is this strategy not replicated in Chhattisgarh? The key problem is jurisdictional. The central government controls military and paramilitary forces. The state government controls the police. Since the police have failed in Chhattisgarh, and since another Rajasekhara Reddy cannot be implanted there, Chidambaram has brought in central troops. But this is the wrong solution.

ॐ

# 24

# Our Freedom was Born with Hunger, We're Still Not Free

*M. S. Swaminathan*
Interview by Saira Kurup*

★

On 15 August 1947, 22-year-old Monkombu Sambasivan Swaminathan famously headed for Auroville even as almost everyone else in Madras seemed to be bound for Marina Beach to celebrate the birth of a free India. Later, he would choose to study agriculture rather than medicine, rightly judging that plentiful food production had an important role to play in keeping a country independent. He went on to play a leading role in India's Green Revolution of the 1960s. In 1999, he was one of only three Indians to be on TIME magazine's list of the 20th century's 20 most influential Asians. The other two were Rabindranath Tagore and Mahatma Gandhi. Swaminathan, 85, was in the capital recently and spoke to Saira Kurup about India's many revolutions — those past and still to come.

◉

*Saira Kurup (SK)*: It's [65] years since India became independent. But we are still fighting for freedom from hunger and poverty. Is this a battle we might never win?

* This article was previously published as 'Our Freedom was Born with Hunger, We're Still Not Free', *The Times of India*, 15 August 2010. The Times of India. © Bennett, Coleman & Co. Ltd., 2011. All Rights Reserved.

*M. S. Swaminathan (MSS):* Our freedom was born with hunger. It was born in the backdrop of the Bengal famine. If you read the newspapers dated 15 August 1947, one part was about freedom, the other was food shortage. This is why Jawaharlal Nehru said after Independence that everything else can wait but not agriculture.

The battle against hunger is a battle we have to win. It requires a fusion of political will, professional skill and people's participation. Our country is fortunate to have fairly good water resources, reasonably good rainfall, [and] a hardworking farming population. We must bring about a marriage between brain and brawn in rural professions. We need a large number of educated young people to go into farming using science and new eco-technologies. We have all the necessary ingredients for progress. But the gap between scientific knowhow and field level do-how is large.

The green revolution was the product of four things: the first was technology. The genetic technology of the 1960s was transformational and changed people's understanding of wheat and rice yields. The second was services that took the technology to the field like extension services, credit and insurance; third was public policies of input–output pricing like the prices commission, and lastly, the farmers' enthusiasm. Today, unfortunately, the most important thing is missing — farmers' enthusiasm. A revolution cannot come from a government programme. A National Sample Survey study says 40 per cent of the farmers want to leave farming. It's important to revive that enthusiasm.

There's no shortage of food in terms of production. Why are people going hungry then? There are three parts to the problem. First, availability of food in the market, which is not bad; second, access to food or purchasing power. Under [the] NREGA, a worker gets ₹ 100 a day for 100 days, i.e., ₹ 10,000 a year. If he has a family of five, it means ₹ 2,000 a year per person. When *dal* [lentil] is selling at ₹ 80 to ₹ 90 a kilo, how do they buy it? Third, is the absorption of food in the body, which means getting clean drinking water, sanitation? Otherwise, it means a leaky pot — a child would keep getting infections.

*SK*: How do you view the green revolution now, when the widespread use of pesticides in Punjab is being linked to increase in cancer rates in some areas?

*MSS*: In 1966, I had said the green revolution should be an 'evergreen revolution', which is enhancement of productivity in perpetuity without ecological harm. I had warned against overuse of pesticides and fertilisers and against converting the green revolution into a greed revolution.

*SK*: What can be done to set things right?

*MSS*: There are two aspects of the green revolution — farm ecology and farm economy. But if farm ecology goes wrong, nothing else will go right. Soil quality must be taken care of, water quality must be ensured. We should also be ready for climate change. I call it a two-pronged strategy — get the best of a good monsoon or climate and second, minimise the adverse impact of unfavourable weather.

*SK*: Why are you objecting to Bt brinjal?

*MSS*: I didn't oppose it. I supported Jairam Ramesh's moratorium. I chaired a committee in 2004 and recommended in a report the setting up of a regulatory authority, which would have its own testing facilities. The Genetic Engineering Approval Committee has no such facility. I advocate safe and responsible use of biotechnology particularly in the case of human nutrition. Some long-term residual toxicity tests should be done. If you introduce some good-yielding hybrids, farmers will grow only those. So I said, '[u]se the moratorium to collect all the genetic material or germ plasm'. We also need a literacy programme for the public.

*SK*: You have been influenced by the philosophy of the Mahatma and Sri Aurobindo. In an age when technology is the new god, do you think there can be a meeting point for science and spirituality?

*MSS*: There can be no science without spirituality. It gives purpose to science. Vivekananda said, '[t]his life is short, the vanities of the world are transient, but they alone live who live for others'. That's my personal philosophy. My father was a doctor. He died when I was 10. My mother wanted me to go into medicine. But the papers were full of Bengal famine and I asked myself how I could serve my country better. I got calls from a medical college and an agricultural college. After I joined, the principal of the agricultural college asked me why I took up agriculture because the subject was not considered as important as medicine!

*SK*: Do you have any unfulfilled dreams?

*MSS*: My only dream is a hunger-free India. Every fourth child here is born underweight. We are denying our own children opportunities for a fulfilled life. I wanted to see a hunger-free India in 2007 when we celebrated our 50th year of Independence. But it has not happened. That's why I accepted nomination to the Rajya Sabha because in a democratic country much depends on the political system. Fortunately, when I was Farmers' Commission chairman, we recommended a food guarantee Act. Now I am in the National Advisory Council and am working on the Right to Food Act. It's the last chance to make food a legal right. Gandhiji said in Noakhali in 1946 that the first and foremost duty of independent India is to see that no child, woman or man should go to bed hungry, because to the hungry, bread is god.

৵

# 25

# The Wrong Diagnosis

## Chetan Bhagat*

✪

Violent images from Kashmir filled television screens last week. So let's look at the tally. Seven Naxal-affected states, disturbances in all seven north-eastern states and, of course, the ever-present strife in Kashmir — 15 of India's 28 states have violent internal conflicts at present. In addition, we also have religious/caste/regionalism-based violence in other parts of the country. If that's not enough, add honour killings to that list. While no one strife dominates, we are probably living in one of the most violent times in independent India. This in 2010, when India is one of the fastest growing economies in the world, when we have a relatively stable government and we see more affluence around us than any other time. Three questions come to mind: What's going on? Where will all this lead to? Most importantly, what can be done about it?

The answer to the first question — what's going on? — can be the same cynical response that this is what India is. Blame the politicians, corrupt officials, illiterate voters and that seems to answer the question. The question can also be answered by a usual 'who cares', especially for us city dwellers who don't really see the impact of these 15-odd conflicts. The Naxalites haven't attacked our five-star hotels, cinemas and train stations (yet) and the north-east movements are tucked away too far to be noticed.

---

* This article was previously published as 'The Wrong Diagnosis', *The Times of India*, 17 July 2010.

However, we have to care. Because the next question — where will all this lead to? — is simply not being discussed enough.

Fact is, despite liberalisation, the benefits are not reaching Indians. Yes, they reach the top 10 per cent of Indians. However, they do not reach the other 90 per cent. In fact, these Indians get the worst of badly implemented capitalism — inflation kills their savings and purchasing power, their land gets stolen by corporates, their politician cares only about the rich guys. They are no advertiser's target group, so the media dismisses them and they don't get a voice. Every now and then, a politician comes and tosses cheap rice or wheat at them, keeps them alive on drip-feed, and hopes to swing some votes. Our rural poor never see the benefits of liberalisation.

Add to this poor education, archaic caste-based social dis-crimination, poorly-implemented welfare policies and a general lack of job opportunities, and it leads to a kind of passive frustration that urban people can never understand. The leaders of these movements apparently do, and that is why a youth with his whole life ahead of him takes up guns against the state and becomes a rebel.

So while we might debate endlessly on whether the CRPF is adequate to fight the Naxals, and whether the army is doing a good job in Kashmir or not, the fact is that in these discussions we are only addressing the symptoms. We are trying to bring the fever down while the infection is what needs to be cured. We don't need Crocin, we need strong antibiotics. And unless the rural or underprivileged Indian youth sees a better life coming, the infection is only going to grow. From 15 states, we could have all 28 states infected. Trouble is brewing, and the cities are ignoring it.

The final question — what can be done about it? — is what we need to spend most of our time on. For one, better politicians who are committed to developing their local areas need to be elected. However, currently they can't. In the interiors, the single-most important criteria for voting is caste. No matter how capable a candidate, if you aren't matching the voter's caste, you will not get his vote. In such a scenario, there is no incentive for a candidate to do a good job. Managing his caste alliances is the only real qualification. And since most of our candidates come from the interiors, we end up with a bunch of politicians that give us the India we have today. How will this change? The city–rural connection needs to be made significantly stronger. Our most educated and modern-thinking people are in the cities. While still a small proportion of the total population, these educated people can be ambassadors for a new India in the villages.

One suggestion is to use the massive youth student population. A radical move — such as exchange programmes between city and rural colleges — where every city student spends time in the villages, and vice versa, will help a lot. This needs to be done on a massive scale. The city students will spend time in the villages and infuse modern values there, and come back home with a better understanding of rural issues. There can be other similar ideas — incentivising MNCs to base themselves in smaller towns is another one. Sure, there will be lots of challenges but, frankly, there is no other way out. Unless we truly reform the core of our country, things will never really change.

One insurgency curtailed will turn into another, TV anchors will scream, politicians will offer a Crocin and the infection will continue to spread. Surely, that's not the India we want to leave behind for the next generation. It's time to pop the antibiotics and, most importantly, stay and complete the course.

ॐ

# 26

# Force Should be Met with Force

## Swapan Dasgupta*

★

Earlier this year, a fashionably 'progressive' essayist lauded India's Maoist terror squads as 'Gandhians with a gun', a description that is about as persuasive as 'celibate rapist'. Not that either mockery or public anger plays any role in tempering the perversity of those who flaunt democracy only to subvert it. In the wake of the second massacre in Dantewada in two months, the experts of terror have raised their sophistry to bizarre heights.

Take the justification of the 17 May [2010] blast that killed 44 bus passengers — all local inhabitants and all poor. Since the earlier claim of paramilitary forces being a legitimate target is clearly untenable, it has been suggested that the presence of a few off-duty special police officers in the bus was a direct provocation. 'If there were indeed civilians in the bus', writer Arundhati Roy told *The Times of India*, 'it is irresponsible of the government to expose them to harm in a war zone by allowing police and SPOs to use public transport'.[1]

The logic is revealing: anyone remotely connected with the state, even [an] SPO drawing a pathetic ₹ 3,000 allowance each month, is an enemy and must face the bloody consequences. It is

---

* This article was previously published as 'Force Should Be Met With Force', *The Times of India*, 23 May 2010. The Times of India. © Bennett, Coleman & Co. Ltd., 2011. All Rights Reserved.

[1] *The Times of India*, 'Cops shouldn't have Used Public Bus: Arundhati', 19 May 2010.

further implied that by using public transport, these functionaries are inviting collateral damage on fellow passengers. The real Mao once wrote that 'revolution is not a dinner party';[2] his disciples have reminded us that there is no place for squeamishness and table manners.

How the conduct of these armed 'Gandhians' squares with the Mahatma who called off the Non-Cooperation movement in 1922 after an angry mob killed 23 policemen in Chauri Chaura, is best brushed aside. For the moment, it would be unwise to disregard the menacing overground message from the underground.

Those who can conduct military operations with such ruthless efficiency have long lost the right to be called 'misguided ideologues' and treated with benevolent indulgence. What is the difference between [Ajmal] Kasab and the Maoists who ambushed the CRPF *jawans* on 6 April and detonated a deadly explosive under a bus last week? Kasab believed that he was part of God's army and that every Mumbai resident was a legitimate target for murder. The Maoists too believe they are a People's Liberation Army waging war on the state and its flunkeys.

The only obvious difference is that while Kasab came from Pakistan, the foot soldiers of the Red army are Indian by birth. In every other respect, the Islamists and the Maoists are the same: both have transformed grievance and utopia into inhumanity. They may well have had a place in the statecraft of preceding centuries; judged by contemporary norms, they have forfeited all claims to human rights.

It is important to stress the mismatch between Maoist insurgency and Indian democracy, if only to drive home the necessity of a unified response from both the state and civil society. The argument that equitable economic development will blunt the anger of those who resent their marginal status is true only up to a point. However, if the benefits of state welfare and the market economy are to reach every corner of India, it is necessary for the

---

[2] Mao Zedong, *Report on an Investigation of the Peasant Movement in Hunan* (Peking: Foreign Languages Press, 1953).

state to be in physical control of territory. The Maoist approach is not to present the wretched of the earth with a revolutionary alternative that can compete with bourgeois politics on equal terms. It aims to exercise a military stranglehold over a region and either intimidate or eliminate dissent. Maoists don't believe in choice; they are committed to total control.

It's literally a chicken and egg situation. Sonia Gandhi may feel that NREGA and a Food Security Act will deliver the deviants to the Indian Constitution and isolate the doctrinaire Maoists. However, the district administration and the panchayats need to be physically present to undertake good works. To undertake Bharat Nirman in a large chunk of forested, central India, the state must uproot an illegal military presence first. The development route to counterinsurgency is, ironically, prefaced on a military victory. Reduced to essentials, the difference between the hardliners and the appeasers is one of articulation. It may be tactically prudent to keep the language of retaliation less robust and peppered with piousness but there is no escaping the fact that the Maoist leadership will not be moved by either persuasion or bribery. To make Maoism unattractive to frightened villagers, force will have to be met with force. Siddharth Ray showed the way in West Bengal in the 1970s.

Unlike separatist movements that can be coerced into compromise, there is no halfway house in confronting communist insurgencies. In the war for state power, it's either us or them. One side has to yield. The choice is stark: it's either Maoism or the democratic way of life.

ॐ

# 27

# Grow Up

## M. S. Swaminathan*

✪

The India Meteorological Department has predicted that the 2010 South-West Monsoon is likely to be normal. A recent article in *Nature* points out that the current national emission targets are not sufficient to limit global warming to 2° celsius during this century as called for in the Copenhagen Declaration.[1] Present pledges, including that of India, are likely to lead to a world with global emissions of 47.9 to 53.6 gigatonnes of $CO_2$ equivalent per year by 2020. This is about 10–20 per cent higher than today's levels. A 1° celsius rise in mean temperature will lead to a reduction in wheat production in India by 6–7 million tonnes per year.

A climate-resilient agriculture, which we urgently need, will have to be based on a two-pronged strategy: maximising farm productivity and production during a normal monsoon period; and minimising the adverse impact of unfavourable weather as witnessed during 2009. Unfortunately, we are yet to develop an anticipatory research and extension programme to minimise damage during unfavourable monsoon periods. For example, the deficiency in rainfall during the South-West Monsoon of 2009 was 23 per cent. The growth in agriculture and allied sector gross

---

* This article was previously published as 'Grow Up', *Hindustan Times*, 5 June 2010. © HT Media Ltd.

[1] Joeri Rogelj, Julia Nabel, Claudine Chen, William Hare, Kathleen Markmann, Malte Meinshausen, Michiel Schaeffer, Kirsten Macey and Niklas Höhne, 'Copenhagen Accord Pledges are Paltry', *Nature*, vol. 464, no. 7292, 22 April 2010.

domestic product (GDP) was -0.2 per cent last year. The highest growth rate in agriculture GDP of 5.2 per cent was observed during 2005–06 when the growth in total GDP was 9.5 per cent. Had we had a scientific monsoon management strategy, we could have minimised the loss last year. Similarly, if we have a strategy for maximising the benefits of a good monsoon, we can hope to achieve at least a 5 per cent growth rate during 2010–11 in agriculture and allied sectors. In parts of China like the Yunnan province, which has experienced 60 per cent less rainfall than normal, there is a move to grow different crops together in the same field, thereby distributing the risk arising from monoculture. It is time to develop a proactive monsoon management strategy in India consisting of the following five components:

One, we must improve soil health and help farmers to benefit from the nutrient-based subsidy regime that was introduced [on] 1 April 2010. If used properly, this revised approach to fertiliser subsidy should promote balanced fertilisation with concurrent attention to both macro- and micro-nutrients as well as soil organic matter. To benefit from this revised approach, farmers should have access to soil health cards (SHCs) containing credible information on the chemistry, physics and microbiology of their soils. Some states like Gujarat have started the practice of empowering farm families with SHC. Factor productivity is low now because of the lack of attention to micro-nutrients and soil organic carbon content.

Two, we must maximise the benefits of all available water sources: rain, ground, river, treated effluents and sea water. The lessons learnt from the over-5,000 farmer participatory projects designed to maximise yield and income per drop of water organised by the Ministry of Water Resources should be extended to all farms. Every farm in rain-fed and dry farming areas — that constitute 60 per cent of our total cultivated area — should have a farm pond, a bio-gas plant and a few fertiliser trees. This will help to build soil carbon banks (SCBs) and also farm-level water banks that will help to undertake crop life, saving irrigation when needed. Energy management is another important requirement for irrigation water security. Electricity and diesel are essential for both groundwater use and for lift irrigation.

Three, we should launch a programme for spreading the best available technologies including the most appropriate seeds in the 128 agro-climatic zones of our country. During June 2010, the faculty and post-graduate students of agricultural and animal sciences universities, the staff of the various departments of government related to agriculture and irrigation and representatives of lead banks and the National Bank for Agriculture and Rural Development (NABARD) should go from village to village in every zone to check whether seeds and other essential inputs are available or not.

Such monsoon management teams may be constituted jointly by the state government, financial institutions, state agricultural and animal sciences universities, concerned Indian Council of Agricultural Research (ICAR) institutions, farmers' associations and panchayati raj bodies. If these teams are constituted immediately, they can plan their visit to every village in each one of the 128 agro-climatic zones during June, so that farmers can benefit from an intensive exposure to new technologies and climate-resilient agronomic methodologies. June 2010 may be declared as 'Monsoon management month'.

Four, both credit and insurance agencies should do their best in taking credit to the last mile and last farmer and get them the benefit of the 5 per cent interest rate for farm loans announced by the finance minister. Similarly, insurance companies should deliver the benefits of insurance to every farm family. Under the Mahila Kisan Shasakthikaran Pariyojana, all women farmers should be enabled to have access to credit, technology, inputs and market.

Finally, the economic viability of farming will depend upon access to assured and remunerative markets. The minimum support price announced for nearly 25 crops must be enforced. A national grid of grain storages starting with the 'pusa bin' (silos made of earth or sun-dried bricks with a capacity of 1–3 tonnes) at the farm level, storage godowns at the village level and modern silos at the regional level should be established without further delay. It is painful to observe the spoilage caused to food grains and perishable commodities due to poor storage conditions.

Many of our problems in the field of food and nutrition security are not related to the lack of schemes, but to the over-abundance of disjointed programmes operated by different ministries. There is, for instance, little coordination among large national programmes like the Rashtriya Krishi Vikas Yojana, the Food Security Mission, the Horticulture Mission, the National Rural Employment Guarantee Programme and many other projects. If there is convergence and synergy among these programmes, our progress in improving the productivity, profitability and sustainability of small farm agriculture will be fast.

The South-West monsoon is just beginning. We have only a few weeks to launch a '[m]aximise the benefit of a good monsoon movement' and for ensuring last mile and last farmer connectivity with reference to knowledge, technology, seeds, credit, insurance and market. Unless the central and state governments take immediate action in organising monsoon management teams in each of the 128 agro-climatic zones, the finance minister will have serious problems in linking outlay with outcome when he presents the budget next year.

There is no time to relax and every day lost will be a blow to the food security of our country, which is already suffering from extensive malnutrition. The future belongs to nations with grains and not guns. Guns can be purchased easily in the global market. But grains, as our efforts to import pulses to contain food inflation revealed this year, cannot be purchased.

꙰

# 28

# No Ifs or Buts, Defeat Maoist Violence

## Gurcharan Das*

✪

Arundhati Roy writes seductively. Recently, I picked up her new book, *Listening to Grasshoppers* [2009],[1] and was mesmerised by her luminous prose but I disagreed profoundly with her conclusion. I was revolted, in particular, by her support for violence. She regards Naxalism as armed resistance against a sham democracy. I call it terrorism.

Roy thinks that India pretends to be a democracy in order to impress the world. I think our democracy is as real as my grandson's thumb. Yes, it has many flaws but it is legitimate. We need to reform the police, speed up justice, make babus accountable, stop criminals from entering politics, etc. Yet, this democracy has done a colossal amount of good. It has raised the prospects and self-esteem of the lowest in our society and protected us from the great genocides of the 20th century. Gujarat, to its disgrace, may have killed 2,000 people but Mao's China killed more than 50 million, according to the Marxist historian, Eric Hobsbawm. One may be justified in taking up arms against a loathsome African or Latin American dictator but not against the Indian state.

---

\* This article was previously published as 'No Ifs or Buts, Defeat Maoist Violence', *The Times of India*, 25 October 2010.

[1] Arundhati Roy, *Listening to Grasshoppers: Field Notes on Democracy* (London: Hamish Hamilton, 2009).

Like many in the 1960s, I was a Leftist and admired Charu Mazumdar who had founded the Naxalbari movement. Although one belonged to that idealistic middle class generation, I was not tempted to abandon all and join the Maoists. Perhaps, it was because I lived in sensible Bombay rather than Calcutta. The Naxalite movement died in the 1970s but it revived subsequently and today it operates in over 200 districts across 20 states and controls huge Indian territory. The prime minister [Manmohan Singh] thinks it is the greatest security threat to India, and I agree.

Soon after the Maoist leader, Kobad Ghandy, the police in Hazaribagh got another prize catch. On 10 October, they captured Ravi Sharma and his wife, B. Anuradha. Top-level Naxalites, they hailed from Andhra Pradesh but were running the Maoist movement in Bihar and Jharkhand for the past 10 years. On their laptop the police found their strategy and plans. Ravi Sharma is an agricultural scientist and a member of the Maoist Central Committee. As he was being led by the police to the court in Hazaribagh, Sharma told reporters that he did not regret killing thousands of people. 'During a revolution',' he spoke honestly, 'one does not care how many are killed; only the goal should be achieved'.

Ravi Sharma, thus, raised the old dilemma of means and ends. Vidura posed the same question in the Mahabharata when he justified sacrificing an individual for the sake of a village and a village for the sake of a nation. Vidura, like Sharma, judges an act to be *dharmic* if it produces good consequences for the greatest number of people. Yudhishthira, however, is concerned with means rather than ends. Having given his word to Dhritarashtra, he refuses to give in to Draupadi's insistent demand that Pandavas raise an army and win back their kingdom which was stolen in a rigged game of dice. No matter how great the goal, Yudhishthira would not condone the Maoists' use of violence.

I usually agree with Vidura but on this one I am with Yudhishthira. Marxists have never valued human life and have always found it easy to take the gun. Mao and Stalin easily justi-fied killing millions for the sake of the revolution. They never understood that violence in the end brutalises both the oppressor and the victim. Neither should we let the Indian state get away by using wrong means for the sake of good ends. I agree with Arundhati Roy that the state should not get away with unlawful detention or killing people in custody. I applaud her and human rights activists for raising these issues.

The Naxalite movement has always found sympathy in our influential, leftish upper middle class. Like most people, I was aghast at the beheading of police officer Francis Induwar on 30 September by the Maoists, and expressed my horror to an elegantly dressed friend who was visiting me. She is with an NGO and has sentimental feelings for Maoists. She said, 'Yes, it is wrong, but we need development as well as force to defeat Maoists'. I could not disagree with her, but was appalled at the ease with which she dismissed the beheading. Mamata Banerjee, the leader of Trinamool Congress, had the same response.

For once we have a home minister [P. Chidambaram] who understands the Maoist threat to our nation and is determined to act with courage. It is pathetic that he should be slowed by endless debate on development versus police action; or whether helicopters should fire on rebels and risk civilian casualties. We have talked for two decades. Enough is enough. No ifs or buts, you cannot negotiate with someone with a gun. Now is the time for action.

ॐ

# 29

# Maoism is Terrorism

*Shankkar Aiyar**

✪

Denial was decimated at Dantewada [on 17 May 2010]. The massacre of 76 lives demands Indians face the harsh truth. Maoism is terrorism. By definition, terrorism is the use of force or violence to intimidate. Maoism is terrorism draped in a fig leaf of virtuous intent, in Marxist–Leninist ideology. It was in November 2004 when Prime Minister Manmohan Singh first declared Maoism as the biggest threat to India. For six years Maoists have been 'enemy number one' and grown without fear of retribution. The Maoists are thriving because India has been hostage to romantic notions of a band of do-gooders chased by evil in uniform. Make no mistake; Maoists are extortionists and terrorists masquerading as modern day Robin Hoods aided by a thick fog of sentiments. Yes. Every third person in India — or nearly 400 million people — lives below the poverty line. It is deplorable and a reflection of failed politics and stalled governance. Maoism has flourished because the vote has become a four-letter word that impales decisions, a disincentive for political parties from doing the right thing. Poor road connectivity, the fading writ of law, [and] abject poverty are all allies of Maoism.

Circumstance of poverty though cannot be an alibi for violence, nor a justification for terror. Not in a democracy which affords citizens many avenues to seek justice. Like fashion victims some

* This article was previously published as 'Maoism is Terrorism', *India Today*, 9 April 2010.

commentators find reason to sympathise with the cause of Maoists, to condone criminality and intellectualise the indefensible. Let's not forget the goal of Maoists is to overthrow the Government through an armed struggle. Eloquence is not a substitute for rationale. Those presenting poverty and oppression as justification for stoking terror are ideologically in the company of Osama bin Laden.

Dantewada is just another milestone on the Maoist agenda. Since 2004, India has suffered over 7,000 incidents involving Maoists in which over 5,000 have been killed. In 2009, Maoism claimed a life every eight hours. Apologists for Maoism cite lack of development even as Maoists wrecked over 1,700 schools in just two years — in 2008 and 2009. More lives have been claimed by Naxal violence than *jihadi* terror in the past decade. Maoist guerrillas have described the state as the 'enemy' and the conflict as a 'war'. A war is being waged against India in 220 of its 600 districts, or one in three districts.

Home to the argumentative billion, India also seems to be the emerging refuge of the banal babel. Every Maoist attack triggers in its wake a tedious tide of rhetoric on the need for a political approach to tackling Naxalism. A day after 76 *jawans* bled to death, the Government [was] trapped in a debate on whether it will deploy the army or not, whether it will use air power or not. How can we use force on 'our own' ask[ed] the pacifists in the system, forgetting that never [had] India been so bloodied by its 'own'. This [was] not the occasion for semantics-military or paramilitary, air power or air force. And the war can't be won with just 7,000 trained men. It call[ed] for a new strike force and drafting of trained ex-servicemen. The operative phrase should be 'fitting response'.

Every inch of India is ruled by the states and war will essentially have to be waged by states. The Centre can at best be a catalyst, the evangelist. If state governments are not delivering, they should be named and shamed. Yes, the war will not be won by bullets alone. If India truly aspires to be a superpower then it needs to reclaim both the landscape and the mindspace. It could be a public private partnership. Corporates could be invited to adopt the

100 worst districts under the social responsibility banner to help deliver social infrastructure. On its part, the Government could create a special mechanism to ensure implementation of programmes like NREGA and Bharat Nirman under the supervision of senior bureaucrats and young ministers of state. As Home Minister P. Chidambaram has said: 'We need a strong head, a stronger heart and staying power to win.'[1] The massacre has forged a political consensus across the political spectrum. It is a rare moment that must be leveraged. India must respond. India must declare a war, on the conditions which foment Maoism and Maoists.

‌ॐ

---

[1] 'Fighting Naxals Primary Job of States: Chidambaram', *Indian Express*, 15 April 2010.

# 30

# Arms over People: Maoists in Bastar

*Nirmalangshu Mukherji**

✪

The Indian state has amassed nearly 100,000 paramilitary forces — code-named Operation Green Hunt — ostensibly to confront an armed rebellion organised by the Communist Party of India (Maoist) in the Dandakaranya forests in the Bastar region of Chhattisgarh. As the forces raise their guns at each other, massive and protracted violence is breaking out in these hills and jungles affecting the lives of several million tribals inhabiting the area. [Among] these was the killing of nearly 40 civilians and trainee special police officers by the Maoist forces in Dantewada [17 May 2010]. After exploding a civilian bus carrying 50–60 persons, they opened fire on those who survived the blast. This atrocity [was] preceded by a series of other atrocities, the most notable being the killing of 76 CRPF personnel on 6 April while they were walking back to their camp. The attack on the civilian bus shows that the Maoists have escalated the scale of 'revolutionary violence' in response to Operation Green Hunt to the point that they are prepared to inflict massive 'collateral damage' to innocent civilians. This is clearly a warning to the government of the shape of things to come if Operation Green Hunt continues. While the cabinet committee on security, the army chiefs, the home ministry, and counter-insurgency experts prepare for even more aggression with

* This article was previously published as 'Arms over People: Maoists in Bastar', *Outlook*, 19 May 2010.

an 'expanded mandate' for the home minister, a crucial factor is systematically missed in the raging debates on this issue in the mainstream media (there is some discussion in the alternative media, especially the internet).

There is overwhelming evidence that the Maoist forces at the frontline — the militias and the guerrilla army — consist entirely of tribal youth. While the orders for a specific action could be emanating from the essentially non-tribal leadership hiding safely in their secured bases, it is the tribals on the ground that carry out the explosions and the killings. According to reports [examined further in the chapter], there are about 50,000 armed militias and 10,000 guerrillas operating basically in the Bastar area; *all these people are young tribals*. The Maoists have been able to raise this huge force because a vast majority of tribals in Bastar have sided with the Maoists for reasons [that will be discussed later in the chapter]. The massive presence of tribals in the Maoist scheme of things has led commentators such as [Arundhati] Roy[1] to conclude that there is no difference between the tribals and the Maoists. I will evaluate the factuality of this conclusion.

For now, it is evident — yet systematically overlooked — that any armed operation to flush out the Maoist leadership will have tribals, *armed or unarmed*, as the direct target. There are layers and layers of tribal human shields between the government forces and the Maoist leadership. Further, as the ill-fated and murderous Salwa Judum campaign showed, any attack on tribals not only results in immense calamity for the tribals, it in fact helps increase Maoist base of support including expansion of guerrilla forces. The essentially non-tribal veteran leadership from Andhra [Pradesh] and Bihar have carefully planned all this for decades after poring over maps and demographic profiles.

To understand why even the militias and the guerrillas — not to mention the millions of unarmed tribals who support them — ought to be viewed as victims requiring protection, we need to understand the real character of how the (upper class) Maoists,

[1] Arundhati Roy, 'Mr Chidambaram's War', *Outlook*, 9 November 2009.

driven out from Andhra [Pradesh] and Bihar, went about constructing their base of support in Bastar.

## The Documents

We have four important documents in the public domain to study this issue. Two of these are based on recent travels inside the Maoist territory by two public intellectuals from Delhi;[2] the others are detailed interviews of the general secretary of the Maoist party [Ganapathy][3] and the Maoist spokesperson [Azad].[4]

The [latter] two are Maoist documents by definition. As for the other two, it stands to reason that the Maoists wouldn't have allowed the intellectuals, accompanied by guerrilla forces, to travel extensively in their territory in times of war unless the intellectuals showed prior sympathy to the Maoist movement. It is beyond belief that the Maoists would invite people, including other Naxalites, who are opposed to them to travel with the guerrillas, take photographs, make audio recordings, visit the headquarters at Abujmaad to interview the general secretary, and inspect documents of Maoist administration.[5]

As it turns out, there is not a single remark in the two (very) long pieces written by the intellectuals that questions the basic objectives of Maoist strategy. (For records, ['Mr Chidambaram's War'][6] did contain some well-tempered critical remarks; they are now totally absent from ['Walking with the Comrades']).[7]

---

[2] Arundhati Roy, 'Walking with the Comrades', *Outlook*, 29 March 2010; Gautam Navlakha, 'Days and Nights in the Heartland of Rebellion', *Sanhati*, 1 April 2010.

[3] Jan Myrdal and Gautam Navlakha, 'In Conversation with Ganapathy, General Secretary of CPI(Maoist)', *Sanhati*, 12 February 2010.

[4] 'Edited text of 12,262-word response by Azad, Spokesperson, Central Committee, CPI (Maoist)', *The Hindu*, 14 April 2010, http://www.thehindu.com/multimedia/archive/00103/Edited_text_of_12_2_103996a.pdf (accessed on 29 February 2012).

[5] Navlakha, Gautam, 'Days and Nights in the Heartland of Rebellion'.

[6] Roy, 'Mr Chidambaram's War'.

[7] Roy, 'Walking with the Comrades'.

Furthermore, each article is strewn with political remarks of the authors themselves, some of which directly support the basic Maoist goals and practices. Take just one of those remarks: 'Charu Mazumdar was a visionary in much of what he wrote and said. The party he founded (and its many splinter groups) has kept the dream of revolution real and present in India. Imagine a society without that dream'.[8] As a matter of fact, lip-service notwithstanding, most 'splinter groups' of the erstwhile Naxalite movement no longer share Charu Mazumdar's 'vision'; for example, that 'vision' strictly forbade participation in electoral politics, as the Maoists rightly emphasise. Charu Mazumdar's — and Kanhai Chatterji's — 'vision', in its original form, is currently upheld essentially by the Maoists. Away from the propaganda of the Indian state, then, this study is based on pro-Maoist documents.

The Maoist spokesperson Azad[9] asserts that 'the welfare of the masses is the first priority for the Maoist revolutionaries'.[10] The media-savvy Kishenji (Koteshwar Rao) offers to talk to any party that 'worked for the good of the common people'[11] suggesting that the Maoists had devoted themselves to the 'common good' of tribals in Bastar forests. The Maoists had already entrenched themselves in these forests for about 25 years before the first of the major attacks by the state began in 2005, in the form of the Salwa Judum campaign. So, what did the Maoists accomplish *for the tribals* in that quarter of a century?

## Maoist Control

The ability of an organisation to engage in the welfare of a given population is obviously a function of the influence of that organisation in the concerned area. As the writers report, the Maoists entered the Dandakaranya forests in small groups — two

---

[8] Roy, 'Walking with the Comrades'.
[9] 'Edited text of 12,262-word response by Azad', *The Hindu*.
[10] Ibid.
[11] 'Stop Green Hunt: Kishanji', *The Times of India*, 18 May 2010, p. 19.

squads,[12] seven squads[13] — back in 1980. (The puzzling issue of why they chose Dandakaranya of all places in this vast country will be taken up later.) Having secured the confidence of the local, predominantly tribal population, they set about organising them so that they can realise their rights — for example, rights of land, forest produce, and the like. Needless to say, vested interests, such as tribal chiefs in cohort with the local police and forest officials, attempted feeble interventions initially. There were more determined attempts in 1991 and 1997 that were easily dispelled because a large number of tribals had benefitted from the movement by then: 'killing a few of the most notorious landlords'[14] did the job. As the remnants of state representatives were driven out of the area, things seem to have proceeded smoothly till about 2005.

During this period, the Maoists were able to build up a substantial organisational base both in terms of participation of people and coverage of area. The peasant-worker front, Dandakaranya Adivasi Kisan Mazdoor Sangh (DAKMS), currently has nearly 100,000 members. The women front, Krantikari Adivasi Mahila Samity (KAMS), has nearly 90,000 members. Even the cultural front, Chetna Natya Manch, has over 10,000 members.

From 2001 onwards, Dandakaranya is directly administered by Revolutionary People's Committees (Janatanam Sarkars [JSs]). Each JS is elected by a cluster of [three to five] villages whose combined population can range from 500–5,000; 14–15 such JSs make up an area JS, and [three to five] area JSs go on to constitute a division. There are 10 divisions in Dandakaranya. So, the general picture is that the party's authority 'now ranged across 60,000 square kilometres of forest, thousands of villages, and millions of people'.[15] I must emphasise that these are Maoist numbers as told to the visiting intellectuals. Assuming, in the absence of

[12] Navlakha, 'Days and Nights in the Heartland of Rebellion'.
[13] Roy, 'Walking with the Comrades'.
[14] Ibid.
[15] Ibid.

contrary evidence, that these numbers are not inflated to impress the outsiders, we can now ask what the Maoists have achieved for these millions of people.

The travelogues attempt to paint an impressive general picture of Dandakaranya. Away from the ugly inequalities of the rest of India, with its filthy towns and failed countryside, we get a picture of a land of pristine rivers and lush green forests. There live a population of beautiful people in colourful attires going about happily with their daily lives, armed with their newly-found dignity and self-reliance in a largely egalitarian society. According to Vandana Shiva,[16] peace and tranquillity prevailed in Bastar before the Indian state attacked the people. Despite grinding poverty and historical neglect by the state, tribal areas usually present a sense of serenity on the surface. A very different and disturbing picture emerges when we scratch the surface.

## Maoist Welfare: Wages and Agriculture

Consider the issue of wages. On a seasonal basis, much of tribal livelihood in the concerned area depends on collection of forest produce such as *tendu* leaves and bamboo culms, among other items. A bundle of 50 *tendu* leaves — 70, according to Gautam Navlakha[17] — currently fetches one rupee. To earn about 30 rupees, then, a tribal has to collect and bundle nearly 2000 *tendu* leaves per day! No doubt this is a substantial increase from a meagre 3 paise per bundle in 1981.[18] Similarly, the wage for a bundle of 20 bamboo culms has been raised from 10 paise in 1981 to 7 rupees now. So, a tribal has to cut, collect and bundle 100 bamboo culms to earn 35 rupees a day. These figures are roughly corroborated by Kobad Ghandy who reported that daily wages have been raised [to three to four times the 10 rupees that it had been some years ago].[19]

[16] Vandana Shiva, speaking to NDTV, 13 April 2009.
[17] Navlakha, 'Days and Nights in the Heartland of Rebellion'.
[18] Roy, 'Walking with the Comrades'.
[19] 'Kobad Ghandy 2008 Interview', *BBC News*, 23 September 2009.

It is difficult to compare wages on an absolute scale since they vary widely with respect to nature of work, location, caste, gender, etc. It is well-known that tribals occupy the bottom of economic ladder. Given their atrocious exploitation in the past by the state and private operators, the wages sketched above signal 'huge achievements for tribal people';[20] the impoverished tribals never knew anything better. The documents report, without furnishing data that these wages — negotiated by the Maoists with private contractors—are higher than those announced by the Chhattisgarh government. The Maoists were also able to eliminate traditional social evils such as free first day labour for tilling the land of the village chief. These measures explain why tribals feel indebted to the Maoists.

But the mere surpassing of highly exploitative wages announced by a particular state government to satisfy the greed of private contractors does not by itself qualify as an 'alternative development model' that others allegedly preach but the 'Maoists have been practicing for last thirty years among millions of Indians'.[21] Even if absolute comparisons are difficult, it is evident that these wages are much, much lower than the minimum wages enforced across the nation; the tribals in Bastar 'make just enough to stay alive until the next season'.[22] For agricultural labour, minimum wages typically vary between 60–80 rupees a day in the rest of the country. In a 'high-wage' state like Kerala — perhaps one model the Maoists would wish to compete with — wages under the rural employment guarantee scheme range up to 150 rupees a day.[23]

The other side of this problematic picture is that, having negotiated what I consider to be merely subsistence wages for the tribals, the Maoists themselves collect 120 rupees per bag of *tendu* leaves from the contractors (each bag contains 1,000 bundles). The contractors are allowed to collect up to 5000 bags per season per contractor. This means that for a big contractor with 5,000 bags,

---

[20] Roy, 'Walking with the Comrades'.
[21] Navlakha, 'Days and Nights in the Heartland of Rebellion'.
[22] Roy, 'Walking with the Comrades'.
[23] Personal interview with Utsa Patnaik.

the party makes about 600,000 rupees. Arundhati Roy reports that, at a conservative estimate, such a contractor makes about 5,500,000 rupees per season.[24] The documents do not state how many contractors operate in the Dandakaranya area; in general, it is said that the *tendu* leaf business itself runs into hundreds of crores of rupees. A similar story obtains for bamboo culms, tamarind, and other forest produce that generate 'royalties' for the party, and huge profits for contractors.

As for agriculture, the Maoists did encourage the tribals to grab about 300,000 acres of forest land which they had been cultivating 'illegally' in any case for generations. The task was relatively easy since there were no landlords from the outside and tribal societies have insignificant class structure. As the Maoists realised, the issue was basically to grab forest land of the state at will since there was no real intervention of vested interests. In fact, something like a class-structure developed as tribal chiefs and other elements with muscle-power grabbed disproportionate portions of land. The problem was subsequently solved by killing a few of the more notorious landlords, as noted. The net picture, it is claimed, is that 'there are no landless peasants in Dandakaranya'. The Maoists also organised the tribals to construct some harvesting structures such as ponds and wells, and encouraged the nomadic tribals to learn proper cultivation techniques. There's an attempt to introduce multicrop and shifting cultivation. Gautam Navlakha presents some details about the grain and vegetable items cultivated, and their yields, as recorded in a given JS.[25] There's some mention of using tractors and buffaloes for ploughing in some areas in recent times. None of this sounds anything more than routine and — compared to other regions of the country — primitive agricultural practices.

It is difficult to form a picture of the extent of these efforts and their role in improving the quality of life of the tribals. Recall that we are talking about an area of 60,000 square kilometres and a

[24] Roy, 'Walking with the Comrades'.
[25] Navlakha, 'Days and Nights in the Heartland of Rebellion'.

time-span of a quarter of a century. In general terms, Roy writes: '[o]nly 2 per cent of the land is irrigated. In Abujhmad, ploughing was unheard of until 10 years ago. In Gadchiroli on the other hand, hybrid seeds and chemical pesticides are edging their way in [Gadchiroli is in adjacent Maharashtra]. 'We need urgent help in the agriculture department', Comrade Vinod says. 'We need people who know about seeds, organic pesticides, permaculture'.[26] Why is Comrade Vinod asking for these absolutely basic things now? What have the Maoists been doing for close to three decades?

## Maoist Welfare: Health and Education

A more concrete picture of the food-situation emerges when we look at the health sector. There is no mention of even a single health centre initiated by the Maoists in that vast area. All we are told repeatedly is that people have been advised to drink boiled water; apparently, this method reduced infant mortality by 50 per cent.[27] Navlakha reports that lately the JSs have initiated a scheme of 'barefoot doctors' in which some tribals are trained to apply some medicines (distinguished by their colour) for afflictions such as malaria, cholera and elephantitis, the three most dreaded illnesses.[28] Again, we do not know the extent of these efforts.

However, Roy reports a doctor she met — a doctor was visiting that area after many years. The doctor said that most of the people he has seen including those in the guerrilla army have a haemoglobin count between five and six (when the standard for Indian women is 11).[29] There is extensive tuberculosis caused by more than two years of chronic anaemia. 'Young children are suffering from Protein Energy Malnutrition Grade II. Apart from this, there is malaria, osteoporosis, tapeworm, severe ear and tooth infections and primary amenorrhea — which is when malnutrition

---

[26] Roy, 'Walking with the Comrades'.
[27] 'Kobad Ghandy 2008 Interview', *BBC News*.
[28] Navlakha, 'Days and Nights in the Heartland of Rebellion'.
[29] Roy, 'Walking with the Comrades'.

during puberty causing a woman's menstrual cycle to disappear, or never appear in the first place'.[30] 'It's an epidemic here, like in Biafra,' the doctor said. 'There are no clinics in this forest apart from one or two in Gadchiroli. No doctors. No medicines'.[31]

Notice that most of the severe conditions are caused by acute malnutrition — especially in women and children — suggesting what the 'alternative model' of agriculture and other efforts at Maoist 'development' has done to the people of Dandakaranya. Words like 'famine' and 'sub-Saharan condition' are frequently used in the documents under study.[32] The words are of course polemically directed at the state: 'Look, what the Indian state has done to the tribals'. Any index on quality of life certainly brings out what the Indian state has done to its people, not just the tribals. But the area at issue concerns essentially the Maoists 'with a history of more than two decades where the party has been able to create an alternative structure, virtually uncontested'.[33]

As with the almost complete absence of health centres, the documents do not provide any evidence for any new and regular school for the tribal children in the vast area. *The rare schools that exist are all provided for by the state.* By now, a large number of these impoverished schools have either been occupied by the security forces or blown up by the Maoists to prevent the security forces from doing so. Lately, the JSs under the Maoists have initiated a mobile school programme; there's also a mention of some evening schools operating in some areas. The mobile schools are 'in nature of camps where children attend schools for anywhere between 15 to 30 days, depending upon how tense the situation is in a particular area. Classes last for 90 minutes for each subject with four subjects taught in a day. There are between 25–30 students and three teachers. They have begun to employ certain teaching

---

[30] Roy, 'Walking with the Comrades'.

[31] Ibid.

[32] Navlakha, 'Days and Nights in the Heartland of Rebellion'; 'Edited text of 12,262-word response by Azad' *The Hindu*.

[33] Navlakha, 'Days and Nights in the Heartland of Rebellion'.

aids from globe, torchlights to CDs to teach history and science'.[34] Again we do not know the extent of these efforts. In any case, beyond these rather primitive and grossly inadequate efforts, the documents do not explain why the Maoists failed to introduce thousands of *regular schools* in the 10 divisions under their control during at least two decades of *non-tense* situation.

## Alternative Model

In so far as tribal welfare is concerned, could the Maoists have done better on wages, agriculture, health, and education? Given their vast command area with visible support from millions of tribals, it is not difficult to conceive of real alternatives to the measly 'development' programmes they initiated. With thousands of villages under their control, they could have dominated thousands of *gram sabhas* and hundreds of panchayats in the Bastar area.

Under the auspices of these tribal-controlled panchayats, they could have formed hundreds of democratically-constituted cooperatives to administer the livelihood of tribals. For example, cooperatives devoted to forest produce such as *tendu* leaf could have competed — with massive popular support — for the tenders floated by the state each year. This way the system of greedy contractors would have been eliminated from the scene and the entire profits — after paying 'Kerala'-type wages — would have remained with the tribals. Similar efforts could have been directed at other forest produce and agricultural land.

Add to this the state funding that would have been allocated to these panchayats, and the ability to draw rural credit from local banks. One can only imagine what good could have been done for the tribals with the funds so available: schools, colleges, technical institutes, health centres, tractors, buffaloes, tubewells, irrigation canals from rivers, safe source of drinking water. In time, these people's organisations could have made full use of the National Rural Employment Guarantee Scheme, the Forest Rights Act,

---

[34] Navlakha, 'Days and Nights in the Heartland of Rebellion'.

the Right to Information, the Education Act, and other schemes of the state.

There are other advantages with strong and legal people's bodies. For example, it is mandatory for corporations to secure consent of the local people before they can start operations. To that end, Tata Steel authorities organised a public hearing for their planned steel plant on 12 October 2007. The corporation 'secured' the required consent by hiring an audience of about 50 people in a meeting far away from the concerned area. It is doubtful if they would have dared to do so if vigilant people's committees, under the auspices of panchayats, were in place. In fact, Roy reports on a wonderful initiative by the women's mass organisation, KAMS, in which members of KAMS immediately surround a police station after someone is falsely arrested, and get the person released before the police is able to file charges.[35] One wonders if such initiatives can be expanded with legal people's institutions in place.

None of this of course was going to be easy. The alternative just sketched would have required creative economic initiatives backed by democratic movements; it would have also involved legal battles with the state and the contractors, as every people's movement in the rest of the country know[s]. Nonetheless, in Dandakaranya, the Maoists enjoyed unprecedented advantages, as noted, to pursue these democratic goals. There is no evidence that the Maoists even contemplated these obvious steps. Why not?

## Primacy of Warfare

A disturbing answer begins to emerge when we look at what else the Maoists have done in the area during the same period. The basic idea, as the General Secretary Ganapathy told his visitors, is that 'it is important to guard against getting bogged down in legalism and economism and forget that masses have to be prepared for seizure of power'.[36] So, 'seizure of power', and not the welfare of the tribals, was the central goal. In this light, it is seriously

[35] Roy, 'Walking with the Comrades'.
[36] Myrdal and Navlakha, 'In Conversation with Ganapathy'.

questionable if the Maoists entered the forests of Dandakaranya three decades ago with tribal welfare in mind at all. The documents suggest the following story. After considerable setbacks to their armed struggle in Andhra, the Maoists decided to enter these forests way back in 1980, as noted. The basic goal was to 'build a standing army, for which it would need a base. Dandakaranya was to be that base, and those first squads were sent in to reconnoitre the area and begin the process of building guerrilla zones'.[37] Dandakaranya offered a variety of advantages. It was a vast densely forested area spanning across several provinces such that people can cross state boundaries through the forest itself. After the refugees from the erstwhile East Bengal left the area, it was inhabited almost entirely by the tribal population who have been there for ages. The state had only a rudimentary presence in some areas, while it was almost totally absent in others. Also, as noted, 'there was a class society here, but due to the tribal traditions, unlike plains the Mukhia/Manjis exploitation did not appear sharp'.[38] Finally, due to their historical isolation and exploitation from the outsiders, tribal traditions have been compelled to acquire some degree of militancy to defend themselves. Much before the Maoists entered the scene, tribals in Bastar had a history of resistance against the British, landlords and moneylenders. Dandakaranya was virtually a 'blank slate' on which the Maoists decided to inscribe Charu Mazumdar's — and, later, Kanhai Chatterji's — 'vision'.

The first task was to create enough guerrilla *zones*, and the second was to secure guerrilla *bases* in the zones so created. Navlakha explains the distinction: '[g]uerilla zone is a fluid area in the sense that there is contention for control and the State is not entirely absent, even if it be in shape of its police or armed force. However, there are spots in these guerrilla zones which are demarcated to ensure that some work can carry on relatively uninterrupted. These are "bases" which are not easily penetrable or accessible'.[39]

[37] Roy, 'Walking with the Comrades'.
[38] Navlakha, 'Days and Nights in the Heartland of Rebellion'.
[39] Ibid.

The current plan is to 'intensify and expand guerrilla war . . . we have to utilize cleverly the tactics of hit and run basically'.[40] Ultimately, however, 'we have to develop guerrilla war into mobile war and guerrilla army into a regular army'.[41] That's the goal. The tribals are essentially cannon-fodder in this elaborate military strategy.

To pursue it, one-third of the guerrilla forces of the erstwhile People's War Group were transferred to Dandakaranya from Telengana in Andhra back in 1988 after some support from the tribal population had been secured. The squads from Andhra started organising village militias from the very beginning. Militias consist of 20 to 30 young people armed with anything from bows and arrows, muzzle loaders, home-made pistols to genuine rifles and rocket launchers (10 per cent of the used stock is distributed from the central army headquarters to the militias each year). Their basic task is to 'guard' a group of villages. Apparently, the best of the fighters from the militias are incorporated into more professional guerrilla squads whose members sport combat uniform and carry 'serious' weapons such as Insas rifles, AK-series rifles, self-loading rifles, pistols, revolvers, hand grenades and other forms of explosives; some carry light machine guns, mortars and rocket launchers. In December 2001, the People's Liberation Guerrilla Army (PLGA) was formally constituted. By now, the PLGA has 'moved from platoons to companies, and are now moving towards battalion formation'.[42] The writers report that there are about 50,000 members of militias and 10,000 in PLGA.

Once guerrilla zones expanded and covered much of the area, the task of constructing guerrilla bases started in earnest in 2001. Two or three spots were selected for guerrilla bases in each division, and in this shape 10–12 spots were concentrated upon to form the guerrilla bases. Abujhmad forms the Central Guerrilla Base. To ensure that these bases are not 'easily penetrable or accessible', a

---

[40] Myrdal and Navlakha, 'In Conversation with Ganapathy'.

[41] Ibid.

[42] Navlakha, 'Days and Nights in the Heartland of Rebellion'.

complex system of landmines and IEDs punctuate every road, approach, landmark tree or rock formation throughout the forest areas. Needless to say, all of this requires an elaborate structure of informers, lookouts, technical experts, technical equipment for secure wireless communication, laptop computers, solar-charged batteries, electronic and other devices for triggering IEDs, vehicles such as hundreds of motorcycles, well-concealed factories and workshops for manufacture, repair and refitting of weapons, and so on. Except for the supply of human power — young men and women — to the militias and PLGA (we return), the tribals are nowhere in the picture.

## Allocation of Funds

The documents do not explain sufficiently where the money for this elaborate military structure comes from. Some weapons and related ammunition have been seized/stolen from police stations and armouries; some have been removed from the corpses of security personnel after ambushes. It is unclear if the total amount of these seizures explains almost battalion-level weaponry. Navlakha does report, in general terms, the source of money: party membership fee, levy and the contributions of the people, confiscation of the wealth and the income sources of the enemy, and taxes collected in the guerrilla zones and base areas.[43]

Presuming that most members are famine-stricken tribals themselves, party membership fees are not likely to amount to much. Later in the essay, Navlakha informs that 'revenue accruing from looting of bank or confiscation of wealth are far less' than the money collected from royalties on forest produce such as *tendu* leaf.[44] So, it is really the royalties/levies from forest produce and taxes on contractors and companies that constitute the bulk of the funds. (What is 'contributions of the people'? Are there remittances from abroad from wealthy sympathisers as with LTTE

---

[43] Navlakha, 'Days and Nights in the Heartland of Rebellion'.
[44] Ibid.

[Liberation Tigers of Tamil Eelam] and similar organisations?)
It is anybody's guess how much money is so collected and how
it is divided between military work and 'mass work'.

An apparently disjointed bit of information throws some light
on the issue. Navlakha reports on the budget for 2009 of one area
RPC [Revolutionary People's Committee] (recall that there are
about 50 area RPCs in Dandakaranya).[45] The income side showed
about 11 lakh rupees. It is interesting that, although the income
includes about 360,000 rupees from taxes on contractors, it does
not directly mention the 'royalties' — the real money. About half
of the income comes from allocation by the JS; it is unclear what
it means. Does it mean that some of the other income, including
royalties, is partly distributed by the divisional RPCs to area
RPCs? Or, does it mean that most of the real money remains with
the party itself for military work?

An indirect evidence for the latter conclusion emerges when
we look at the expenditure side of the budget. It is reasonable
to expect that the income of a given RPC is primarily meant for
development work in the concerned area. It turns out though that
over 50 per cent of the (meagre) income is allocated to 'defence',
about 12 per cent for agriculture, 9 per cent for health, and 0.9 per
cent for education. It is important to note that 'defence' means
providing just the kits for the militias and PLGA (three pair[s] of
uniform, oil, soap, toothpaste, washing soap, comb, gunpowder,
bows and arrows, and food). [The] RPC budget does not pay
for the *weapons* and related military needs; so, the astronomical
money needed for that purpose must be controlled directly by the
party itself. Is that where rest of the money including the 'royalties'
goes? The answer is likely to be in the positive since most of the
development money is diverted to military preparations.

Now that we have some idea of where the money from the
taxes, royalties, and 'contributions from people' basically go, it is
clear why the system of greedy and rich contractors — and similar
characters — must continue to operate freely even in the 'liberated

---

[45] Navlakha, 'Days and Nights in the Heartland of Rebellion'.

zones', while the tribals continue to toil at subsistence wages to survive until the next season. In other words, these contractors and other concealed characters are allowed to cheat the tribals all the way — 'the slippery arithmetic and the sly system of measurement that converts bundles into *manak boras* [standard bags] into kilos is controlled by the contractors, and leaves plenty of room for manipulation of the worst kind' in a business running into several hundred crore[46] — because they basically fund the war against the state for seizure of power. One wonders if the 'rapacious plunder by the tiny parasitic class of blood-sucking leaches'[47] includes these contractors who fund the 'war of liberation'.

The preceding perspective also explains why the Maoists never even contemplated alternative and genuine development plans based on panchayats, cooperatives, etc. For one, as noted, those plans would have driven the system of private contractors out of Dandakaranya resulting into a massive loss of revenue for the party. For another, those plans would have raised the condition of the tribals from mere subsistence to the threshold of decent living. Having tasted decent living by their own cooperative enterprise, would the tribals continue to clutch on to the Maoists; most importantly, would they allow their young people anymore to join the militias and PLGA to die violent deaths at a young age?

Finally, once real economic development with the associated democratic process unfolded, Dandakaranya would have teemed with state officials, other political parties, functionaries of banks and other funding agencies, agents of companies supplying a variety of goods, expansion of communication within the area, etc. — Dandakaranya would have opened up to the outside world. This would have seriously compromised the secrecy, security and inaccessibility of the network of guerrilla bases. It is no wonder that the Maoists *do not* allow development activities of the state in the areas they control.[48] The ostensive reason given is that, in those areas, they themselves 'undertake reforms that benefit people'; by

---

[46] Roy, 'Walking with the Comrades'.
[47] 'Edited text of 12,262-word response by Azad', *The Hindu*.
[48] Navlakha, 'Days and Nights in the Heartland of Rebellion'.

now we have a fair idea of the character of those 'reforms'. In sum, then, the tribals cannot be allowed to prosper beyond subsistence because it will interfere with the plans for seizure of power.

## Children for War

The Maoists complain that the state uses 'school children as SPOs (special police officers) and as police [i]nformers'.[49] Given the character of the state, as noted, this — as with other horrors — might well be true. What is the Maoists' own record with respect to children?

Even if we set aside earlier, unconfirmed reports of children being snatched away from tribal families at gunpoint, the documents provide a range of evidence about extensive involvement of children in the war. Roy describes a young boy, Mangtu, who appears to be one of the conduits between nearby towns and the guerrilla army.[50] Next, she describes another 'slightly older' person, Chandu, with a 'village boy air', who actually belongs to a militia and can handle every kind of weapon except an LMG. Then, of course, there's this much talked about (and photographed) young girl, Kamla. At the time of reporting, she is 17, and is already a hardcore member of the PLGA with a revolver on her hips and a rifle slung on her shoulder. We can only guess about her age when she joined the armed forces. She had taken part in a number of ambushes; in fact, watching 'ambush videos' is her favourite form of entertainment. Yet she has a captivating smile; that's the human design of a 17-year-old which even the addiction to ambush videos cannot disfigure.[51]

These are not isolated examples. Roy's narrative and the accompanying photographs furnish the distinct impression that most, if not all, of the people in the militias and PLGA are aged

[49] 'Edited text of 12,262-word response by Azad', *The Hindu*.
[50] Roy, 'Walking with the Comrades'.
[51] Ibid.

between mid-teens to early 20s, and most of these have been part of the armed forces for several years. Roy's motherly instinct wells up as she prepares to sleep in the forest amidst hundreds of armed guerrillas: 'I'm surrounded by these strange, beautiful children with their curious arsenal'.[52]

Recruiting children for warfare seems to be an established practice in the Maoist scheme of things. Comrade Madhav, who has now risen to be a commander of a PLGA platoon, joined the Maoists at the age of nine in Warangal in Andhra Pradesh.[53] The entire thing is carefully organised. The mobile schools mentioned earlier (perhaps the only Maoist effort at education of tribal children), are not meant to provide education to tribal children in general. While the general tribal child has no school to go to, these specialised schools, called Young Communist Mobile School (or, Basic Communist Training School), host select groups of 25–30 children in the age group 12–15. These children receive intensive training for six months in a curriculum consisting of basic concepts of Marxism Leninism and Maoism, Hindi and English, maths, social science, *different types of weapons*, computers, etc.[54] Once they pass out, 'they trail the PLGA squads, with stars in their eyes, like groupies of a rock band'.[55]

Navlakha also reports that, as with any regular army, recruitment drives are conducted with meetings and leaflets.[56] One of the leaflets, directed at 'unemployed boys and girls of Bastar', says 'you will not get any salary but food, clothes, personal needs will be fulfilled and your families would be helped by the Janatam Sarkar'. Elsewhere in the essay, Navlakha reports on the food supplied to the guerrillas: 'Breakfast can vary between "poha", "khichri", etc., mixed with peanuts and followed by tea. Lunch and dinner

---

[52] Roy, 'Walking with the Comrades'.
[53] Ibid.
[54] Navlakha, 'Days and Nights in the Heartland of Rebellion'.
[55] Roy, 'Walking with the Comrades'.
[56] Navlakha, 'Days and Nights in the Heartland of Rebellion'.

consists of rice with *dal* [lentils] and *subzi* [vegetables]. Food is simple but nutritious. Once a week they get meat. Sometimes more than once if fish is available or there is pork, which is provided by the Revolutionary People's Committee'.[57] Even with this impressive food intake, most of the guerrillas have less than half of the normal count of haemoglobin, as noted. One can only imagine with horror the condition of these children when they joined the forces.

With no schools to go to, no opportunities in hand, and with sub-Saharan conditions prevailing in their families, which able-bodied tribal child can resist the temptation of assured food, clothes, peer company, and the ability to roam the forests with a rifle slung on shoulders? Naturally, when the state attacks and the economic lives of tribals are further disrupted, enrolment for militia and PLGA increases sharply. The more the repression by the state, the bigger the 'people's army' of starving children.

As mentioned, the total strength of the militias and PLGA currently adds up to about 60,000, with many more in the waiting. Assuming as above that most of them joined the forces when they were children, it follows that the Indian state and the Maoist leadership — consisting of Ganapathy, Koteshwar Rao, Kobad Ghandy, Azad, and others in their politbureau and central committee — conspired to deny normal childhood to a vast number of tribal children. They never went to school, learned about life outside the forests, glimpsed the pluralistic complex of Indian society, [or] acquired the skills to become a participating citizen, [and were] never allowed to make up their mind. All they know is how to fashion an IED, how to clean and fire a rifle, how to ambush, how to kill. They form the frontline — and get maimed and killed — when the police, the greyhounds, the CRPF and special operations forces encircle them. As for Kamla, 'if the police come across her, they'll kill her. They might rape her first. No questions will be asked'.[58] Kamla won't be the only one.

---

[57] Navlakha, 'Days and Nights in the Heartland of Rebellion'.
[58] Roy, 'Walking with the Comrades'.

The basic picture is abundantly clear from Maoist documents themselves. In an act of palpable cowardice, the defeated Maoist leadership from Andhra [Pradesh] and Bihar abandoned the struggling people there, and entered the safe havens of Dandakaranya forests. Taking advantage of the historical neglect and exploitation of the tribals by the state — the 'root cause' — the Maoist leadership ensured the support of hapless tribals with token welfare measures while directing most of the attention secretly to construct guerrilla bases. In the process, they lured a large number of tribal children with assurances of food and clothing. These children have now grown into formidable militia and guerrilla forces. After committing atrocious crimes in the name of 'revolutionary violence', these youth brigades are now facing the wrath of the mighty Indian state. It is reasonable to infer that millions of tribals continue to side with the Maoists largely because their children are with them.

Should the tribals now pay the price with their lives and livelihood because of the evil designs of a handful of men such as Ganapathy, Koteshwar Rao, Kobad Ghandy, Azad, and others in their politbureau and central committee? Whose vision is the Indian state supposed to satisfy, Charu Mazumdar's or Gandhi's? How does Mrs Sonia Gandhi address the 'root cause' by attacking the tribals?

The tribals can be saved only if:

(a) The state dismantles Operation Green Hunt since its immediate victims are unarmed tribals under mental and physical seize.

(b) The state announces total and universal amnesty to the young tribal people in the militias and the PLGA — and a safe and concrete programme for their rehabilitation — once they surrender (only) to a citizen's body comprising of individuals such as Yash Pal, Swami Agnivesh, Kuldip Nayyar, Mohini Giri, Medha Patkar, Rajender Sacchar, Himanshu Kumar, Binayak Sen, Jean Dreze, Aruna Roy, Vandana Shiva, and others.

(*c*) The essentially non-tribal leadership of CPI (Maoist) is brought to justice for their crimes against humanity.

In the face of immense calamity unfolding on millions of tribals in Bastar, historical and humanistic decisions are urgently needed beyond routine and failed 'counter-insurgency' operations.

৯৫

# 31

# 'Halt the Violence! Give Me 72 Hours'

## P. Chidambaram
## Interview by Shoma Chaudhury*

✪

*With rare candour, P. Chidambaram tells Shoma Chaudhury he is willing to engage with all aspects of the Naxal problem.*
At the core of the Maoist crisis lie some of the thorniest questions that confront Indian democracy. It poses a mirror to ourselves and asks, is there really any intention to deliver? Are elections merely a smokescreen to preserve the status quo? But brute violence has an uncomfortable way of usurping a show. Recently, India has been convulsed by high-voltage drama as the Maoist 'debate' suddenly erupted [and took] centre stage. As news of Operation Green Hunt, a major central government offensive against the Maoists, gathered steam, activists began to raise alarmed flags about the 'collateral damage' that would inevitably flow. The Maoists themselves retaliated with an even more brazen show of strength: kidnappings, beheaded cops, blasted police stations. In all the competitive and belligerent rhetoric that followed, the real topography of the argument was lost.

In a sense, the man at the heart of this sudden eruption was Home Minister P. Chidambaram. Having taken over a comatose ministry from his predecessor Shivraj Patil, in the wake of the devastating 26/11 attack, over the last year [2008] Chidambaram has

---

*This article was previously published as 'Halt the Violence! Give Me 72 Hours', *Tehelka*, 21 November 2009.

gone about joining many 'missing dots' in the security apparatus, as one of the men in his ministry puts it. One of these joined dots was the decision to spearhead a coordinated strategy between the Centre and Naxal-affected states to 'wipe out the Naxal menace'.

Unlike his predecessor, Chidambaram is not a man you can ignore. In his own words, he started out as a 'flaming communist', a man who, in his youth, hurled idealistic slogans against the capitalist might of the State, until he realised the trade union leaders he was revering were cutting deals on the side. 'I'm done with that murky world', he says in an incidental conversation. In a political career spanning 25 years then, he has moved from being a staunch socialist to being one of the chief architects of the new liberalised economy. Despite some key pro-people steps, including granting a ₹70,000 crore farm loan waiver, (as well as his consistent defence of reservations as affirmative action), in both his stints as finance minister, Chidambaram has largely been perceived as a champion of corporates. His controversial briefs as a lawyer, especially for companies like Vedanta and Enron, have added to his ambiguous aura. A man firmly opposed to SEZs [Special Economic Zones], yet firmly committed to mining. A man, who, even his worst detractors would grant, is highly intelligent and unafraid of taking action. For a society still in transition, inevitably then, for many people, Chidambaram has come to seem a distillate of many contemporary anxieties about power and big money. To find him at the centre of a 'coordinated strategy' therefore seemed hugely reassuring to some, hugely dismaying to others.

About two weeks ago, however, Chidambaram replaced the threat of an 'all out war' with an offer for peace talks. Abjure violence, he appealed to the Maoists, and the government was willing to discuss all the key issues: land acquisition, forest rights, industrialisation, and local forms of governance. In a line: how the State should relate to its people. As it stands, this offer is unimpeachably worded. What's more, it lowers the temperature enough for one to examine what really is at stake.

Physical violence is the simplest part of the argument. Of course physical violence is heinous. Whether it's Francis Induwar beheaded by the Maoists or the 19 tribals shot by the police in

Singaram. Or the 14 in Nandigram. Or in Kalinganagar. What's much more difficult to grapple with is the ideological violence that underpins all of this.

On the one hand, there is the deep, embedded 'structural violence' of the Indian State. What this means is that though in an inspired move our founding fathers granted universal adult suffrage to every Indian citizen at the moment of Independence, the Indian State itself has remained intensely feudal and oppressive in many ways.

On the other hand, though the Maoists seem to champion the cause of the people and are indeed creating a crucial awareness amongst the poor about their rights, they are not interested in reform or resolution. Their political ideal is to overthrow Indian parliamentary democracy and replace it with a dictatorship of the people. Catalysed by armed struggle. Unfortunately, the history of Stalinist Russia and Maoist China is not a pretty sight. Nor are they visions of the utopian equal society anyone would want to live in. The Maoists' rejection of Chidambaram's plea to abjure violence as an 'absurd and irrational demand' and a 'betrayal of the people' is of a piece with this ideology.

In its coverage of the Naxal riddle, *Tehelka* has consistently tried to angle the spotlight at the dispossessed and be a watchdog against State excesses: that is part of its commitment to the Constitution and the idea of the Indian State. However, none of its positions are doctrinaire. Chidambaram's invitation for talks is a huge opportunity: the Maoists' initial rejection, a big disappointment. But there is a much more important interlocutor in this dialogue: the people of India.

In this unusual interview, Home Minister Chidambaram makes many important and hopeful statements. If the people of India can hold him and his government to some of it, it would be a tiny step in the direction all stakeholders claim they want.

Justice and the dream of an equal society is a slow, painful, dialogic process. To imagine anything else is hubris. We have an imperfect system, let's protest against it, let's fix it, let's fight about it, says the Home Minister, but don't throw the whole system out.

And don't kill over it. As a conversation starter, that seems an irreproachable place to begin.

'I am ready to review all the corporate MoUs'

*Home Minister P. Chidambaram tells Shoma Chaudhury everything he is willing to do to de-escalate violence.*

**Shoma Chaudhury (SC)**: In the past few months there's been an escalated rhetoric from the State about Operation Green Hunt and 'an all-out war against Maoists'. Now, with your offer for talks, a lot of that rhetoric has been toned down. What lay behind this sudden escalation and this toning down? And what, according to you, is really the best way to dismantle Maoist violence?

**P. Chidambaram (PC)**: Everybody, especially the media, loves a war. You find this in every country — in the US after 9/11, in India after 26/11. You must not underestimate the gravity of the situation. The CPI (Maoists) have virtually taken control of many districts in seven states and completely paralysed the civil administration. Despite this, there was no conscious effort on the part of the government of India to raise the level of the rhetoric. We went about it in the only manner that we have to address a problem, namely, consulting the states. We consulted the states in January, we consulted the states in August and, necessarily, we put out a statement on what the consensus was. The consensus was that there should be coordinated action to take on the CPI (Maoists), which I think is perfectly right. So the Central Government offered paramilitary forces, real-time intelligence inputs, training, technical equipment and technology to the states. Show me one statement on the part of the Central Government, or me specifically, where I have raised the rhetoric against the CPI (Maoists). So I don't agree that the rhetoric was raised and then toned down. The toning down, in fact, is again a perception. When we were asked if we will talk to the Maoists, I said yes, if they abjure violence we will talk to the Maoists. That's been our stand from day one. The Prime Minister has said this, I've said it. So the so-called escalated rhetoric happened after the consultation with the chief ministers and the so-called lowering is after we said we'll talk to the Maoists. Each event is simply how the media perceives it.

*SC*: There's been a key shift in phrase from asking Maoists to 'lay down arms' to merely asking them to 'abjure violence'.

*PC*: I never asked the Maoists to lay down arms because I know they will not. It is against their ideology. I have merely asked them to abjure violence. Unfortunately, much of the media did not notice the difference.

*SC*: Many government functionaries have spoken of Operation Green Hunt to the media, but both you and Home Secretary Gopal Pillai have recently made public statements that it is a media creation. Are we to take it that this Operation does not exist? And if so, what are we to expect in the months to come?

*PC*: There is no Operation Green Hunt. Name me an officer who has said this and I will take action. I have not seen a single paper or a single document in the Ministry of Home Affairs that uses the phrase Operation Green Hunt. It's a pure invention of the media. What you can expect in the months ahead is merely a more coordinated effort by the state police to reassert control over territory or tracts of land where regrettably the civil administration has lost control. And for that purpose we will assist them in whatever manner is possible, particularly by providing paramilitary forces and sharing of intelligence.

*SC*: There have been some other disturbing statements recently. At your interaction in the *Indian Express* office, you said, if need be, you would call in the army or the Rashtriya Rifles. You have also been saying that civil society is abetting a 'climate of terror' and must 'choose'. Raising one's voice against State violence, excess or failure is the legitimate duty of a citizen; by doing that it does not mean one is supporting Maoist violence. Why trap people in this fatal binary? Why must we choose between two evils? Why would you want to outlaw democratic voices and lump them with Maoists?

*PC*: I don't blame you for inaccurate quotations. That's something I've learnt to live with. You have quoted three parts of my alleged statements. All three are wrong. Let's take the first one. At *Indian Express* I was asked, will the army be called? I said, no, the army will not be called for these internal security operations. I said, if necessary, the special forces in the army, which is the commando unit, may have to be called in for a special situation. That commando unit is meant for anti-terrorist operations and will be used with utmost caution.

Second, you quoted me as saying that civil society has to choose. Show me where I have ever said that. In my statement I outlined the Maoists' history of violence and spelled out their policy of seizing state control through armed struggle. Having done this I said we are wedded to a democratic republican form of government, so civil society has to choose whether we want this form of government or an armed liberation struggle and a dictatorship of the proletariat. That's a stark choice that you cannot duck. You are an Indian citizen living in India and you, I, and everyone has to make that choice. Now Kishenji, Kobad Gandhy and others like them have made that choice. They have the right to make a choice and they have. I have also made my choice. Imperfect as it is, I want a democratic republican form of government. I have taken an oath under the Constitution and I am obliged to defend this form of government that you, I and our forefathers, rightly or wrongly, chose and agreed to abide by. All I say is that all others too have to make that choice. This has got nothing to do with choosing between two kinds of violence. Therefore when you say that I told civil activists to make a choice, you must also provide the context — between what did I say make a choice.

*SC*: Fair enough. Few would argue with targeted operations against Maoist leaders who, per se, do not believe in parliamentary democracy and want to overthrow it through armed struggle. As you say, we have made a choice about living in a democratic republic. But that cannot stop us arguing over its imperfect nature. When we point to state oppression or collateral damage or structural violence, as home minister can't you engender a greater climate of justice? In so far as moral rhetoric drives action, can you not send out a message that violation by either the police or paramilitary will not be tolerated?

*PC*: I entirely agree. We are an imperfect democracy; in fact our imperfections are growing every day. And we must debate, struggle and strive to keep perfecting this system. All I am saying is that no matter how frustrated we feel, no matter how slow the process is, let's not throw out the system itself. I cannot make our democracy perfect overnight. There are other institutions which are required by the Constitution to see that the structures of governance work. There are the courts. There are the Human Rights Commissions at central and state level. There are commissions for minorities, scheduled castes and scheduled tribes. There is the RTI [Right to Information Act] and the information commissioners and election commissioners. There's a CAG [Comptroller and Auditor General] and an accountant general to ensure money is correctly spent. If many [of] these institutions work reasonably well, we'd have a system that works. The frustrating thing is many of these institutions are either faltering or paralysed. This is why our imperfections are growing.

Still, within my authority and power, there are certainly some rules I can ensure. For example, since I took over this ministry, I have made it very clear that anyone who is arrested by the police — State or Centre — must be produced before a magistrate within 24 hours. I am totally opposed to staged encounters. It's possible that in a gun battle between the police and those who take to the gun, people could get killed, but that's unfortunately a battle. But if you arrest a person, he must be produced before a magistrate. There's no question of tolerating an encounter, and I can say with complete confidence that since 1 December 2008, no one who has been arrested by the police has died in an encounter.

Likewise, I can ensure that certain norms are observed. For example there's talk of torture chambers. I have made a thorough investigation and, to my knowledge, there is not a single torture chamber under the control of the central agencies. If you think there is one, if you suspect there is one, let me know where it is, and I know how to locate it and dismantle it.

In the same way, in our coordinated strategy against the Maoists, I have given instructions that there should be no firing unless we are fired at, there should only be intelligence-based operations, not broad sweeping cordon-and-search operations that could alienate local populations. I have been in Punjab, I understand the pitfalls. My point is every organ of government in this country — and I use government with a capital G — must discharge its responsibilities. If you had a strong district judge and a set of very strong, fearless magistrates, very little would go wrong in the criminal justice system.

*SC*: The problem is things are going wrong. In Manipur apparently there have been 285 false encounters this year alone. Tehelka itself exposed one shocking one in July. In the offensive against Naxals too, civil activists like Himanshu Kumar have been trying to highlight the fact that Salwa Judum SPOs [Special Police Officers] have been burning down tribal homes, stealing hens and goats, raping women. There is a complete breakdown of trust because tribals can't even get their FIRs [First Information Reports] filed. Civil rights groups are saying that for the peace talks to have any meaning, we have to restore people's faith in the justice system. Can't you send out a message to the administration that just because this is a conflict zone, excesses will not be tolerated? Arrest some of the SPOs against whom there are complaints…

*PC*: I'm glad you think I have so much power and authority. Law and order is a state subject. All that you have spoken about in the last couple of minutes falls under the jurisdiction of the state governments, the chief minister and home minister of the state. You must take up cudgels with them. If I interfere too much they are likely to throw List II of the Constitution at me.

*SC*: You are washing your hands of it.

*PC*: No, I am saying raise your voice and take up cudgels with the relevant authority. Nevertheless, to answer your question, when

I took over, one of the first issues that came up was the Salwa Judum and I made myself very clear, publicly as well as privately to the chief minister, I do not approve of non-state actors taking things into their own hands. That's a function of the police. And to my knowledge, over time the activities of the Salwa Judum have virtually wound down.

*SC*: No, the SPOs are still armed. The Supreme Court has directed that the villages that were evacuated under the Salwa Judum must be rehabilitated but the SPOs are apparently interfering with this.

*PC*: Quite possible, but the SPO is an agent of the state government. We have them in Jammu and Kashmir, we had them in Punjab. In a sense, they are employees of the state government, so the state must bear responsibility for what the SPO does. If the SPO exceeds his authority or indulges in gratuitous violence, he should be punished. But law and order is a state subject and when there are duly elected governments, beyond prevailing upon the states to change their attitude towards law enforcement, beyond urging them, nudging them, prevailing upon them, there is not much I can do. It falls entirely within the jurisdiction of the state chief ministers to meet the requirements of the Constitution, justice and fair play.

*SC*: To focus on your offer for peace talks. As it stands, your offer is unimpeachably worded. Crucially, you have offered to discuss all the key issues: land acquisition, mining, industrialisation, forest rights, forms of local governance. But the Citizens' Initiative for Peace feels that for the offer to have any meaning on the ground, you must make some gestures to restore people's faith in the justice system. One of the things they suggest is, even if only as a confidence building measure, why don't you hold a *jan sunwayi* or people's hearing in Naxal-affected areas?

*PC*: If any civil rights group or tribal representative will organise it, I am ready to come.

*SC*: Is that on record? Activists like Himanshu Kumar say you don't even need to speak to the Maoists, just start speaking to the people directly — that will wean them away and restore their faith in the Indian State. In these places it's not just that poverty alleviation has been absent, but that the State has only shown its most oppressive or malign face.

*PC*: A group that owes allegiance to Sri Sri Ravi Shankar came to see me. Even though I may not adhere to their politics, I told them if you want to work in these areas and convince tribals to invest faith in the State and eschew support to violence, I will extend all the support I can give, I will ask the states to support and, if necessary, I will come myself to speak to them. But I have not heard from them since.

*SC*: In another context, you've mentioned that because there's President's Rule in Jharkhand, you've been able to achieve a lot, even though it's a Naxal-affected region. So if you had a free hand in Chhattisgarh and Orissa and Bengal, or if there were Congress governments in these states, what are some of the remedial measures you would take?

*PC*: While we can argue about this, I'm very clear in my mind, the first step is to ensure that there is no violence in an area. In a climate of violence, no one will listen to anyone else, no one will trust anyone else and nothing can be done. Maybe it's out of context to say this, but this is a land where Gandhiji was born and he said violence has no place in civil society. I'm not a saint like him, but I firmly believe there's no place for violence in our democracy. Therefore everyone — including the Indian State — must abjure violence. Then we must agree that the civil administration, however imperfect it may be, will be given the space and the time to do certain things. This is what we got in Jharkhand. Once we got the space and the time to do certain things, in just two and a half months, we achieved a lot. If you don't believe me, just go back to the very same people who were complaining and ask them. A year ago, they were saying that the State has failed. Today you have a functioning PDS in the hands of women's groups, old age pension is being paid, free rations are being distributed to everyone below the poverty line, schools have opened, teachers have been appointed. Just the day before polls were announced, I ensured that over a 1,000 doctors and paramedics were appointed, boys and girls in the tenth standard were given cycles, thousands of petty cases for violation of forest rights were cast out. All this was possible in two and a half months because we had broadly asserted control over these areas and, for reasons that I do not know, while the Maoists were indulging in acts of violence here and there, they did not interfere with what we were doing on the ground. At least in these districts.

*SC*: That's exactly the point many concerned citizens are making. You have not had a big military operation in Jharkhand. You did not need it. You just took the initiative to reactivate civil administration on the ground. The Maoists have not had the temerity to harm that because they know if they attack anything that is bringing genuine well-being to the people, local populations will get alienated. Why not take the same initiative in Chhattisgarh or elsewhere?

*PC*: This is not to say Maoists have been not been violent in Jharkhand. They have been particularly violent in instances like the Francis Induwar case. And now they have called for a boycott of the elections and put out a statement saying they will 'target' and 'punish' Congress and JMM [Jharkhand Mukti Morcha] in particular. The point here is, instead of arguing over who is responsible for the violence or who should stop the violence, why don't the CPI (Maoists) heed my appeal and say, 'yes, we will halt the violence and let us hear the Home Minister's response'. Give me two or three days to respond, because I need to consult others in government and state governments. I am not a dictator, I have to consult everyone. Once they say, halt the violence and they actually halt the violence, between their statement and my response which will surely come in about 72 hours, if there is actually no violence, you will find that I am in a position to respond in a manner that violence can be ended once and for all and development can take place, and talks can also be held with the CPI (Maoists). But the first step is to say, 'we halt the violence'.

*SC*: That's a big statement. No one at any end of the spectrum can argue with that position. To get back to your offer for talks: You have offered discussion on all the key issues: land acquisition, forest rights, industrialisation, local governance. While this is an important gesture, why hand over the "rights discourse" to the Maoists? Why don't *you* spell out better more equitable ways of doing all of this? Especially mining. There is a real misgiving that much of the military offensive planned in these areas is to take control over mineral-rich land. Companies like Tatas and Essar have signed MOUs with the state. Do you believe these MOUs directed the Salwa Judum or the urgency with which the state now wants to regain control of this land?

*PC*: I think you are looking for a sinister design that does not exist. I think these MOUs have been signed over a period of time with different governments, long before Maoist violence escalated to this level. Be that as it may, I am prepared to request the Prime Minister to freeze all these MOUs and order a comprehensive review of all the MOUs that have been signed in Jharkhand, Chhattisgarh, Orissa and South Bihar, and then decide which MOU should be implemented, with or without modification. I am prepared to request the PM to do that.

*SC*: That is on record.

*PC*: Yes, it is. But I don't think that is the main issue. It may be the issue foregrounded but the real issue is — and this is something that I am at pains to draw everyone's attention to — the real issue is that the Maoists are not merely champions of the people, defending their rights and challenging the Indian State to function better. Their real thesis is that the parliament system is a rotten system. They believe, and I quote, that 'Parliament is a pigsty' and therefore an armed liberation movement is the only way to destroy the Parliament and establish the dictatorship of the people. Now, that's an intrinsic ideological position. Who can argue with them and tell them they are wrong? If someone holds that position I can't do anything about it but . . .

*SC*: (Overlapping) . . . I want to sideline the focus on the Maoists and focus on the Indian State —

*PC*: — but even if they hold that position and don't indulge in violence and are willing to talk to the government on issues that concern them, I'm still okay with that. I will persuade the state governments and I'll facilitate talks on forest rights, industrialisation, land acquisition and development. But so far, the Maoists response to my offer for talks has been to say that asking them to abjure violence is irrational, absurd and tantamount to betraying the people they defend! Just two days ago, they killed four policemen in Bengal. They weren't even part of a search patrol. Who gave the Maoists the right to be judge, jurist and executioner?

*SC*: I'm back to my question. Why leave it to the Maoists to describe an equitable and pro-people way of doing things? Mining practices is one of the biggest faultlines in our country today. What are *your* thoughts on the matter? You are someone who believes mining is intrinsic to development.

*PC*: Yes, I do. In my mind, I am completely convinced that no country can develop unless it uses its natural and human resources. Mineral wealth is wealth that *must* be harvested and used for the people. And why not? Do you want the tribals to remain hunters and gatherers? Are we trying to preserve them in some sort of anthropological museum? Yes, we can allow the minerals to remain in the ground for another 10,000 years, but will that bring development to these people? We can respect the fact that they worship the Niyamgirhi hill, but will that put shoes on their feet or their children in school? Will that solve the fact that they are severely malnutritioned and have no access to health care? The debate about mining has gone on for centuries. It is nothing new.

*SC*: History has very few examples to show that local communities have benefited from mining.

*PC*: I can point to a dozen examples where the harvesting of mineral wealth has brought about development for the people who lived there. Neyveli in Tamil Nadu is one example. Ask the vaniyars — who by the way are the poorest of the poor — if Kamraj and the lignite mining there has improved their life or not. Jamshedpur is another example.

*SC*: There are double the number of bad examples. Jamshedpur is a turn-of-the-century example. Since then, a lot has changed. Today, private companies, both Indian and international, are literally bleeding the land for private gain.

*PC*: Yes, there are bad examples. These are issues that have to be discussed and we have to find a model where mineral wealth can be exploited without detriment to the environment and without affecting the livelihood of the people. We think — and let me say this with a certain amount of caution — we think we have a good land acquisition and rehabilitation policy. Now private companies have to access 70 per cent of land directly and only then can the State intervene to take over the remaining 30 per cent. If that requires improvement, we can again talk about it. (In fact, Mamata Banerjee has already raised flags. She says the State should not acquire land for private companies under any circumstances. We are discussing that.) We also think we have a good compensation policy that assures jobs, houses and resettlement. But if that requires improvement, we can talk about it. I think the Prime Minister has made it very clear that he is open to any suggestions to improve the system.

Let's go back to where we started. We have an imperfect system; imperfect systems throw up imperfect solutions. So we can talk about how to make both the system and the solution more perfect. But surely we don't need to kill each other because of this!

I am again stating this, I don't know the content of these MOUs but I have no hesitation in saying if somebody wants these MOUs comprehensively reviewed, we can review them. All of you know that I have a critical view on SEZs. Many of these SEZs are falling by the wayside now thanks to the global recession. In a sense, I am happy. So if you want a comprehensive review of the SEZs that have been licensed, I am prepared for that too. But the starting point of that dialogue has to be that violence must stop. Otherwise that dialogue just gets derailed.

*SC*: I agree with you and it's very heartening to hear you say all this. But the Land Acquisition Act was only sent for amendment after the Nandigram resistance. Ditto for the SEZ Act. Ditto for the Rehabilitation Bill. Until these flashpoints are engendered by frustrated people, the State doesn't spend time thinking these things through. This is why some people have begun to feel that until you pick up a gun or cut roads or protest violently, the Government of India is not willing to listen. As journalists, at a pinch, we can access ministers, the common man can't. So why don't legislators spend time thinking through the most fair laws in the first place?

*PC*: Elect better legislators!

*SC*: That's a bad argument.

*PC*: That's not a bad argument! Why don't the people elect someone worthy? I can understand they elect him the first time, why do they elect him the second time if he's corrupt or a knave?

*SC*: The UPA has been entrusted with a second mandate.

*PC*: Yes, but the people have not trusted us with a complete majority, which is okay. They require us to work with others. When we work with others who are elected legislators, we have to accommodate their points of view. Take the Forest Dwellers' Rights Bill. I know the long hours and agonising arguments the prime minister personally chaired with various stakeholders before that bill took shape. Despite that, it was again amended in the floor of the House to accommodate Brinda Karat's concerns — who was then an ally. Now if you tell me that law is still imperfect, we have no choice but to debate it again. This is the way laws are made in our country; if the method is imperfect, the result will be somewhat imperfect. We can keep debating and improving upon the law, but to say we are callous or heartless or deaf to the pleas of civil society or affected people — I don't think that is right.

*SC*: Let's return to mining. The Bellary Brothers, Madhu Koda, Jagan Reddy, Vedanta are just a few obvious examples of the corruption. Then there are problems with effluents, health hazards and pricing. We are also handing over national wealth to private companies who can mine and move on with no concern about national interest. Our mining is not need-based, it's market-based. Tribals are being evacuated from ancestral land without being made stakeholders in these projects. No CSR [Corporate Social Responsibility] clauses are being worked into mining leases. Leave the Maoists aside, what do *you* think is the blueprint for more equitable and sustainable mining?

*PC*: When you say 'you', I suppose you are meaning the Government, because the Government functions through ministries and ministers. The point is, every single concern you have mentioned is already accommodated under the present law. No one can mine unless a mining plan is approved by a competent authority. How much you can mine, how you'll restore the land, how much you'll be taxed, all these things are stipulated and worked out. There's nothing wrong with the mining plan itself. The point is, we don't enforce what we lay down. People get away with impunity by cheating or bribing or violating the plan because the executive is weak. I am back to my basic point. See, the law is not as imperfect as you think it is. It's the application and enforcement of the law which is. If someone points out that this company is violating a mining plan, there are other organs of government which must discharge their duties. Why are these organs silent? Why does everybody look up to a minister? These organs exist in the governance structure so that each one can exercise its authority independently and be a kind of check and balance. The vigilance commission; the information commission; the consumer court; the environment court; the court of law, the CAG, the legislature. More than anyone else, the legislature. Why don't they exercise their powers? Why do they feel emasculated and enfeebled?

*SC*: Unfortunately, we all know graft is driving everything in this country.

*PC*: I agree. Graft is driving a lot, but to say everybody's hand is in the till is wrong.

*SC*: Many activists feel concerned about the fact that you have represented many mining companies as a lawyer. In some cases, you have even argued against the State levying cess on them. There's also discomfort that you were once both lawyer for, and non-executive director of, a company like Vedanta.

*PC*: So what? I have also appeared as a lawyer for many teachers, doctors, government servants and civil rights causes. What's wrong with that? There is utter confusion amongst liberals about this issue. As a lawyer, I am merely executing a professional brief. I might argue the exact opposite point of view for another client. It has nothing to do with my decisions as a minister. I think it is very wrong to casually ascribe motives. I may disagree with your point of view, but I would not ascribe a motive to you unless I am absolutely sure of your *mala fide* intent. I do not claim to be perfect, but I am trying to do my best. If this attitude continues, you will push the good people out of the system. Besides, as a matter of fact, I appeared in an excise law case for a sister company of Vedanta and I recuse myself whenever any Vedanta-related matter comes up before the Cabinet.

*SC*: Recently in Lalgarh, when the OC was kidnapped and the Maoists asked for the release of 14 tribal women, unfortunately they won a major PR [Public Relations] battle. The media kept referring to this as a 'Kandahar swap' and berating the West Bengal government for their 'velvet glove' approach. The truth is the 'velvet hand' of the State should never have arrested these women in the first place. Far from being Naxal terrorists, these women were arrested from a panchayat office where they had gone to complain. There was a 70-year-old widow among them, and many of the others were so poor, their husbands had not been able to visit them in jail. The Lalgarh resistance began because the police randomly picked up dozens of people after the bomb attempt on Chief Minister Buddhadeb. How do you break this vicious cycle?

*PC*: As far as police picking up wrong people goes, I ask, why did the judge remand them? The judge then failed in his duty.

*SC*: But this is the climate of conflict one is cautioning about, with regard to future coordinated police efforts against Maoists or, in another context, Muslim extremists. In this climate, the State has to be extra careful, because it's easy to put away innocent people.

*PC*: I don't agree. The judge could have released them. The point is, I can't sit here in far away Delhi and say release someone who the police is producing before the magistrate in West Bengal. That is why when they released these 14 women I did not utter a word of criticism. I simply said that's a decision the state government is competent to make. But please remember that while there are these 14 women on the one hand, there was another woman who led the attack on the police station and that group killed two police officers and abducted one. That was also a woman. Therefore I don't think you can divide the world into men and women.

*SC*: I agree it's a grey zone, but —

*PC*: The point is these women were obviously victims of circumstances, but I would fault the judge who remanded them to judicial custody. He should have released them on the same day when they were produced before him.

It underscores my point that organs of government in this country are not functioning. There's too much stasis, too much incompetence. The theoretical construct is not wrong, the practice is.

*SC*: A key problem about conflict zones are draconian laws like AFSPA (Armed Forces [Special Powers] Act), MCOCA [Maharashtra Control of Organised Crime Act], the Chhattisgarh Public Security Act. The reason why someone like Binayak Sen could be arrested and kept in jail for two years is that even courts get influenced by the climate of conflict. In the tightrope between security and justice, these laws allow the police or forces to become lazy. Instead of being patient and doing rigorous investigative work that will put away actual perpetrators, they just catch anybody they like. The State is not enjoined to be careful. Such laws increase the cycle of hatred and violence. Manipur is a great example of this.

*PC*: I agree. We have some tough laws but none [tougher] than what was passed by the British Parliament last year, or by the US after 9/11. There, confession before a police officer is admissible. Since I took over, I have made it clear that a confession before a police officer will not be admissible. Tough laws are required under certain circumstances but we have also made it clear that we are willing to repeal these laws once the crisis passes. We repealed TADA (Terrorist and Disruptive Activities [Prevention] Act), we repealed POTA [Prevention of Terrorist Activities Act]. On AFSPA — the Justice Jeevan Reddy Committee recommended repealing it. If they had stopped there, I would have been happy. But they suggested making another law or amending the existing one to virtually incorporate the offending provisions. Anyway, having read that report carefully, I have proposed amendments to AFSPA which will make it a more humane law, and yet serve the purpose when the army is deployed. The army refuses to be deployed in a civil conflict situation unless it has certain protections. There are only two ways to go about the: One, we can say the army will not be deployed: the matter ends there. The other is to say, the army will be deployed if necessary, but we will give them adequate protection, not excessive protection. You have to strike a balance and make a judgement. Right or wrong, it will always be criticised. I have made a judgement and proposed amendments. But can I simply wield a magic wand and bring them into force? No. I have to clear it through Cabinet and Parliament. I may stumble on the way, I may succeed in my effort but at least I am trying to amend [the] AFSPA. I have told everybody in Kashmir and Manipur the amendments are ready, it's before the Cabinet. Now we have to wait and see what we can deliver.

ॐ

# PART V

COUNTER-MAOISM, RULE OF LAW AND CONSTITUTIONAL RIGHTS

# 32

## Plea to Manmohan Singh on Behalf of Binayak Sen

*V. R. Krishna Iyer*\*

✪

Instead of recognising their social contributions, the Indian state, by wrongly branding Dr Sen and many other human rights defenders like him as 'terrorists', is making a complete mockery of not just democratic norms and fair governance but its entire anti-terrorist strategy and operations.

*The text of a letter written by Justice V. R. Krishna Iyer, former Supreme Court Judge, to Prime Minister Manmohan Singh, dated 17 April 2009:*

◉

I would like to bring to your attention a case of grave injustice which is a cause of much shame to Indian democracy: that of Dr Binayak Sen, the well-known paediatrician and defender of human rights.

This good doctor has been incarcerated in a Raipur jail for nearly two years now under the Chhattisgarh State Public Security Act, 2005. Among the charges against Dr Sen, who is renowned worldwide for his public health work among the rural poor, are 'treason and waging war against the state'.

---

\* This article was previously published as 'Krishna Iyer's plea on behalf of Binayak Sen', *The Hindu*, 19 April 2009.

Chhattisgarh State prosecutors claim that Binayak, as part of an unproven conspiracy, passed on a set of letters from Narayan Sanyal, a senior Maoist leader who is in the Raipur jail, to Piyush Guha, a local businessman with allegedly close links to the left-wing extremists. He was supposed to have done this while visiting Sanyal in prison both in his capacity as a human rights activist and as a doctor treating him for various medical ailments.

The trial of Dr Sen, which began in a Raipur Sessions Court late April 2008, has, however, not thrown up even a shred of evidence to justify any of these charges against him. By March 2009, of the 83 witnesses listed for deposition by the prosecution as part of the original charge-sheet, 16 were dropped by the prosecutors themselves and six declared 'hostile', while 61 others have deposed without corroborating any of the accusations against Dr Sen. Irrespective of the merits of the case against Dr Sen, there are very disturbing aspects to the way the trial process has been carried out so far.

As if all this were not enough, Dr Sen has also been repeatedly denied bail by the Bilaspur High Court (in September 2007 and December 2008). And the Supreme Court of India rejected his special leave petition to have the bail application heard before it (in December 2007).

Given the paucity of evidence in the trial of Dr Sen so far, in all fairness the Raipur court should have dismissed the case against him altogether by now. Certainly the weakness of the prosecution's position should entitle him to at least grant of bail. Dr Sen is a person of international standing and reputation, with a record of impeccable behaviour throughout his distinguished career. In May 2008, in an unprecedented move 22 Nobel Prize winners even signed a public statement calling him a 'professional colleague' and asking for his release.

Normally bail is refused only in cases where courts believe an accused can tamper with evidence, prejudice witnesses or run away. In Dr Sen's case none of these apply, as shown by the simple fact that at the time of his arrest he chose to come to the Chhattisgarh police voluntarily and made no attempt to abscond despite knowing about his possible detention.

Today Dr Sen, a diabetic who is also hypertensive, is himself in urgent need of medical treatment for his deteriorating heart condition. In recent weeks his health has worsened and a doctor appointed by the court to examine him recommended that he be transferred to Vellore for an angiography and perhaps, if needed, an angioplasty or coronary artery bypass graft without further delay.

Instead of recognising their social contributions, the Indian state, by wrongly branding Dr Sen and many other human rights defenders like him as 'terrorists', is making a complete mockery of not just democratic norms and fair governance but its entire anti-terrorist strategy and operations.

The repeated denial of bail which results in 'punishment by trial' constitutes an even graver threat to Indian society. The sheer injustice involved will only breed cynicism among ordinary citizens about the credibility and efficacy of Indian democracy itself.

ॐ

# 33

## How Many Deaths
## Before Too Many Die

### Shoma Chaudhury*

✪

*We can physically exterminate the Maoists, but what are we going to do with the big, rebuking questions they have unleashed around us?*

A few weeks after he was released from two years in jail, Binayak Sen, the gentle and now famous doctor from Chhattisgarh, was asked what he thought of the Maoist crisis and the government's response to it. It's like watching two locomotives hurtling towards each other, he replied. Bent upon colliding even when all the warning signals are clearly flashing. And you can do nothing to stop it.

On 6 April, not the first but the loudest of many tragic collisions came to pass. The Maoists ambushed a heavily armed CRPF battalion in the jungles of Dantewada, and blew up an armoured vehicle. Within hours, 76 jawans were dead. The sheer, staggering loss of life — the spiralling pain that would ripple through small anonymous homesteads in UP [Uttar Pradesh] and Haryana and Delhi — took your breath away. Here again, were the poorest of the poor, being sent out to execute the most draconian face of the State. These 76 dead were just a punctuation: more jawans would be sent out, more jawans would be killed. The poor being set to kill the poor. If ever there was reason to rethink strategy, surely, here it was.

---

*This article was previously published as 'How Many Deaths Before Too Many Die', *Tehelka*, 17 April 2010.

But if you watched television studio debates that night or read many of the newspapers the next morning, something more terrifying — and tragic — than the physical image of hurtling locomotives would have become evident: you'd have seen the pistons driving these locomotives to self destruct. Livid, one-sided conversations: ill-informed, deaf, uncurious. And, most damagingly, simple-minded.

Exterminate the terrorists! Wipe them out! The entire nation is united: launch an all-out war. Bring on the airforce. Didn't we pull it off in Punjab? Haven't the Sri Lankans pulled it off with the LTTE [Liberation Tigers of Tamil Eelam]? Why are you 'intellectual sympathisers' talking of root causes and development and urging other approaches? Are you on the side of the savages? Are you condoning Maoist violence? Why are you raising questions about police atrocities and State neglect? How can you equate our violence with their violence? How can you lump the good guys with the bad guys?

On the other side, less loud but equally intractable are voices hurling blanket abuse at the State. Ignoring the slow fruits of 60 years of democracy; ignoring the genuine moral challenges the Maoists present; ignoring the inevitable corruptions of armed rebellion; willing to overlook the dangerous imperfections of one political position to vanquish the other.

Part of the reason why the Maoist debate rouses such anger is that its fundamental cliché is that it is a complex issue. Yet none of the public positions trotted out by its most voluble stakeholders really tell the whole truth. Anger then is inevitable: it arises out of each side finding itself wilfully and inadequately described.

This is why, drowned by the fierce volume of media debates, those who hold a third position feel an added helplessness — the helplessness of being strapped bang centre in the path of rushing trains. Yet if there is anything that can make the collision screech to a halt, it is this position: this saving in-betweenness. Which makes it imperative to outline what the third position is.

And turn up its volume.

The sight of the 76 dead jawans might have some Indians baying for blood: more war, more jawans. For other Indians though, on 6 April, as coffins were loaded on to trucks in the eerie silence of night, and wrapped in the national flag for their moment of pomp the next morning, the image crystallised some of the deepest and most troubling questions that underpin the Maoist crisis. What sort of a society are we creating? What sort of a society have we become? How will this cycle of violence end? The Maoists might have a lot to answer for, but where will we find the answers to the imperfections in ourselves? We can exterminate them physically, but what are we going to do with the big, rebuking questions they have unleashed around us?

This is not the self-flagellation of bleeding-heart liberals that the war hawks make it out to be. In fact, ironically, it is under-scored by the same concern as the death mongers: how can one neutralise Maoist influence in India? Only it seeks deeper answers than merely killing them; it seeks more sustainable strategies. Strategies more introspective and self-transformative.

It is true the State could exterminate the Maoists. As Home Minister P. Chidambaram said a few hours after the bloodbath in Dantewada, 'We might lose more people, many more may die, but the State will ultimately prevail. It might take two or three years, but we have to give them a firm response. If they have declared war on the State, we will launch an all-out offensive against them'. Set aside the disturbing assumptions in that statement. Ask merely the common question at hand: but will this 'wipe them out'? The curious thing is, according to insiders, the Maoist politburo itself feels that Operation Green Hunt might eliminate one-third of their cadres. But will this really 'wipe them out'? The State has crushed the Naxal movement thrice before — in Bengal, in Bihar, in Andhra Pradesh. Each time thousands of Indian citizens have been killed; each time the Maoists have resurrected themselves. This is the fourth big wave. Are we finally going to accept their challenge and address 'root causes', or are we going to content ourselves with killing tens of thousands of our poor every decade?

Part of the mounting ironies around Operation Green Hunt is that, contrary to the broad brush with which the Home Ministry and others in the Establishment have taken to tarring civil society, many activists and concerned citizens stretching deep into the far left are extremely disturbed by the growing militarisation of the Maoist movement. 'I am completely unequivocal about this', says Binayak — a man the State had jailed as being a 'big Naxal leader' — 'violence cannot be the answer. This growing militarisation cannot be the way forward'. Others too, both underground and overground who might otherwise share Maoist views on social transformation, are murmuring disapprovingly about 'Left adventurism'. As a former member of the People's War Group and close aide of their towering leader Kondapalli Seetharamaiah says, 'I have lived in the jungles. I have been in jail. I have been tortured by the police. And I have seen the idealism and zeal with which the Maoists work in the jungles. But I no longer believe violence can be the path'.

Yet the big, thorny conundrums persist. Home Minister P. Chidambaram might repeatedly be calling for talks with the Maoists saying he is not asking them to lay down arms but merely asking them to 'abjure violence' — almost flamboyantly urging them to give him just 72 hours to turn the discourse around. But it a measure of the deep scorn and distrust on both sides that even a hint of talks arouses two viscerally cynical reactions: the State says it's merely a ploy on the part of the Maoists to gain time and regroup; the Maoists says it's merely a ploy on the part of the State to bring them over ground and smash their hideouts. The shadow of the failed talks and its bloody aftermath in Andhra Pradesh in 2005 looms large.

At a deeper level, the possibility of talks with the Maoists breaks down prima facie on two genuinely sticky points: How can a State committed to parliamentary democracy (no matter how flawed) broker peace with an armed group whose stated resolve is to overthrow it and seize State power by 2050? Are events in Nepal a possible roadmap for the way forward? Will the Maoists privilege their ideals of social justice over their ambition to seize State power through protracted war? Will they somehow function as a pressure lobby within the framework of Indian democracy, slowly changing the political system from within? As the late and highly respected human rights activist K. Balagopal said, this might contravene the very basis of their ideology, but are the

Maoists right to hostage current generations of tribals to some promise of a future utopia that may never come?

On the other hand, equally, the Maoists might ask, why should we lay down arms and join Indian democracy? Has the Indian State ever demonstrated that it speaks to peaceful people's movements? The only reason tribal welfare has even entered contemporary national discourse — even as mere lip service — is because of the power of the gun. Many civil society and people's movements leaders have been urging Chidambaram to side-step the Maoists and talk to them on the same issues of social justice that the Maoists are raising. They challenge that if they are allowed to work in those areas, they will be able to reduce Maoist influence. But he steadfastly refuses. He is bent on 'area domination' through force. It seems only nuisance value can trigger offers for talks, not ethical consciousness.

(In fact, one of the most disturbing trends triggered by Operation Green Hunt is the way civil rights activists are increasingly being outlawed by the State: mocked, arrested, sidelined, pigeon-holed — merely for seeking answers beyond easy binaries. So it is that Gandhian activist Himanshu Kumar has been hounded out of Chhattisgarh — his ashram demolished by the State in Dantewada and a diktat put out that no one should rent their home out to him; and a Home Ministry dossier on him grows by the day. So it is that in Bengal, just a few days ago, activist Kirti Roy was arrested for organising a people's tribunal on police torture. The police had filed a case against him for attempting to impersonate the judiciary.)

This taunting question about the nature of the Indian State then is one we might well ask of ourselves. If the tribals lay down arms, will the State keep its promises, or will it ride like a storm over them, seizing their lands and stealing their resources as it has done elsewhere? And why does the Indian State have such a dismal record of speaking to people's movements espousing just demands? The Bhopal Gas victims have never taken to arms. For 25 years they have walked the 800 miles to Delhi again and again, camping in Jantar Mantar and asking for justice: have they got it? Far from it. Instead, Dow Chemical was invited to set up shop in

Nayachar in West Bengal. Worse, the Indian government is in the process of signing a nuclear agreement that will excuse foreign investors from paying damages in the event of a leak. And protestors are no longer allowed to camp overnight in Jantar Mantar — Indian democracy's designated site for people's protest.

Unfortunately, the epic list of questions doesn't stop here. Were the people of Nandigram and Singur made stakeholders in the projects that would displace them from their emerald land? Why was the draconian Land Acquisition Act and *mala fide* SEZ Act not thought through in equitable ways, on the sheer basis of the State's benevolent intention? Why was the State ramming its projects through? Why did it take violent people's resistance for these Acts to go back to the drawing board? Why are workers in Delhi being uprooted from colonies they have lived in for 30 years and being pitchforked into far-flung wastelands where there are no schools, no health centres, no toilets, no roads, no public transport, merely to beautify the city for 12 days of Commonwealth Games? Why do the people of Sohanbadra in UP have to walk miles through arsenic sludge and breathe fly ash from thermal plants? Why is it that almost every industrial project in India turns into a human rights violation — either in terms of land or labour or environmental violation or human health?

The truth is, as long as the poor suffer silently, Indian democracy chugs along, doing little. If people protest peacefully, no one cares: not the media, not the government. If they organise themselves in outrage, they are berated for being disruptive and crushed. If they have grown too powerful to be crushed, the State offers talks. As eminent lawyer K. G. Kannabiran, who was part of the Committee of Citizens that brokered the (failed) peace talks between Maoists and the Y. S. R. Reddy government in Andhra Pradesh and is today a faintly dejected man, says, 'We are experiencing the beginning of a long and terrible earthquake. Why doesn't the Indian State follow the Constitution? Why doesn't it act on its own Planning Commission Report on Naxal-affected areas which advocates a development-centric approach? Forget the Maoists. Even Locke and Laski said the right to insurrection arises when constitutional guarantees fail'.

The massacre of 6 April then places us at a potent crossroad. We could choose the path of escalated violence that will lead to a bloody civil war in the heart of the country. Or we could step back and choose the long march to social transformations that will leach away the attraction the oppressed have for the Maoists. On the first path, pain and futility stretches vast on either side. Increasing Maoist violence on one side: more police stations attacked, more jawans dead, more informers executed. Amplifying mistakes of the State on the other. Set aside 60 years of neglect, just three years of the Salwa Judum had notched up a terrifying roster of violence: 640 villages forcibly evacuated, lakhs of tribals forced to flee or live in camps, tribals set against tribal, homes burned, chickens and grain stolen, women raped, young boys dead. The Judum might now officially be declared a misadventure but it increased tribal disenchantment with the Indian State and pushed thousands more into Maoist arms.

Now Operation Green Hunt is doing exactly the same: for every 'genuine' Maoist ideologue arrested or killed, hundreds of ordinary people — minors, old folk, just adults scratching out a survival — are being arrested or killed. It enrages many in political and media circles when this is said, but the truth is, quite apart from 'root causes' — the structural violence in Indian society that stretches back through time — every cluster of deaths, every crisis in the contemporary Maoist saga has an irretrievably muddied chain of cause and effect.

As G. N. Saibaba, a Delhi University professor and an activist 'black-marked' by the intelligence apparatus, says, 'Ultimately nobody wins a war. You can only win in an ideological and social domain'. So which route will India choose now? The knee-jerk, short-term logic of violence and counter-violence? Or the statesman's game?

At one level, 'the flags of our fathers' draped around the dead jawans remind us of the soaring ideals on which India was founded, the articles of faith that keep us together as a nation. Few — positioned anywhere on the political spectrum — can deny that the Indian Constitution is a shining document and a real existential and political counter-challenge to the Maoists.

Every deformity in the Indian polity today is a corruption of the Constitution. But as organising principles for society go, there can be very few documents in the world that are more sophisticated and far-seeing. And more capable of reconciling India's inherently mammoth contradictions. Yet, at another level, 'the flags of our fathers' recalls the Clint Eastwood film that exposed the empty gestures and faux patriotism of war-torn America in the 1940s. Like the flag hoisted merely for a photo-op in the film, beneath the saber-rattling talk of 'our jawans' and calls for retaliation, there lurks a terrible cynicism.

Like those they have been sent out to battle with, these jawans are the weakest links in the Indian chain. They are merely another face of the poverty they have been sent out to vanquish. In the same breath that they speak of the terror of the Maoist attack on them, they speak of the inhuman conditions they live in, the lack of training, the lack of basic living facilities.

Besides, what is the SOP the jawans are being berated for not following? SOPs — 'standard operating procedures' — dictate that jawans should walk single file or ride on motorbikes in Maoist territory. That way, if a mine goes off, only a couple of jawans will die: not enough to embarrass the State, not enough to make the evening news. After all, 76 jawans dying over 76 days is not as insupportable as 76 jawans dying in one day. It's not human life and sorrow and 'the deaths of innocent men' that's got us in a twist then: it's an imagined slap on the imagined face of the nation. And to avenge that slap, we are willing to trot out more cannon fodder: more ill-equipped jawans, more terrified boys. Caught between poverty and duty.

Also, the uncomfortable truth is, the Maoists may have a lot to answer for, but tragic as it is, the massacre of 6 April 6 is not the most damaging of them. Sections of the media might call them 'terrorists' and 'savages' for the attack in Dantewada, but if terrorism is defined as anonymous hits on civilians, the Maoists' night-time massacre of sleeping villagers in Jamui in Bihar last year counts as a much worse blot. The 6 April attack was an episode between combatants — an inevitable by-product of a poorly addressed conflagration. And the worst part is it could well happen again.

For this reason alone, contrary to the almost colonial outrage about 'savages' burning the airwaves, for many patriotic Indians, the death of these 76 jawans could be read as a catalyst for turning up the volume on the third position on the Maoist debate. (It might soothe those baying for escalated State action to remember that top cop K. P. S. Gill — the hero of Punjab — and Ajit Doval, former Intelligence Bureau chief, both feel that, in its current form, Operation Green Hunt is something of a strategic misadventure.)

Of the many half-truths on the back of which the Maoist crisis is currently escalating, the biggest lie is that there is political unanimity on Operation Green Hunt. For the moment, Home Minister P. Chidambaram may be the loudest voice from the UPA [United Progressive Alliance] government and he may (ironically) enjoy the fervid support of the BJP [Bharatiya Janata Party] and CPM (Communist Party of India [Marxist]) in treating the Maoists as merely a 'law and order problem' and declaring an 'all-out offensive' on them, but Chief Ministers Shibu Soren and Nitish Kumar, and Union Railway Minister Mamata Banerjee are not the only politicians uncomfortable with this stance. The Congress party itself is richly and positively divided on this. And though their silence so far is baffling, the heartening fact is that many of its most powerful leaders hold the third position. Or variants of it. As one particularly powerful Congress insider says, 'There has to be a middle way between the zero strategy of the Home Ministry in UPA 1 and the George Bush-like utterances of the Home Ministry in UPA 2. It's getting more ludicrous by the day'.

What is this third position then? The first and primary relief of the third position is that it is not a monolithic one: it is no soundproof room blocking out all argument that challenges its notions. It recognises that India is a complex country to run. It recognises that Home Minister Chidambaram is partially right in saying a State cannot let 234 districts slip out of its hands and some targeted use of force is called for to re-dominate those areas. But in the same breath it recognises that military action alone is suicidal. 'Compassionate governance' cannot be a verbal frill attached to a machine gun. It has to be the primary soldier, the captain of the guard. In the third position, courage lies in rethinking fundamental directions of our society. It lies in acknowledging that Maoists are not merely demonic outsiders but a complex grid of Indians driven in equal parts by ideology, desperation and new political awakening.

As veteran Congress leader Mani Shankar Aiyar says, 'It is ridiculous to attack everyone just because they have a view on the Maoist issue as anything more than just a "menace". While there's no alternative to a State defending itself to a challenge by insurgents, we have to ask ourselves why this insurgency is confined to 5th Schedule Areas (i.e., tribal) areas. And as long as our ideas of development is restricted to gains for people like Vedanta and POSCO and Tata and Essar and the Mittals, and we allow them to exploit tribal resources, the tribals are bound to see this development not as desired but disruptive. The point is, we have to define the difference between "participatory development" and "aggressive development"'.

For those who find the prospect daunting, Aiyar has an inspiring list of simple measures, constitutional provisions and visionary legislations that can begin to effect change. Read the 73rd Amendment along with Article 243G and 243ZD of the Constitution, he urges. Let all states governments implement PESA — Provisions of the Panchayat (Extension to Scheduled Areas) 1996 — on the ground. Invoke the provisions of the Forest Act to give full ownership of forest produce to tribals. And watch the miracles start to flow.

For middle-class audiences, PESA is probably the least known piece of legislation, yet it is sheer genius in its simplicity. It prescribes that no proposal of a Panchayat, no disbursal of funds, and no use of common property resources can be sanctioned without the permission of the Gram Sabha. Unlike the Panchayat which has elected members, the Gram Sabha includes every adult member of a village community. This consultative process is the most elemental step of a democracy and it effectively ensures that tribals can take full control of their lives, finances and functionaries — cutting out the corruptions of an alien bureaucracy.

Aiyar is not alone in these views. Congress veteran Digvijay Singh has written pieces in the media on the same lines. Rural Minister C. P. Joshi, who was handpicked by Rahul Gandhi (and whose ministry report on 'State Agrarian Relations' spoke of Operation Green Hunt as the 'biggest land grab in the history of India') also has similar views. 'There is a failure of governance, a real crisis of credibility among the lower level functionaries. The whole judicial system, for instance, relies on the *patwari* and *thanedar*. If they tamper with an FIR or land paper, how can the system work? We have to think of alternative forms of governance. We have 32 states — let there be 10,000 forms of local government in them. We have to take the traditions of each community and work within that to implement democratic ideals'. At a press conference in Chhattisgarh, asked about the Maoist crisis, Rahul Gandhi himself said, 'When governance fails to reach people, such movements are bound to gain strength'.

These ideas however cannot be postponed to some future utopia — a time when 234 districts have been recovered from Maoist control. 'It is misleading to suggest all these areas have slipped out of government control', says Aiyar. 'Even in Naxal-affected areas, only some *thanas* are under their control. The rest are all under State control. We should immediately implement full-fledged Panchayati Raj and PESA in these *thanas*. We can win this only if we construct a real and shining alternative to the Maoist-led government'.

For that to happen, at the very least, in a sort of first sign of good intention, Prime Minister Manmohan Singh needs to retrieve the Ministry of Tribal Affairs and Panchayati Raj from the ciphers [that] now control it and give it to someone at par with the incumbent Home Minister. In fact, in the sort of neat ironies life sometimes offers, Home Secretary Gopal Pillai, who is seen as an able lieutenant to Chidambaram's security-driven hard line, is married to Sudha Pillai, one of the country's top civil servants on Panchayati Raj. Since, so far, governance has been promised at the heel of security — with disastrous consequences, for a while, perhaps, the wife should be foregrounded over the husband.

There are other urgent areas of redressal. As Aiyar says, 'If the Tatas and Ambanis can own vast tracts of land and the government deems private property as sacred, how is it that we think of community property as something that the government can take over? The tribals have owned these forests since time immemorial. This tradition was only disrupted when the British entered the forests of Dandakaranya. Can't democratic India restore the rights over this forest back to its own people? Finally, if middle-class Indians can have shares in corporate projects, why can't tribals be made stakeholders in projects that usurp their land?'

So before the memory of the 76 jawans fades, here's the question again: what route is India going to take now? When you ask the Home Minister — or chief ministers of Naxal-affected States — to seize the high moral ground and send out a message to their police and paramilitary forces that no excesses will be tolerated, they snap back: why are you pointing fingers at the State? What about the 55 CPM cadres the Maoists have killed in Bengal this year? What about the 11 jawans they have killed in Koraput? The trap of binary conversations.

It is futile to remind them that they are our elected representatives and democracy demands we hold them more accountable than the Maoists; futile to remind them that we expect the State to have a greater morality than the outlaws they are combating. Futile to assert that our constitutional concern about the nature of the Indian State does not equate to support for the Maoists. Violence can only legitimise itself by painting broad pictures of Good and Evil, by painting itself the Avenger. This is why, for defenders of Operation Green Hunt, condemnation of Maoist violence must ride on silence about the State's.

In a telling detail, however, the widow of beheaded policeman, Francis Induwar understood that death does not come in different colours. Barely weeks after her husband's gory murder at the hands of Maoists, she was pleading with the government not for revenge but a non-military approach to resolve the Maoist crisis. A cardinal rule of leadership that leaders often forget is the powerful symbolism of taking the unilaterally ethical stand. Not contingent on the good behaviour of others. As Abraham Lincoln famously said, 'I am not bound to win, but I am bound to be true'.

Maybe the death of these jawans will bring that message home to those men and women who wield most power in this country.

ॐ

# 34

# Bastar, Maoism and Salwa Judum

*Nandini Sundar**

✪

Visitors to the official Bastar website[1] will 'discover' that Gonds 'have pro-fertility mentality', that 'marriages . . . between brothers and sisters are common', and that 'the Murias prefer "Mahua" drinks rather than medicines for their ailments'. 'The tribals of this area', says the website, 'is famous for their "Ghotuls" where the prospective couples do the "dating" and have free sex also'. As for the Abhuj Marias, '(t)hese people are not cleanly in their habits, and even when a Maria does bathe he does not wash his solitary garments but leaves it on the bank. When drinking from a stream they do not take up water in their hands but put their mouth down to it like cattle'. Some of the tribals are 'leading a savage life', we are told, 'they do not like to come to the outer world and mingle with the modern civilisation'. Into this charming picture of 'savages' who 'shoot down strangers with arrows', one must unfortunately bring in a few uncomfortable facts.

What used to be the former undivided district of Bastar (since 2001 carved into the districts of Dantewada, Bastar and Kanker) is currently a war zone. The main roads, in Dantewada in particular, but also in parts of Bastar and Kanker, are full of CRPF [Central Reserve Police Force] and other security personnel, out on combing operations. The Maoists control the jungles. In the

*This article was previously published as 'Bastar, Maoism and Salwa Judum', *Economic and Political Weekly*, vol. 41, no. 29, 22 July 2006, pp. 3187–92.

[1] http://www.bastar.nic.in/ (accessed 22 July 2006).

frontlines of this battle are ordinary villagers who are being pitted against each other on a scale unparalleled in the history of Indian counterinsurgency. The officially year-old Salwa Judum, is touted by the government as a 'spontaneous people's movement' and a 'peace mission'. Villagers go in procession to other villages and 'convince' them to join. However, as a wireless message from the former SP [Superintendent of Police] of Bijapur, recorded by the Maoists and released to the press shows, 'The *janjagaran* people are telling very clearly to villagers "you come with us first time, or second time. If you do not come third time, we will burn your village"'.

At least five different investigative teams have confirmed that of the nearly 46,000 people living in camps strung along the main road, the majority have come to pre-empt attacks or been forcibly brought in by the Salwa Judum and the security forces. Some of them are now being permanently settled by the road, with plans to establish 581 new villages. But no provision has been made for suitable employment or access to land. Rendered desperate by the lack of food, they resort to looting when set loose on other villages. The Government has appointed some 3,500 Special Police Officers [SPOs], many of them minors, equipped them with lathis, bows and arrows and .303 rifles, supposedly to counter the Naxalites. Many were attracted by the promise of ₹1,500 a month, the machismo of weapons, and the hope of getting permanent employment in the police force. However, several now regret joining, feeling immensely vulnerable to retaliatory action by the Maoists. Those not in camps are hiding out with the Maoists in the jungles, while an equally large number is said to have fled to neighbouring states. Fields lie abandoned, taken over by feral cattle. Entire villages are divided, each side resentful of the other for the choices they are being forced to make.

Deaths have become so commonplace that nobody bothers to talk about them anymore, and nobody knows what the real figures are. Government figures list 268 civilians killed (including some 50 SPOs) and 706 injured by the Maoists since June 2005; the Maoists have released a partial list of 116 civilians killed by the Salwa Judum till March 2006. In addition 72 police personnel and

30 Naxalites have died. The killings by the Salwa Judum are simply not recognised either by the government or the media. What
the newspapers report is only a total count of deaths and violent
attacks, mostly by the Maoists of civilians and police personnel,
and some by the police/CRPF of Maoist guerrillas, creating the
impression of endless one-sided violence. What they don't report
at all is the scale of state terror on civilians. Initially the Salwa
Judum seems to have targeted the mass front members or *sangham*
(compelling co-villagers to inform on them), but given the atmosphere of suspicion, anyone can be described as a Naxalite and
killed. There is complete impunity. For their part, the Maoists
initially picked out individuals active in the Salwa Judum, but since
February 2006, they have resorted to large scale 'counter-terror'.

Rumours that women are being used as sexual slaves in Salwa
Judum camps are rife. Citizens Initiative got testimony from one
woman in jail, charged under the arms act. She said she had been
pulled off the backseat of her brother's cycle, and gangraped by
the CRPF on the road. Her brother had been shot. She was taken
to the local *thana* and raped repeatedly over the next 10 days. The
other women in jail said she was so bruised when she came, she
could hardly walk. Other prisoners said that they had been picked
up on their way to market or simply while working on their fields.
A number of sangham members have been forced to 'surrender' and
are being kept in chains. The Salwa Judum has burnt houses —
nearly 2,000 according to a Maoist list — but this doesn't include
villages like Arlempally in Konta *tahsil*, where the entire village
is said to have smouldered for weeks. One Salwa Judum activist
confessed to the Citizens Initiative that he had participated in the
burning. When we tried to go there, the Salwa Judum chased us,
turned us back and beat up our young guide. We saw a house in
Asirguda village where even the pigpen had been burnt to ashes.
Villagers on the 'Maoist side' of the Indrawati river are completely
cut off, unable even to visit the weekly markets for fear of the
Salwa Judum. Whatever authority the government exercised over
the villages and small towns on the main road, has now been ceded
to the Salwa Judum. Camp leaders, mostly non-tribals, give orders

to the *thanedars* and to SDMs [Sub-Divisional Magistrates], passing vehicles are repeatedly searched and local people fear that even
if the government were now to suspend its support to the Salwa
Judum, it would be too late.

Senior officials told Citizens Initiative they had received no
complaint about the Salwa Judum, but conceded that there may
be some 'anti-social elements'. To men who think that Gonds are
'primitive and promiscuous' or that Abujhmarh is populated by
'Bhils and Bustars', no doubt what is happening is merely 'anti-
social.' As the Pioneer so helpfully exhorts us, why worry about
the Constitution and some dead adivasis when the Naxalites have
to be finished off?

## Competing for the Legacy of the Bhumkal

The leader of the Salwa Judum, Mahendra Karma, Congress
MLA [Member of the Legislative Assembly] from Dantewada,
and Leader of the Opposition, told Citizens Initiative in an interview that the Maoists had opposed modern development. Since
there was a limit to how long adivasis could live under terror, they
had now chosen to rebel in a 'repeat' of the 1910 rebellion against
the British known as the Bhumkal. The Maoists have also laid
claim to the Bhumkal. On 10 February 2004, they held what they
claimed was their biggest rally ever to commemorate the event,
with 10,000 people in attendance. Footage of the rally shown on
Sahara Samay television channel certainly indicates massive attendance, not all of it possible under the shadow of the gun, and all
of it completely unknown to the authorities. To decide which of
these two contenders, if any — Karma or the Maoists — is a more
appropriate heir of the Bhumkal, one must look at both the history of Bastar and the stated positions of the two parties regarding
their vision of development.

Forest reservation in Bastar (then a feudatory state in the Central
Provinces) began in the early 1900s. People's shifting cultivation,
hunting and collection of forest produce was restricted, land taxes
were raised, a number of villages were displaced from the reserves,
and the influx of officials, policemen, foresters and *malguzars* led
to a rise in the demand for corvee. In February 1910, the entire

area rebelled, led by their *majhis* and village headmen. Bazaars were looted, the houses of officials, traders and police stations — all those associated with the state — were burnt and robbed and grain redistributed. Then too, villages which did not join in the rebellion were threatened by the others. In the months it took the British to suppress the uprising, many villagers escaped into the jungles.

For several decades after this, the administration of the area was kept deliberately light, yet the advance of capitalism showed in the commercial exploitation of forests. The two major projects post independence, the Dandakaranya resettlement project and the Bailadilla iron ore mines which started exporting to Japan in 1966, provided neither land nor employment to the locals. Instead, the rivers Sankini and Dankini ran red with effluent. In the 1960s, under the leadership of the ex-Raja, Pravir Chandra Bhanj Deo, people protested asking for land, access to forests and cheaper rice. Pravir was killed in 1966 and the protests eventually faded out.

Even as people's access to forests was restricted, senior officials and politicians were allowed to decimate tree cover under the Malik Makbuja scam. Influential people would buy land cheap in order to profit from the sale of trees on it. Trees on forest land were fudged as being on private land. In response to a case filed by two NGOs in 1997, the Supreme Court ordered a Lokayukt enquiry. The final report of the Lokayukt states:

> On scrutiny of the case records it is found that the purchasers of land have purchased it for a paltry sum not commensurate with the value of land with trees standing thereon . . . The Committee came across a number of such cases in which even the full amount agreed upon between the parties was not paid and payment of part amount was deferred on some pretext or the other. . . Revenue case Nos. 107-A-63/1995-96, 108-A-63/95-96, 155-A-63/95-96 all of one applicant namely Rajkumar Mandavi and 132-A-63/1993-94 in which applicant is Mahendra Karma may be cited as examples of such cases.[2]

---

[2] Final Report of the Lokayukt Committee on the Felling of Trees on Malik Makbuja and Other Government Land in Bastar District, Madhya Pradesh, p. 16.

These officers (Forest and Revenue officials responsible for supervising sales) granted permission freely in favour of other influential persons also like Mahendra Karma (the then Member of Parliament), Rajaram Todem (presently Dy. Leader of Opposition in M.P. Legislative Assembly) and other influential merchant families like Suranas, Awasthis, Brij Mohan Gupta and many others who have entered in this trade of purchasing land with standing trees and selling the timber.[3]

On the basis of the Lokayukt's calculations, Karma made a profit of almost [Rs] 16 lakh on the sale of the trees in just six months. A CBI FIR [Central Bureau Of Investigation First Information Report] was filed against him and others in 1998, but no further action appears to have been taken.

In the 1990s, especially following the formation of Chhattisgarh, there has been a concerted emphasis on industrialisation, taking advantage of the region's rich mineral deposits. Despite a token gesture to tribal entrepreneurs, what is quickly emerging is that the process depends on how easily adivasis can be forced into parting with their land. In 1992, when the Bharat Jan Andolan demanded proper rehabilitation and shares for adivasis who were to be displaced by a steel plant at Maolibhata village, its leader and former Collector of Bastar, the 65-year-old Dr B. D. Sharma, was pulled off the pillion of a scooter by BJP activists, stripped and paraded through the streets of Jagdalpur with a garland of shoes around his neck. A decade later, the residents of Nagarnar village were beaten up and arrested for protesting against land acquisition for another steel plant. When the *gram sabha* rejected the proposal (under the Panchayat Extension to Scheduled Areas Act, 1996, the gram sabha has to be consulted before land is acquired), the authorities rewrote the minutes of the gram sabha meeting. Justice Bhargava, who investigated the incident, also noted several serious violations of environmental and other procedures. Similar fake gram sabhas (consisting of shopkeepers and mining employees rather than villagers) and threats by gangs of goons are

---

[3] Ibid., p. 22.

being reported from the areas around Dhurli and Bhansi villages, near Dantewada, where Essar is currently trying to acquire 900 ha for its steel plant. The 267-km Essar slurry pipeline connecting Bailadilla and Visakapatnam has apparently cut down forests in a 20 m width as against the 8.4 m width it was sanctioned. The Tata Steel plant at Lohandiguda, for which the company wants 4500 acres, has run into opposition by 10 villages whose lands will be acquired. The recently revived Bodhghat Hydroelectric Project, the Jagdalpur–Dalli Rajhara railway line and the Polavaram dam, will also involve large-scale forest diversion and displacement.

The issue is not so much whether such steel plants should be built (although one may legitimately debate how many are needed and whether they should trump all other land uses) but how the benefits and losses will be distributed, and why a colonial law like the Land Acquisition Act should be used to compel villagers to sell their lands, at throwaway prices, to private companies. The people who are rooting for these projects most strongly are the non-tribals settled in urban centres like Jagdalpur and Kanker, traders who came with little but grew rich on the profits of minor forest produce, illegal tin smelting, illicit felling, etc. The non-tribal population in the area has expanded so dramatically in less than a decade (1991–2001) that moves are on to de-reserve Jagdalpur and Kanker constituencies. While many unemployed tribal youth want jobs, the government has not invested anything in their education that would enable them to get anything more than menial jobs in these projects. Proper information, compensation or shares in the project are not 'sops', but constitutional rights. However, to those used to thinking of adivasis as expendable 'primitives', even this begins to seem an affront.

When Citizens Initiative asked Mahendra Karma, what he thought about shares for adivasis in projects using their land, he laughed contemptuously and said, 'all this sounds good on paper'. As for employment for the locals, 'since tribals will consume any compensation they are given, they should be given work in ancillary industries. Instead of tractors, use them for land levelling'. The Naxalites, on the other hand, argue for a 'new democratic economy' based on increasing agricultural production through

242 | Nandini Sundar

co-operatives, education, health, etc., rather than large projects which displace people.

Where does the Salwa Judum come into this? The following 'orientation' program for Salwa Judum activists and SPOs observed by [the] ACHR [Asian Centre for Human Rights] in Konta camp is revealing. Mr Achla (Konta SDPO [Sub-Divisional Police Officer] telling the villagers): 'You leave your forests and shift to the road sides. You will be adequately compensated by the industrialists and commercial concerns, who are ready to take your land and develop it. You will get employment and other provisions. But if you stay back in the forest, Naxalites will kill you'. At a minimum, no one would dispute that 'sanitising' the area of Maoists and ensuring 'peace' is necessary to lure investors.

So far, if one reads the 1910 Bhumkal as a movement by the people of Bastar to defend their rights, the balance of the legacy is in the Maoist favour. Yet the Maoist vision, for all its talk of 'people's democratic authority organized in the form of Gram Rajya Committees' appears peculiarly self-serving in its conception of base areas: 'A base area, besides certain military aspects, would (and must) necessarily have a self sufficient economy. Without that, it can neither sustain itself, nor can it provide the ever growing needs of the Party and people's armed forces'. It is debatable how practical or realistic such autarky is in today's context of advanced capitalism, and how useful to its inhabitants.

## The Maoists in Bastar

The Maoists claim to include 60 lakh people in the 'organisational sweep' of their Dandakaranya 'guerrilla zone' (comprising Gadchiroli, Bhandara, Balaghat, Rajnandgaon, undivided Bastar, and Malkangiri), which is headed by a Special Zonal Committee. Their mass organisations, the most prominent among which are the Dandakaranya Adivasi Kisan Mazdoor Sanghatan (DAKMS) and the Krantikari Adivasi Mahila Sanghatan (KAMS), are colloquially called sanghams. In 1995, after the sanghams had practically overthrown the traditional village leadership, the Party set up Gram Rajya Committees elected by the gram sabha, which settle disputes and delegate developmental work to other sub-committees. From 1993 onwards, the People's War Group began to form special guerrilla squads and in 2000, the People's Liberation Guerrilla Army was formed. Militias have been formed on a large scale in villages. Indeed, after the Salwa Judum started, there appears to have been a spurt in recruitment to these militias. The degree of weaponisation, however, seems no match for the government — with about 7,300 weapons for 10,500 armed cadre.

Maoist literature claims that they have engaged in considerable development work over the last 20 years. For instance, in south Bastar and Gadchiroli they say they have established 135 people's clinics, started six primary schools, 10 night schools, built 25 huts for government teachers to persuade them to come, set up 10 village libraries, etc. The maximum work has been in the field of agricultural and livelihood improvement: 81 tanks in Dantewada district, 400,000 fish seedlings distributed in the Konta squad area, 16,200 saplings distributed (of which, like any government document, they note that only 30 per cent survived because the people did not take sufficient care), bullock carts built in 10 villages, diesel pumpsets introduced in nine, 268 cattle detention yards built, five rice mills introduced, people trained in forest protection, cooperative paddy banks set up and agricultural co-operatives created in 220 villages.

While these figures, assuming them to be true, do not match what the state could achieve, it shows more commitment to people's development than the government. Doctors willing to work in rural areas may be difficult to find, but surely the government could do better than 112 primary health care centres (PHCs) in this vast area. To blame the lack of basic facilities and the starvation deaths on the Naxalites simply echoes the excuse that many staff, including teachers, employ to shirk work. To argue, as some officials do, that regrouping people on the roadside is actually meant to benefit them by making it easier to provide services is an even worse insult to intelligence. If this logic held, how come government schools in urban slums are so badly provisioned?

However, in the drive to establish their own 'Janata Sarkar' the Maoists have resisted even genuine government initiatives.

**Table 34.1:** Bastar, Kanker and Dantewada, Census of India 2001[4]

|  | *Bastar* | *Dantewada* | *Kanker* |
|---|---|---|---|
| Area (sq. km) | 14,974 | 17,634 | 6,506 |
| Population | 1,306,673 | 719,487 | 650,934 |
| Population Density | 87 | 41 | 100 |
| Number of Villages | 1,461 | 1,220 | 1,068 |
| Literacy Rate (Total) | 43.9 | 30.2 | 72.9 |
| Percentage of Scheduled Tribe Population | 66.3 | 78.5 | 56.1 |
| Number of PHCs | 57 | 34 | 21 |
| Number of Primary Schools (from Government Website) | 1,473 | 918 | NA |

*Note*: NA= Not Available.

While recognising that traders cheat adivasis over minor forest produce, they have defended them against government attempts to introduce co-operatives to buy tamarind and *tendu* [*Diospyros melanoxylon*]. The grounds given are that the government is more impervious to price struggles, they offer lower rates than private contractors, and these co-operatives engender corruption. This logic may work in areas where the Maoists are strong and they keep prices up, (which has been a genuine help to people) but elsewhere as soon as the co-operatives stop, the traders drop their prices and resume cheating. If made to work, the co-operatives can offer much needed employment to village youth or women. The dependence on immigrant traders also has other negative spin-off effects — they are the very constituency that has been responsible for support to Hindutva, displacement and Salwa Judum. Even in the unlikely event that the government introduced co-operatives only to 'ensure that the revolutionaries will stop being able to levy taxes on the thekedars', it would be well within its rights, since it is scarcely obliged to help fund its enemy. While 'extortion' is not the appropriate word, the relationship between big thekedars and the party is unhealthy, based on mutual and simultaneous mistrust

---

[4] Government of India, *Census of India 2001* (New Delhi: Office of the Registrar General, India, 2001).

and dependence. The Maoists are dependent on the thekedars for funds, and the thekedars are dependent on the Maoists to work in their areas or get contracts, yet scared of their dictates on proper labour payments or higher rates for forest produce and eager to seize the first opportunity to turn them in.

The Maoists claim to have transformed social relations, though their depiction of the 'ocean of darkness' which Dandakaranya represented, betrays revolutionary reductionism. For instance, take the claim that before the party came 'women were no more than chattels slaving away from morning to night' or that children led 'wasted lives' making armed struggle a better alternative for them. Certainly, in my experience, while people lead miserably poor lives, their lives have meaning even without armed struggle. The festivals that punctuate every agricultural task and which the party sees as needless superstition break the monotony of the year. The fines that are imposed for violating these festival rules (such as eating new mangoes before the rest of the village) are important to maintain the social solidarity that is one of the strengths of adivasi society. Sometimes the expenses are onerous — for the same reason people in other areas convert to Hindu sects or Christianity which do not demand so much — but this is no reason to treat the entire practice merely as evidence of the feudal hold of priests and headmen. Of course children deserve a better life but to think that playing games of cops and Naxalites, mimicking the use of the gun in their games and dances, acting as informers for the guerrillas thus exposing themselves to danger or learning how to use arms from the age of 16 onwards is a great alternative, displays an unacceptable fetishisation of militarism. Indeed, much of the Maoist literature unnecessarily glorifies killing the enemy and dying a martyr's death.

However, unlike the urban elite who rail against 'keeping tribals as museum pieces', the Maoists actually live among the people whose lives they seek to transform. The Krantikari Adivasi Mahila Sangham (KAMS) is said to take up issues of bigamy, forced marriages, and the involvement of women in social and political decision-making in the village. They appear to draw huge crowds to their demonstrations, and to performances of their cultural troupe, Chetna Natya Manch. Unlike the RSS [Rashtriya Swayamsevak Sangh], which is heavily penetrating these areas and which has contempt for adivasi language and religion, the Maoists consciously promote Gondi language and literature.

These achievements, however, have coexisted with brute force. In establishing their Gram Rajya Committees, the Maoists have killed village headmen, sarpanchs, and others who have opposed them. One account lists at least 17 people who have died 'a dog's death at the hands of people'. Anyone producing above 50 quintals is considered a 'landlord', while those producing 30–50 quintals are seen as rich peasants. We are told that only the 'most notorious landlords' have been killed for resisting land distribution, while others have been allowed to live on their smaller plots. As for the rich peasants, only the excess forest land they grabbed during the first phase of forest occupation has been distributed. It is not surprising that this has engendered some support for the Salwa Judum. However, it would require intensive fieldwork to assess how much the Maoist movement has built on existing structures of solidarity and authority and how much it has overthrown them. Indeed, a Maoist representative whom Citizens Initiative met conceded that in the Marh there was little 'rupture' with the traditional headman, whereas there was greater differentiation in the South.

The histories of individual villages would reveal an even more complicated picture of Maoist influence and adivasi agency. For instance, in 2004, I met a rich family from Bheji who had to leave their village because other villagers complained against them to the *dalam* (local guerrilla squad). When that dalam tried to sort it out through a face-to-face meeting, the villagers complained to another dalam. The Bheji family told me that the People's War told them to leave the village for two years and promised to look after their fields for them in the meantime. In another story I was told about Sattuwa village, the Sarpanch (who like others had been forced to resign by the Maoists after being elected in January 2005), drew money for himself from the block office in collusion with the *gram sachiv*. When the village sangham leader complained he was shot. In return the dalam killed the sarpanch and told his family to leave. Eleven other families left with them and were settled by the government elsewhere. Later, after Salwa Judum started, the Naga Battalion forced the rest of the village into camp. In Arlempalli village, Citizens Initiative was told, the village went over entirely to the People's War after they broke the hand of the local CPI [Communist Party of India] leader. Having suffered once, the village refused to join the Salwa Judum, and was destroyed as a consequence.

In keeping with their emphasis on militarism, the Maoists proudly list attacks on police stations, especially during 'retaliation week', the 'annihilation' of CRPF personnel, attacks on the NMDC [National Mineral Development Corporation] explosives depot, and the killing of 'Salwa Judum goons'. Land mines have been indiscriminately laid. The police also see killing Maoists as an occasion for rewards. For both sides to consider each other fair game leads nowhere politically, especially when unemployment or desperation drives recruits on both sides.

While the Maoists promote election boycotts as a way of showing up an electoral system relying on big money, it is not clear what purpose these boycotts ultimately serve, since people end up with representatives like Karma. A visit to Konta *tahsil* during the Lok Sabha elections of 2004 revealed deserted villages and shut polling booths. Yet 'votes' were 'cast' from them — in the Vidhan Sabha elections, for the then ruling Congress, and in the Lok Sabha, for the ruling BJP.

To summarise, the considerable local support for the Maoists — which as K. Balagopal points out demands a political response — has also come with some violence. Their supporters need to debate whether armed struggle was necessary to their positive work, and whether peaceful mass mobilisation would not work better. Certainly, the attempt to defend their guerrilla zone seems now to have overtaken people's needs, including the desperate desire for peace.

## Salwa Judum: Shifting Violence onto Civil Society

The Salwa Judum is perhaps the most egregious example of an increasingly common phenomenon, viz. the use of 'civil society' groups to fight others. The formal structure of government participatory policies and the political reality in which they operate means that for every adivasi movement opposing a project there is often a counter adivasi movement propped up by the ruling party If violence ensues, the government can claim it is helpless, and even better, point to the differences as evidence that the movement in question does not enjoy a mass base.

There have been previous Jan Jagran Abhiyans led by Mahendra Karma, and Salwa Judum too seems to have originated as another such Abhiyan. Local factors at Kutru (in north-west Dantewada district) may have provided the immediate spark in June 2005 but several pieces of evidence suggest that there was prior government planning, including a police video which talks of 'Operation Salwa Judum' initiated from January 2005 onwards, the DGP [Director General of Police] of Chhattisgarh saying that Salwa Judum had been introduced as a 'pilot project' in two blocks of Dantewara district, the Ministry of Home Affairs policy on supporting 'local resistance groups' against militants, and the mysterious phenomenon of letters inviting people to attend Salwa Judum meetings issued in the name of a non-existent Sodi Deva.

The government does not make it easy for people who wish to engage in peaceful struggle. The politics of bans also betray an inherent bias, apart from being pointless. As E. A. S. Sarma points out, parties like the Congress and the BJP which have both engaged in large-scale pogroms (Delhi, 1984; Gujarat, 2002) are never outlawed. Even when there is evidence that the Bajrang Dal is engaged in bomb-making there is no further enquiry or media coverage. If the ruling parties were willing to shun violence, they would have a greater moral right to demand that others do too.

➳

# 35

# Salwa Judum Judgement of the Supreme Court (Decided by B. Sudershan Reddy and Surinder Singh Nijjar, JJ)*

✪

Extracts from 'Nandini Sundar and Ors vs Respondent: State of Chhattisgarh'.[1]

We, the people as a nation, constituted ourselves as a sovereign democratic republic to conduct our affairs within the four corners of the Constitution, its goals and values. We expect the benefits of democratic participation to flow to us — all of us — so that we can take our rightful place, in the League of Nations, befitting our heritage and collective genius. This case represents a yawning gap between the promise of principled exercise of power in a constitutional democracy, and the reality of the situation in Chhattisgarh, where the Respondent, the State of Chhattisgarh, claims that it has a constitutional sanction to perpetrate, indefinitely, a regime of gross violation of human rights in a manner, and by adopting the same modes, as done by Maoist/Naxalite extremists. The State of Chhattisgarh also claims that it has the powers to arm, with guns, thousands of mostly illiterate or barely literate young men of the tribal tracts, who are appointed as temporary police officers, with little or no training, and even lesser clarity

* Writ Petition (Civil) No. 250 of 2007. Reported in (2011) 7 SCC 547.
[1] 2011(6) SCALE 839 (decided on 5 July 2011).

about the chain of command to control the activities of such a force, to fight the battles against alleged Maoist extremists.

As we heard more and more about the situation in Chhattisgarh, and the justifications being sought to be pressed upon us by the Respondents, it began to become clear to us that the Respondents were envisioning modes of state action that would seriously undermine constitutional values. That large tracts of the State of Chhattisgarh have been affected by Maoist activities is widely known. It has also been widely reported that the people living in those regions of Chhattisgarh have suffered grievously, on account of both the Maoist insurgency activities, and the counter insurgency unleashed by the State. The situation in Chhattisgarh is undoubtedly deeply distressing to any reasonable person.

That violent agitator politics, and armed rebellion in many pockets of India have intimate linkages to socio-economic circumstances, endemic inequalities, and a corrupt social and state order that preys on such inequalities has been well recognised. In fact the Union of India has been repeatedly warned of the linkages. In a recent report titled *Development Challenges in Extremist Affected Areas*,[2] an expert group constituted by the Planning Commission of India makes the following concluding observations:

> The development paradigm pursued since independence has aggravated the prevailing discontent among the marginalized sections of the society . . . *The development paradigm as conceived by policymakers has always imposed on these communities . . . causing irreparable damage to these sections. The benefits of this paradigm have been disproportionately cornered by the dominant sections at the expense of the poor, who have borne most of the costs.* Development which is insensitive to the needs of these communities *has inevitably caused displacement and reduced them to a sub-human existence.* In the case of tribes in particular it has ended up in destroying their social organization, cultural identity and resource base . . . which cumulatively makes them increasingly vulnerable to exploitation

---

[2] Planning Commission, *Development Challenges in Extremist Affected Areas* (New Delhi: Government of India, 2008).

*. . . The pattern of development and its implementation has increased corrupt practices of a rent seeking bureaucracy and rapacious exploitation by the contractors, middlemen, traders and the greedy sections of the larger society intent on grabbing their resources and violating their dignity.*[3]

[. . .]

It is necessary to contextualize the tensions in terms of social, economic and political background and bring back on the agenda the issues of the people — the right to livelihood, the right to life and a dignified and honourable existence. *The State itself should feel committed to the democratic and human rights and humane objectives that are inscribed in the Preamble, the Fundamental Rights and Directive Principles of the Constitution. The State has to adhere strictly to the Rule of Law. Indeed, the State has no other authority to rule . . . What is surprising is not the fact of unrest, but the failure of the State to draw right conclusions from it.* While the official policy documents recognize that there is a direct correlation between what is termed as extremism and poverty . . . or point to the deep relationship between tribals and forests, or that the tribals suffer unduly from displacement, the governments have in practice treated unrest merely as a law and order problem. It is necessary to change this mindset and bring about congruence between policy and implementation. *There will be peace, harmony and social progress only if there is equity, justice and dignity for everyone.*[4]

The justification often advanced, by advocates of the neo-liberal development paradigm, as historically followed, or newly emerging, in a more rapacious form, in India, is that unless development occurs, via rapid and vast exploitation of natural resources, the country would not be able to either compete on the global scale, nor accumulate the wealth necessary to tackle endemic and seemingly intractable problems of poverty, illiteracy, hunger

---

[3] Planning Commission, *Development Challenges in Extremist Affected Areas*, paras 1.18.1 and 1.18.2, emphasis supplied.
[4] Ibid., paras 1.18.3 and 1.8.4, emphasis supplied.

and squalor. Whether such exploitation is occurring in a manner that is sustainable, by the environment and the existing social structures, is an oft debated topic, and yet hurriedly buried. Neither the policymakers nor the elite in India, who turn a blind eye to the gross and inhuman suffering of the displaced and the dispossessed, provide any credible answers. Worse still, they ignore historical evidence which indicates that a development paradigm depending largely on the plunder and loot of the natural resources more often than not leads to failure of the State; and that on its way to such a fate, countless millions would have been condemned to lives of great misery and hopelessness.

It is now clear to us, as alleged by the Petitioners, that thousands of tribal youth are being appointed by the State of Chhattisgarh, with the consent of the Union of India, to engage in armed conflict with the Maoists/Naxalites. The facts as stated in the affidavits of the State of Chhattisgarh, and Union of India themselves reveal that, contrary to the assertions that the tribal SPOs are recruited only to engage in non-combatant roles such as those of spotters, guides, intelligence gatherers, and for maintenance of local law and order, they are actually involved in combat with the Maoists/Naxalites. The fact that both the State of Chhattisgarh and the Union of India themselves acknowledge that the relief camps, and the remote villages, in which these SPOs are recruited and directed to work in, have been subject to thousands of attacks clearly indicates that in every such attack the SPOs may necessarily have to engage in pitched battles with the Maoists. This is also borne out by the fact that both the Union of India and State of Chhattisgarh have acknowledged that many hundreds of civilians have been killed by Maoists/Naxalites by branding them as 'police informants'. This would obviously mean that SPOs would be amongst the first targets of the Maoists/Naxalites, and not be merely occasional incidental victims of violence or subject to Maoist/Naxalite attacks upon accidental or chance discovery or infrequent discovery of their true role.

The State of Chhattisgarh has itself stated that in recruiting these tribal youths as SPOs 'preference for those who have passed the fifth' standard has been given. This clearly implies that some, or many, who have been recruited as SPOs may not have even passed the fifth standard. Under the new rules, it is clear that the State of Chhattisgarh would continue to recruit youngsters with such limited schooling. It is shocking that the State of Chhattisgarh then turns around and states that it had expected such youngsters to learn, adequately, subjects such as IPC [Indian Penal Code], Code of Criminal Procedure, Evidence Act, Minors Act, etc. Even more shockingly the State of Chhattisgarh claims that the same was achieved in a matter of 24 periods of instruction of one hour each. Further, the State of Chhattisgarh also claims that in an additional 12 periods, both the concepts of Human Rights and 'other provisions of Indian Constitution' had been taught. Even more astoundingly, it claims that it also taught them scientific and forensic aids in policing in [six] periods.

It is abundantly clear, from the affidavits submitted by the State of Chhattisgarh, and by the Union of India, that one of the primary motives in employing tribal youth as SPOs is to make up for the lack of adequate formal security forces on the ground. The situation, as we have said before, has been created, in large part by the socio-economic policies followed by the State. The policy of privatisation has also meant that the State has incapacitated itself, actually and ideologically, from devoting adequate financial resources in building the capacity to control the social unrest that has been unleashed.

We specifically, and repeatedly, asked the State of Chhattisgarh, and the Union of India as to how, and in what manner they would take back the firearms given to thousands of youngsters. No answer has been given so far. If force is used to collect such firearms back, without those youngsters being given a credible answer with respect to their questions regarding their safety, in terms of their lives, after their appointment ends, it is entirely conceivable that those youngsters refuse to return them. Consequently, we would then have a large number of armed youngsters, running scared for their lives, and in violation of the law. It is entirely conceivable that they would then turn against the State, or at least defend themselves using those firearms, against the security forces themselves; and for their livelihood, and subsistence, they could become roving groups of armed men endangering the society, and the people in those areas, as a third front.

Given the number of civil society groups, and human rights activists, who have repeatedly been claiming that the appointment of tribal youths as SPOs, sometimes called Koya Commandos, or the Salwa Judum, has led to increasing human rights violations, and further given that NHRC [National Human Rights Commission] itself has found that many instances of looting, arson, and violence can be attributed to the SPOs and the security forces, we cannot but apprehend that such incidents are on account of the lack of control, and in fact the lack of ability and moral authority to control, the activities of the SPOs.

In light of the above, we hold that both Article 21 and Article 14 of the Constitution of India have been violated, and will continue to be violated, by the appointment of tribal youth, with very little education, as SPOs engaged in counter-insurgency activities.

Article 14 is violated because subjecting such youngsters to the same levels of dangers as members of the regular force who have better educational backgrounds, receive better training, and because of better educational backgrounds possess a better capacity to benefit from training that is appropriate for the duties to be performed in counter-insurgency activities, would be to treat unequal as equals. Moreover, in as much as such youngsters, with such low educational qualifications and the consequent scholastic inabilities to benefit from appropriate training, can also not be expected to be effective in engaging in counter-insurgency activities, the policy of employing such youngsters as SPOs engaged in counter-insurgency activities is irrational, arbitrary and capricious.

Article 21 is violated because, notwithstanding the claimed volition on the part of these youngsters to appointment as SPOs engaged in counter-insurgency activities, youngsters with such low educational qualifications cannot be expected to understand the dangers that they are likely to face, the skills needed to face such dangers, and the requirements of the necessary judgement while discharging such responsibilities. Further, because of their low levels of educational achievements, they will also not be in a position to benefit from an appropriately designed training programme that is commensurate with the kinds of duties, liabilities, disciplinary code and dangers that they face, to their lives and health. Consequently, appointing such youngsters as SPOs with duties, that would involve any counter-insurgency activities against the Maoists, even if it were claimed that they have been put through rigorous training, would be to endanger their lives.

To employ such ill equipped youngsters as SPOs engaged in counterinsurgency activities, including the tasks of identifying Maoists and non-Maoists, and equipping them with firearms, would endanger the lives of others in the society. That would be a violation of Article 21 rights of a vast number of people in the society.

We order that:

(*a*) The State of Chhattisgarh immediately cease and desist from using SPOs in any manner or form in any activities, directly or indirectly, aimed at controlling, countering, mitigating or otherwise eliminating Maoist/Naxalite activities in the State of Chhattisgarh;

(*b*) The Union of India to cease and desist, forthwith, from using any of its funds in supporting, directly or indirectly the recruitment of SPOs for the purposes of engaging in any form of counter-insurgency activities against Maoist/Naxalite groups;

(*c*) The State of Chhattisgarh shall forthwith make every effort to recall all firearms issued to any of the SPOs, whether current or former, along with any and all accoutrements and accessories issued to use such firearms. The word firearm as used shall include any and all forms of guns, rifles, launchers etc., of whatever calibre.

৵

# Bibliography

Amin, Samir, *L'avenir du maoïsme* (Paris: Éditions de Minuit, 1981).

———, 'Théorie et pratique du projet chinois de socialisme de marché', *Alternatives Sud*, vol. 8, no. 1, 2001, pp. 53–89.

———, *Pour un Monde Multipolaire* (Paris: Syllepse, 2005).

Assadi, Muzaffar, 'Forest Encroachments, Left Adventurism and Hindutva', *Economic and Political Weekly*, vol. 39, no. 9, February 28 2004, pp. 882–85.

Balagopal, K., 'The Limits of Violence', *Himal*, vol. 20, no. 12, December 2007.

Bandyopadhyay, Mouparna, 'It happened in Naxalbari', *Financial Express*, 29 June 2009.

*BBC News*, 'Kobad Ghandy 2008 Interview', 23 September 2009.

Bhatia, Bela, 'On Armed Resistance', *Economic and Political Weekly*, vol. 41, no. 29, 22 July 2006, pp. 3179–83.

Bhattacharyya, Amit, 'Is Lalgarh Showing the Way?', *Economic and Political Weekly*, vol. 45, no. 2, 9–15 January 2010, pp. 17–21.

Bhattacharya, Ravik, 'Kishenji aide quits, says Maoists anti-tribal', *Indian Express*, 8 February 2010.

Carson, Rachel, *Silent Spring* (Boston: Houghton Mifflin, 1962).

Committee on Special Multipurpose Tribal Blocks, *Report of the Committee on Special Multipurpose Tribal Blocks* (New Delhi: Ministry of Home Affairs, Government of India, 1960).

Debray, Regis, *The Revolution on Trial: A Critique of Arms* vol. 1, trans. Rosemary Sheed (New York: Penguin Books, 1977).

———, *The Revolution on Trial: A Critique of Arms*, vol. 2, trans. Rosemary Sheed (New York: Penguin Books, 1978).

Dubey, Abhay Kumar, *Kranti ka Atma Sangharsh* (New Delhi: Vinay Prakashan, 1994).

Duyker, Edward, *Tribal Guerrillas: The Santals of West Bengal and the Naxalite Movement* (Oxford: Oxford University Press, 1987).

Ehrlich, Paul R., *Population Bomb* (New York: Ballantine Books, 1968).

Frasca, Cheryl, Eric Wohlforth and Commonwealth North, 'At A Crossroad: The Permanent Fund, Alaskans, and Alaska's Future', Commonwealth North Study Report, November 2007, http://www.housemajority.org/coms/hfsp/pdfs/CWN_PF_Study.pdf (accessed on 16 March 2012).

Gandhi, Sonia, 'Letter to the Congresspersons', *Congress Sandesh*, May 2010.

Giri, Saroj, 'The Dangers Are Great, the Possibilities Immense: The Ongoing Political Movement in India', *Monthly Review*, 8 November 2009, http://monthlyreview.org/091106giri.php (accessed on 27 January 2010).

Government of India, *Census of India 2001* (New Delhi: Office of the Registrar General, India, 2011).

Guha, Ramachandra, 'Adivasis, Naxalites and Indian Democracy', *Economic and Political Weekly*, vol. 42, no. 32, 11 August 2007, pp. 3305–12.

Guha, Ranajit, *Elementary Aspects of Peasant Insurgency in Colonial India* (New Delhi: Oxford University Press, 1983).

Harrison, Gordon Scott and Alaska Legislative Affairs Agency, 'Article IX, Section 15 — Alaska Permanent Fund', in *Alaska's Constitution: A Citizen's Guide* (Juneau: Alaska Legislative Affairs Agency, 2003).

*Hindu, The*, 'Edited text of 12,262-word response by Azad, Spokesperson, Central Committee, CPI (Maoist)', 14 April 2010, http://www.thehindu.com/multimedia/archive/00103/Edited_text_of_12_2_103996a.pdf (accessed on 29 February 2012).

Hobsbawm, Eric J., *Bandits* (London: Abacus, 2001).

Human Rights Forum, *Death, Displacement & Deprivation: The War in Dantewada: A Report* (Hyderabad: Human Rights Forum, 2006).

*Indian Express*, 'Fighting Naxals Primary Job of States: Chidambaram', 15 April 2010.

Jha, Prashant, 'Complicating the "Naxalite" Debate', *Kafila*, 22 October 2009, http://kafila.org/2009/10/22/complicating-the-naxalite-debate/ (accessed on 24 January 2010).

Kumar, Kundan, 'Dispossessed and Displaced: A Brief Paper on Tribal Issues in Orissa', Discussion Paper, Vasundhara, Bhubaneshwar, Orissa, 2004.

Manrique, Nelson, 'The War for the Central Sierra', in Steve J. Stern (ed.), *Shining and Other Paths: War and Society in Peru, 1980–1995* (Durham, NC: Duke University Press, 1998), pp. 193–223.

Meadows, Donella H., Dennis L. Meadows, Jorgen Randers and William W. Behrens III, *The Limits to Growth; A Report for the Club of Rome's Project on the Predicament of Mankind* (New York: Universe Books, 1972).

Menon, Nivedita, 'Radical Resistance and Political Violence Today', *Economic and Political Weekly*, vol. 44, no. 50, 12 December 2009, pp. 16–20.

———, 'Response to Arundhati Roy: Jairus Banaji', *Kafila.org*, 22 March 2010.

Mitra, Maureen Nandini, 'Red Alert in Chhattisgarh', *Down to Earth*, 31 October 2006.

Mohanty, Manoranjan, *Revolutionary Violence: A Study of the Maoist Movement in India* (New Delhi: Sterling Publishers, 1977).

Myrdal, Jan and Gautam Navlakha, 'In Conversation with Ganapathy, General Secretary of CPI(Maoist)', *Sanhati*, 12 February 2010.

Navlakha, Gautam, 'Days and Nights in the Heartland of Rebellion', *Sanhati*, 1 April 2010.

Nehru, Jawaharlal, Constituent Assembly of India Debates, vol. 2, 22 January, 1947, pp. 316–17, http://164.100.47.132/lssnew/constituent/vol2p3.html (accessed on 27 February 2012).

Nigam, Aditya, 'A Million Mutinies Within', *Tehelka*, vol. 6, no. 26, 4 July 2009.

———, 'Democracy, State and Capital: The "Unthought" of 20th Century Marxism', *Economic and Political Weekly*, vol. 44, no. 51, 19 December 2009.

Paine, Thomas, *Agrarian Justice* (Philadelphia: Folwell for B.F. Bache, 1797).

Planning Commission, *Development Challenges in Extremist Affected Areas* (New Delhi: Government of India, 2008).

Raghuraman, Shankar, 'Ironic? Story of the Great Indian Loot', *The Times of India*, 5 June 2010.

Ray, Partho Sarathi, 'Background of the Movement', *Sanhati*, 13 November 2008, http://sanhati.com/front-page/1083/#1 (accessed on 24 January 2010).

Robinson, Simon, 'India's Secret War', *Time*, 29 May 2008, http://www.time.com/time/magazine/article/0,9171,1810169,00.html#ixzz1lfmF50dx (accessed 7 February 2012).

Rogelj, Joeri, Julia Nabel, Claudine Chen, William Hare, Kathleen Markmann, Malte Meinshausen, Michiel Schaeffer, Kirsten Macey and Niklas Höhne, 'Copenhagen Accord Pledges are Paltry', *Nature*, vol. 464, no. 7292, 22 April 2010.

Roy, Arundhati, *Listening to Grasshoppers: Field Notes on Democracy* (London: Hamish Hamilton, 2009).

———, 'Mr Chidambaram's War', *Outlook*, 9 November 2009.

———, 'Walking with the Comrades', *Outlook*, 29 March 2010.

Russell, Bertrand, 'Why I am not a Communist', in Robert E. Egner and Lester E. Denonn (eds), *Bertrand Russell: The Basic Writings of Bertrand Russell* (London: Routledge, 2010).

Sarkar, Sumit and Tanika Sarkar, 'Notes on a Dying People', *Economic and Political Weekly*, vol. 44, no. 26 & 27, 27 June 2009, pp. 10–14.

Schmid, Alex Peter and A. J. Jongman, *Political Terrorism: A New Guide to Actors, Authors, Concepts, Data Bases, Theories and Literature* (New Brunswick, NJ: Transaction Publishers, 2005).

Sethi, Nitin. 'As Forests Feed Growth, Tribals Given the Go-By', *The Times of India*, 5 June 2010.

Simha, Vijay, 'Public Intellectuals in the Chair 7: "All the News we get is Killing and Getting Killed"', *Tehelka*, 21 January 2006.

Singh, Jaipal, *Constituent Assembly Debates*, vol. 1, pp. 143–4, 19 December 1946, http://164.100.47.132/LssNew/constituent/vol1p9.html (accessed on 27 February 2012).

Sundar, Nandini, 'Bastar, Maoism and Salwa Judum', *Economic and Political Weekly*, vol. 41, no. 29, 22 July 2006, pp. 3187–91.

*The Times of India*, 'Stop Green Hunt: Kishanji', 18 May 2010.

———, 'Cops shouldn't have used public bus: Arundhati', 19 May 2010.

————, 'Maoist Violence Claims 2,680 Lives in 2008–10', 9 March 2011, http://articles.timesofindia.indiatimes.com/2011-03-09/india/28671947_1_incidents-of-naxal-violence-school-buildings-telephone-exchanges (accessed on 19 March 2012).

Union Research Institute, *Documents of Chinese Communist Party Central Committee, Sept. 1956–Apr. 1969*, vol. 1 (Hong Kong: Union Research Institute, 1971).

United Nations Development Programme (UNDP), *Human Development Report 2010: The Real Wealth of Nations: Pathways to Human Development* (Basingstoke: Palgrave Macmillan, 2010).

————, *Human Development Report 2011: Sustainability and Equity: A Better Future for All* (Basingstoke: Palgrave Macmillan, 2011).

Zedong, Mao, *Report on an Investigation of the Peasant Movement in Hunan* (Peking: Foreign Languages Press, 1953).

————, 'A Single Spark Can Start a Prairie Fire', in *Selected Works of Mao Tse-tung*, vol. I (Peking: Foreign Languages Press, 1967).

————, 'Problems of War and Strategy (November 6, 1938)', in *Selected Works of Mao Tse-tung*, vol. II (Peking: Foreign Languages Press, 1967).

————, 'On the Ten Great Relationships (April 25, 1956)', in *Selected Works of Mao Tse-tung*, vol. V (Peking: Foreign Languages Press, 1977).

**Films:**

*La Chinoise*, dir. Jean-Luc Godard, 1967.

*My Name Is Khan*, dir. Karan Johar, 2010.

*Rajneeti*, dir. Prakash Jha, 2010.

# About the Editor

**Santosh Paul** graduated in Economics from Elphinstone College, Mumbai in 1985. He obtained a degree in law from the Government Law College, Mumbai in 1988 and is a practising lawyer in the Supreme Court of India. He has written articles for *Lex et Juris*, *Legal World* and *Supreme Court Cases* (SCC), and presented a paper 'Right to Food' at the All India Seminar on Judicial Reforms organised by the Confederation of Indian Bar in August 2010. He is a trustee of the Society for Economic and Political Reconstruction, and is at present working on a book on judicial appointments.

# Notes on Contributors

**Shankkar Aiyar** is Managing Editor, *India Today*, and specialises in economics and politics with a particular emphasis on the interface between the two. He is currently based in New Delhi and is responsible for the magazine's coverage of political economy, governance, corporate and financial markets.

**Swaminathan S. Anklesaria Aiyar** is a prominent journalist and columnist. He is Consulting Editor for *The Economic Times* and writes regularly for the *The Economic Times* and *The Times of India*.

**Samir Amin** is an Egyptian economist with a PhD in political economy as well as degrees from the Institut de Statistiques and the Institut d'Etudes Politiques. He is the Director of the Third World Forum in Dakar, Senegal and the author of more than 30 books.

**Jairus Banaji** is Professorial Research Associate, Department of Development Studies, School of Oriental and African Studies (SOAS), University of London. His main research interests include agrarian history, Marx's method in *Capital*, modes of production, the fate of the peasantry under capitalism, and labour and capital in India's economy.

**Chetan Bhagat** is an author, columnist and speaker. He quit his international investment banking career in 2009 to devote his entire time to writing. Bhagat is the author of five bestselling novels.

**Shoma Chaudhury** is Managing Editor, *Tehelka*. She has written and covered many prominent contemporary issues in India: communal strife, the Naxalite–Maoist insurgency, and conflicts

262 | Maoist Movement in India

between the Indian government and dispossessed people. She has won several awards, including the Ramnath Goenka Award and the Chameli Devi Jain Award for the most outstanding woman journalist in 2009. In 2011, Newsweek (USA) picked her as one of 150 power women who 'shake the world'.

**P. Chidambaram** is a politician with the Indian National Congress and the current Union Minister of Finance, Government of India. Previously he was Union Minister of Home Affairs (2009–12), and Union Minister of Finance (2004–08). He started his career as a lawyer in 1969 and became Senior Advocate in 1984. He was elected to Parliament from the Sivaganga constituency in Tamil Nadu in 1984 and thereafter held different portfolios in the Congress Party as well as various governments.

**Gurcharan Das** is an author, commentator and public intellectual. He graduated with honours from Harvard University in Philosophy. He was CEO of Procter & Gamble India, and later Managing Director of Procter & Gamble Worldwide (Strategic Planning). In 1995, he took early retirement to become a full-time writer.

**Swapan Dasgupta** is a senior journalist. At various points in his career, he has held editorial posts at *The Statesman*, *The Daily Telegraph*, *The Times of India*, *The Indian Express* and, most recently, *India Today*, where he was Managing Editor till 2003. He has written for *The Pioneer*, *The Telegraph*, *Dainik Jagran*, *The Times of India*, *The New Indian Express*, *Outlook*, *The Free Press Journal* and several other newspapers and magazines.

**Sonia Gandhi** is a politician and the President of the Indian National Congress, one of the major political parties of India. She is also the Chairperson of the Coordinating Committee of the ruling coalition, the United Progressive Alliance.

**Smita Gupta** is Deputy Editor, *The Hindu*. She previously worked as Political Editor with *Outlook*.

**B. K. Handique** is Member of the 15th Lok Sabha of India. He represents the Jorhat constituency of Assam and is a member of the Indian National Congress. He was the Minister of Mines from May 2009 to January 2011, Minister of Development of North-Eastern Region from May 2009 to July 2011, and Minister of State, Chemicals and Fertilisers from 2006 to 2009.

**V. R. Krishna Iyer** is former Judge, Supreme Court of India. He was previously Minister of Law, Power, Prisons, Irrigation and Social Welfare in the Government of Kerala. In 1973, he was sworn in as a Judge of the Supreme Court of India. He was conferred with Padma Vibhushan in the year 1999.

**Prakash Jha** is a film producer-director-screenwriter, who is most known for his socio-political films. He has also made several National Film Award winning documentaries.

**Nitish Kumar** is a politician and has been the Chief Minister of Bihar since 2005. He leads the Janata Dal (United) party. As Chief Minister, he has gained popularity by initiating a series of developmental and constructive activities in Bihar.

**Vinod Mehta** is Editor-in-Chief, *Outlook*, and is regarded as one of the senior-most editors in the country. He was the Founder-Editor of *Outlook*, which was launched in 1995. Mehta previously held the post of Editor at several news publications, including *The Pioneer*, *The Sunday Observer*, *The Independent* and *The India Post*.

**Dola Mitra** is Special Correspondent, *Outlook*.

**Tusha Mittal** is Principal Correspondent, *Tehelka*. She recently won the Chameli Devi Jain Award for reportage of life in deep interior Bengal, Orissa and Chhattisgarh and the Press Institute of India award for best articles on humanitarian issues published in the Indian media. At *Tehelka*, she has written extensively on land rights and displacement struggles.

**Nirmalangshu Mukherji** is Professor, Department of Philosophy, University of Delhi. His publications include *December 13: Terror over Democracy* (2005).

**Aditya Nigam** works in the broad field of social and political theory. He has published extensively on Marxism, nationalism, identity and radical politics in both English and Hindi.

**Surinder Singh Nijjar** is presently Judge, Supreme Court of India. He was the Chief Justice of the High Court at Calcutta.

**Santosh Paul** is Advocate, Supreme Court of India. He is Trustee of the Society for Economic and Political Reconstruction.

**Shankar Raghuraman** is Senior Editor, *The Times of India*, and has spent the last 23 years in journalism as business journalist with the Times Insight Group.

**Shafi Rahman** is Associate Editor, *India Today*. He has worked as a journalist in India and the Middle East, and has widely covered politics and policies from across the region.

**Jairam Ramesh** is an economist and politician affiliated to the Indian National Congress. He is a Member of Parliament representing the state of Andhra Pradesh in the Rajya Sabha since June 2004. He is currently Minister of Rural Development with additional charge of Drinking Water and Sanitation.

**Srinivasa Rao** is Correspondent, *India Today*.

**Sudershan Reddy** is former Judge, Supreme Court of India. He has held several positions including Judge of Andhra Pradesh High Court and Chief Justice of the Guwahati High Court. He is well known for rendering several landmark judgments on various branches of law, in particular on issues of criminal jurisprudence, constitution and human rights.

**Shobhan Saxena** is Editor, *Sunday Times of India*. His interests range from international issues, human rights and politics, to art and culture.

**Nitin Sethi** is Assistant Editor, *The Times of India*, Delhi (national bureau).

**Supriya Sharma** is Special Correspondent, *The Times of India*. She was previously part of the Mumbai reporting team of NDTV.

**Digvijay Singh** is a politician, former Chief Minister of Madhya Pradesh and a senior leader of the Indian National Congress party. He is currently the General Secretary of the All India Congress Committee.

**Nandini Sundar** is Professor of Sociology, Delhi School of Economics and Co-editor, *Contributions to Indian Sociology*. She has previously worked at the Centre for the Study of Law and Governance, Jawaharlal Nehru University; the Institute of Economic Growth, Delhi; and the University of Edinburgh. She has been a member of several government committees concerning the welfare of scheduled tribes.

**M. S. Swaminathan** is an agricultural scientist, and currently serves as a Member of Parliament from the Rajya Sabha, and is member of the National Advisory Council. He is known as the 'Father of the Green Revolution in India', for his leadership and success in introducing and developing high-yielding varieties of wheat in India.

**Madhavi Tata** is Senior Special Correspondent, the Outlook Group. She is a journalist with 15 years of experience in the print media. Currently she is in charge of *Outlook* in Andhra Pradesh.

# Index

For Product Safety Concerns and Information please contact our EU
representative GPSR@taylorandfrancis.com
Taylor & Francis Verlag GmbH, Kaufingerstraße 24, 80331 München, Germany

www.ingramcontent.com/pod-product-compliance
Lightning Source LLC
Chambersburg PA
CBHW050703280326
41926CB00088B/2439

9 781138 662926